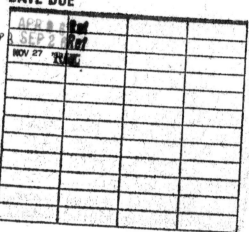

THE BEST SHORT PLAYS 1982

THE
BEST
SHORT
PLAYS *1982*

edited and with an introduction by
RAMON DELGADO

Best Short Plays Series

Chilton Book Company
Radnor, Pennsylvania

Copyright © 1982 by Ramon Delgado
All Rights Reserved
Published in Radnor, Pennsylvania 19089, by Chilton Book Company,
and simultaneously in Canada by VNR Publishers,
1410 Birchmount Road, Scarborough, Ontario M1P 2E7
Library of Congress Catalog Card No. 38-8006
ISBN 0-8019-7144-6
ISSN 0067-6284
Manufactured in the United States of America

1 2 3 4 5 6 7 8 9 0   1 0 9 8 7 6 5 4 3 2

For Christian H. Moe
and Eelin Stewart-Harrison

BOOKS AND PLAYS BY RAMON DELGADO

The Best Short Plays 1981 (*with Stanley Richards*)

The Youngest Child of Pablo Peco
Waiting for the Bus
The Little Toy Dog
Once Below A Lighthouse
Sparrows of the Field
The Knight-Mare's Nest
Omega's Ninth
Listen, My Children
A Little Holy Water
The Fabulous Jeromes
The Jerusalem Thorn

CONTENTS

INTRODUCTION

With this volume we celebrate the fifteenth anniversary of Chilton Book's publication of *The Best Short Plays*. This annual anthology, revived in 1968 by Stanley Richards, was a resumption of *The Best One-Act Plays* series, edited by Margaret Mayorga from 1937 until her retirement in 1962.

As an added feature to this anniversary edition, I have compiled a cumulative index to aid the reader in locating the plays in these fifteen volumes. Thus, 191 individual plays, listed alphabetically under the author's last name, may be located by yearly volume. A glance through this list reveals a veritable roll call of the outstanding established playwrights and the most promising of the emerging playwrights, who perhaps fifteen years hence are likely to be as renown.

From the scores of short plays read and seen for consideration in this series, I have selected eleven for the 1982 volume which represent the best writing of both British and American playwrights. Sources utilized in finding these plays have been myriad and include: submissions from individual playwrights, agents, and publishers; plays first produced at play festivals, the American Theatre Association Playwrights' Workshop, Dale Wasserman's Midwest Playwrights Laboratory and the Eugene O'Neill Theatre Center; and the recommendations of teachers of playwriting in colleges throughout the country.

Notable among the theatre festivals featuring short plays in the past year have been Jon Jory's Actors Theatre of Louisville's two events—*Shorts*, featuring nine new one-act plays and the *Fifth Annual Festival of New American Plays* with seven short sketches and five fully developed one-act plays. The New York area was well served with thirty-nine short play entries in the *6th Annual Off-Off Broadway Original Short Play*

Festival, sponsored by the Double Image Theatre, Helen Waren Mayer, Artistic Director, with William Talbot as Festival Coordinator. Curt Dempster's Ensemble Studio Theatre continued in its series of one-acts with *Marathon 1981,* presenting thirteen different short plays. Even the venerable Lincoln Center engaged its Mitzi E. Newhouse theatre in a six-week run of three one-act plays selected by Edward Albee (including Jeffrey Sweet's *Stops Along the Way* in the 1981 collection of *The Best Short Plays,* and John Guare's and Percy Granger's plays in this volume). Five of the plays in this collection were first produced at one of these festivals.

The continuing interest in the short play is evident not only from the amount of production activity, but from the calibre of playwrights who, though successful in longer forms, continue to write one-act plays. Lanford Wilson and John Guare are two notable examples in this year's collection, both recipients of the highest honors and commercial success in American theatre and both returning on occasion to the short form which initiated their careers.

In the two years that I have been associated with this series, I have not detected any unusual trends in the development of the short play. Certainly those plays included here contain a variety of theatrical and dramatic techniques, viewpoints, and topics. There are fewer satiric comedies offered than I might have suspected, and a large number of plays submitted or viewed have dealt with lonely strangers reaching out to one another, searching for values, identity, and self-fulfillment. Family ties—father-and-son, mother-and-daughter relationships—have been examined frequently, not with conflicting values as they might have ten years ago, but with efforts to reconcile differences. There appears to be less experimentation in non-linear form than a few years ago, and there is a deep concern with character relationships and vivid language.

There are many people whose assistance is indispensable in putting together a collection of this calibre. I would especially like to thank William Talbot and Lawrence Harbison of Samuel French, Inc.; F. Andrew Leslie and James C. Throneburg of Dramatists Play Service, Inc.; Michael Feingold, critic for the *Village Voice;* and Christian H. Moe, Professor of Theatre, Southern Illinois University at Carbondale, for their cooperation and helpful suggestions. In addition my gratitude

is without end for Laura Woodson-Hammond, who first stim-
ulated my involvement with this series. Tribute is due also to
the scores of playwrights and agents who submitted plays and
waited patiently for decisions. Finally, let me thank the directors, actors, producing groups, and readers, who with their
productions and patronage make this publication a worthy
and satisfying undertaking.

RAMON DELGADO
Montclair, New Jersey

Lanford Wilson

THYMUS VULGARIS

Lanford Wilson

Reviewing Lanford Wilson's *Brontosaurus* (which appeared in *The Best Short Plays 1979*), Rob Baker of the New York *Daily News* wrote "Lanford Wilson is probably our greatest functioning American playwright."

Since that assessment in 1977, Wilson has written his most ambitious project to date: three plays depicting the Talley family of Lebanon, Missouri. In 1979, New York's Circle Repertory Company produced *Talley's Folly,* a two character romance between Sally Talley and Matt Friedman set on July 4, 1944. Walter Kerr, in the *New York Times,* raved about the subsequent production on Broadway, "a charmer, filled to the brim with hope, humor and chutzpah." The play won the 1980 Pulitzer Prize for Drama, the Theatre Club Inc. Award for Best American Play of 1980 and the New York Drama Critics' Circle Award. The second play in the series, *5th of July,* set in 1977, depicts the next generation of Talleys attempting to piece together their lives after a disruptive decade of social change. The third Talley play, *A Tale Told*—Wilson's 29th production directed by Marshall W. Mason—again takes place on July 4, 1944, showing the family that Sally wanted to escape. Julius Novick in the *Village Voice* responded to *A Tale Told:* "What an old-fashioned play Lanford Wilson has written; and what a good one!" . . . . Mr. Wilson writes in his "customary Chekhovian fashion, bringing very specific selves and viewpoints and relationships with them . . . . the people of his trilogy go on living when they are offstage." It is reported that there may be as many as five more plays forthcoming in the Talley saga.

Lanford Wilson was born in Lebanon, Missouri, in 1937, and was educated at San Diego State College and the University of Chicago, where he started writing plays. His professional career began at the now defunct Caffe Cino in Greenwich Village. After presenting ten productions at this pioneer Off-Off-Broadway cafe-theatre and six at the Cafe La Mama, he moved to Off-Broadway in 1965 with *Home Free!* at the Cherry Lane Theatre. In 1966, Mr. Wilson again was represented Off-Broadway, this time with a double bill, *The Madness of Lady Bright* and *Ludlow Fair,* at the uptown Theatre East. *This Is the Rill Speaking,* another of his short plays, was seen during that same season at the Martinique

Theatre in a series of six works originally presented at the Cafe La Mama.

In 1967, Mr. Wilson won a Drama Desk-Vernon Rice Award for his play, *The Rimers of Eldritch,* a lyrical study of life in a small town in the Middle West. This was followed by another full-length play, *The Gingham Dog,* which opened in 1968 at the Washington Theatre Club, Washington, D.C., and was presented on Broadway the following year. The author returned to Broadway in 1970 with *Lemon Sky,* which drew the following comment from Clive Barnes: "Mr. Wilson can write; his characters spring alive on stage; he holds our attention, he engages our heart."

In 1972 Mr. Wilson received considerable praise for his libretto for the operatic version of Tennessee Williams' *Summer and Smoke.* The opera, with music by Lee Hoiby, was performed by the New York City Opera at Lincoln Center.

The highly acclaimed play *The Hot L Baltimore,* written under a Guggenheim Fellowship, originally was presented by the Circle Repertory Company in January, 1973, then transferred in March to Off-Broadway's Circle in the Square Downtown for a commercial engagement, ran for 1,166 performances and won the New York Drama Critics' Circle Award for Best American Play of the 1972–73 season; the Outer Critics' Circle Award; and an Obie award for Best Play.

Among the author's other works for the theatre are *Balm in Gilead; Wandering; So Long at the Fair; No Trespassing; Serenading Louie; The Mound Builders; The Great Nebula in Orion,* introduced in *The Best Short Plays 1972;* and *The Sand Castle,* in *The Best Short Plays 1975.*

Mr. Wilson has been the recipient of Rockefeller, Yale, and Guggenheim Fellowships, as well as an award from The American Academy of Arts and Letters for "the body of his work as a playwright." In the fall of 1981 the University of Missouri at Kansas City awarded Mr. Wilson the honorary degree Doctor of Humane Letters.

Mr. Wilson's new one-act, *Thymus Vulgaris,* was commissioned by Edward Albee for New York's Lincoln Center One-Act Festival at the Mitzi E. Newhouse Theatre. Here Wilson creates a memorable portrait of a Cinderella "showgirl" about to marry into wealth. Her expectations are contrasted against the common social and economic background of her long-suffering mother.

Presented by the Circle Repertory Company in January of 1982, *Thymus Vulgaris* was directed by June Stein with the following cast:

RUBY Pearl Shear
EVELYN Katherine Cortez
THE COP Jeff McCracken

The Characters:

RUBY *is somewhere between fifty and sixty-five. Not thin and with the bleached ends of a rather vivid hairstyle. She is in a blue slip or housecoat.*

EVELYN *is between thirty and forty—probably thirty-five. Not thin, very like her mother. Her hair is a vivid color. She wears a very expensive bright yellow silk dress or slacks a size too small.*

THE COP *is in his twenties, none too bright, tall, well built and blonde.*

The Set:

In the center of the stage is a raised platform perhaps two feet high that is the size and general shape of a small house trailer. The platform is furnished as a trailer might be, everything quite close together, and perhaps painted in only two colors—yellow and blue for a choice. There are plenty of counters to duck behind and vanish from sight. At rise there are perhaps a few pillowcases or laundry bags stuffed with clothes. All this need not be more realistic than is necessary to convey the subject. No roof, windows, walls, background, etc.

Ruby is suddenly discovered in the center of the platform. She immediately reacts to the audience—acute embarrassment. She starts to step off the platform, doesn't know which way to turn, quickly puts three or four things away, pillowcases stuffed with clothes, which gives her the chance to duck behind a counter. She grunts from the effort.

RUBY: Oh, dear God. Oh, goodness. Oh, my goodness.
EVELYN: (*Calling from off*) Momma? Momma? (*She appears striding on*) Momma, I'm here. Can you believe your eyes? (*As she makes it to the platform, and yells off-stage*) It wouldn't kill you to have left that step here. (*On the platform, in doorway*) Momma, I'm here! Could we lose the music?
(*Ruby has been bending over and is out of sight. She raises up now and looks at Evelyn blankly*)
RUBY: Huh?

EVELYN: Momma! Why aren't you ready?

RUBY: What?

EVELYN: Look at you. Oh, God, Momma.

RUBY: Evie! It's my baby! Out of the blue!

EVELYN: Why aren't you ready? Didn't you get my letter? (*Pause. Devastated*) You didn't get my letter. Oh, Momma, it's a red letter day.

RUBY: Well, maybe that explains why you sashay into my trailer like this. Catching me before I have time to do. (*Sotto voce*) This isn't for me, honey. I can't stand up here with the lights on me and everybody watchin'. I mean I don't even go to shows.

EVELYN: Momma, these days you just got to let 'er roll right off your back.

RUBY: I'm okay for a person, honey, but I'm no good for a character.

EVELYN: Momma, we're not people like us no more. In the last year, Momma, I've made a complete three hundred and sixty degree turn. (*Preparatory to a major announcement*) Momma, sit down.

RUBY: I will not sit down till I've hugged my baby. (*Running to her*)

EVELYN: (*Being hugged*) I can't believe you didn't know. I wrote you everything. It took me six hours to compose a letter. I wrote eight pages, Momma.

RUBY: (*Arms length*) Of course she did.

EVELYN: Is this the same trailer or did you trade it for a smaller one?

RUBY: This is the same trailer you know.

EVELYN: I can't hardly move in here.

RUBY: God almighty, let me make us some coffee.

EVELYN: (*Same*) Momma . . . sit down! (*Announcement*) Momma. I'm getting married.

RUBY: Ohhhhhh. My little baby. (*Running to her, hugging her again*) I almost didn't forgive her for catching me off guard. And now she's getting married. You tell me, honey, while I do.

EVELYN: Momma, there's no time to do. Oh, you didn't get my letter. You don't know the particulars. I'll tell you in the taxi to Hollywood.

RUBY: You know how much it is to taxi from Palmdale to Hollywood . . . ?

EVELYN: I know how much it is. I just did it. It's one hundred and twenty-five cookies.

RUBY: Oh, my God! That's a cleaning lady for two months. I wouldn't have to turn my hand.

EVELYN: You ain't ever gonna have to turn your hand again, Momma.

RUBY: Normally this place is spotless, honey. I mean, if I'd known.

EVELYN: What is that you got growing all around the trailer? I just walked through it and I've got its smell all over me.

RUBY: Oh. That's thyme.

(*Beat*)

EVELYN: That's what?

RUBY: Thyme.

EVELYN: It stinks like I don't know what. Smells like medicine. Is that a drug?

RUBY: No, honey, that's an herb.

EVELYN: Well, some drugs come right from herbs. It smells like Vicks Vapo Rub.

RUBY: It's used in cooking.

EVELYN: Two hundred fifteen dollars a half-ounce, I bathed in *Mon Plasir*. I smell like someone doped me up for coming down with the croup.

RUBY: (*Looking off*) I should maybe trim it off the path, neaten it up—what is that? Is that a cop?

EVELYN: Oh, no. What have you done now? Good lord, yes. That's a highway patrolman. Don't let him see you.

RUBY: What did you do that you'd be wanted by the highway patrol?

EVELYN: Momma, the only motor cops I've seen in a year are the ones Solly bribes to get him to the airport on time.

RUBY: Would they follow you from Hollywood?

EVELYN: They don't follow me, Momma, unless they want my picture . . . Oh, he's coming here.

COP: (*Enters, looks for a place to get up, finds it, stands in the door*) Excuse me.

RUBY and EVELYN: How do you do? Hello. What can we do for you?

COP: Is this the Bentley ur—uh—trailer? I'm looking for a Mrs. Ruby Bentley.

RUBY: No. No . . .

EVELYN: No. No . . .

RUBY: This is the Gonzales' residence. We don't know a Mrs. Bentley.

EVELYN: (*Annoyed with Ruby, but making do*) See—no—habla—anglay.

COP: They said over there that this was the Bentley trailer. I got . . .

RUBY: People in this particular trailer park don't really know other people in this particular trailer park too good.

EVELYN: We're mostly just prominent citizens who are innocent by-standers.

COP: Well, see, I got this urgent . . . (*He notices the audience and freezes*) Oh, my lord.

EVELYN: You got a what? (*Snaps her fingers in front of his face. The cop stands transfixed*) Well, that's done it.

RUBY: (*Sotto voce*) This isn't gonna turn out good, honey. This isn't for people like us.

EVELYN: Look at him.

COP: (*Coming out of it, slipping on a pair of sunglasses. From here on, he is "acting" and very badly*) Well, uh, you see, I have this urgent and important official police business communication with a party by the name of Bentley.

RUBY: We're very sorry we can't help you.

EVELYN: (*Nudging him out*) You call again, though, any time.

RUBY: Any time. Such a nice, strong, clean looking young man.

COP: Yes, well, actually six feet four. Natural wave. A hundred ninety-five.

RUBY: And such a nice smile. That's very important in an occupation where you meet people.

EVELYN: Momma.

RUBY: You work close by, do you?

COP: Right here in Palmdale, Miss. Uh, Mrs . . . uh . . .

EVELYN: Sanchez.

RUBY: And you drive a motorbike.

COP: Yes.

EVELYN: You're the real article, no doubt about it. It's been fun.

COP: It's a Honda brand bike. Honda is a . . . good bike. I get good . . . mileage. Good check-ups.

EVELYN: That's fine. Goodbye now.

COP: Well, I better not stay from my appointed rounds. (*Backing out*) It's been a privilege.

RUBY: Oh, yes. There's always a demand for someone of your vocation and appearance on the uh . . . media.

COP: Yes, ma'm, I appreciate the exposure . . . er . . . uh . . . the time.

RUBY: Any time. You never know.

EVELYN: Any time.

COP: Yes, ma'm. I appreciate it, ma'm. (*Falling off the platform. Backing out*) Good day . . . good day.

RUBY: Sorry we couldn't be more help.

EVELYN: (*As the cop backs out saying "Good day, ma'm"*) Good lord, I thought he was gonna unbutton his shirt.

RUBY: Goodbye. (*Sotto voce*) Some of them, especially men, I think it kinda goes to their head. Bye-bye.

(*The cop is finally gone*)

EVELYN: (*In a flurry*) Throw something in a bag and let's get out of this soup can before he gets wise to whatever you've done.

RUBY: Honey, I'm not like that no more. I'm completely changed.

EVELYN: Cops don't inquire at the homes of people who are completely changed.

RUBY: I've become a conscientious citizen.

EVELYN: Momma, conscientious citizens don't live in a trailer flat straddling the San Andreas Fault at the smack damn edge of the desert. Ten more feet that way, you'd be parched by noon. People who have changed don't have their trailer crawling over with a cooking herb that smells like Vicks and motorcops, Momma. And any minute, he could be coming back. I'll phone for a taxi while you put something on, (*Takes the phone book*) and let's blow this joint. Taxi, taxi—taxidermist, dear God, right in Palmdale, it just makes you creep. (*Dials. Ruby is putting on a white blouse*) Momma, don't wear white; either one of us shows up at a wedding in white, the roof would fall in on the church. (*Phone*) Yes, I . . . uh . . . (*Hangs up*) What do I care if that cop comes back? I'm just sittin' here with my momma.

RUBY: Honey, your momma doesn't really feel up to being busted just today. Your momma isn't as spunky as she used to be, honey.

EVELYN: I hung up because that girl was gonna say what

was my destination. And I don't want to hear that right now. Aww, Momma, I wrote you such a beautiful letter. I wrote you like poetry—that's how moved I was to be writing to you after all this time. I know you think I'm just terrible and selfish and heartless—off God knows where—but sometimes I get so *moved*—just thinking all the things I'd like to tell you and do for you. Only I never go ahead and tell 'em to you or do 'em for you. I really always have been full of wonderful and beautiful things. Sometimes I think of myself as an un-tapped person. I'll bet I have so many things in me that are beautiful. Only for some reason I never seem to be able to let anyone see.

RUBY: They're just blind if they can't see.

EVELYN: I really have such a wonderful . . .

RUBY: I always have known that.

EVELYN: . . . poetic . . .

RUBY: You don't have to tell me, honey . . . And now she's getting married.

EVELYN: Well . . .

(*Pause*)

RUBY: Let me get the coffee before it boils away.

EVELYN: I maybe better call Ed and Nora and see if Solly's got there.

RUBY: Where are you supposed to be?

EVELYN: Oh, Solly's got these two wonderful friends in Hollywood.

RUBY: Ed and Nora.

EVELYN: Yeah. We're meeting at their place. They got a real nice place. I was there and Ed was there and Nora was there and the preacher—but when Solly didn't come and you didn't come . . .

RUBY: Well, he's there by now.

EVELYN: Oh, I don't want to know. If he is or not. If he's showed or not. I want to believe. It's been wonderful believ-ing. (*Drinks coffee*) That's the first thing I've had in my stom-ach all day from worry.

RUBY: You seem to have put on a little weight since I saw you.

EVELYN: What are you talking about? I've never been in better shape in my life. This is how Solly likes me.

RUBY: Do you think he found out? Is that what's got you upset?

EVELYN: Found out what?

RUBY: What?

EVELYN: That he found out what?

RUBY: About your . . .

EVELYN: You mean my work? (*Ruby nods gratefully*) Momma, I met him at the . . . "Club."

RUBY: At the where?

EVELYN: At the . . . "Dance Hall." (*Beat*) The . . . "Place." (*Beat*) The house. He was a regular customer. Momma, it's the love of the century. We've been in columns.

RUBY: My goodness.

EVELYN: In newspapers.

RUBY: Oh, my goodness.

EVELYN: I'm not the person I was, Momma.

RUBY: What did they say?

EVELYN: (*Digging in her purse, hands Ruby two or three news-paper clippings*) They said: Bliss! They said: The love of the ages. They said: Romeo and Juliet. They said: Grapefruit King and Showgirl! "Showgirl!" Twelve times if it was once I drag-ass up to that two-bit Sands for an open call for the chorus. Six times if it was once to Caesar's Palace for an interview for cocktail waitresses. They said I couldn't walk. I won't tell you what they said I walked like. I mean they aren't even polite to a person. They said I had too much personality.

RUBY: Well, of course you do.

EVELYN: Not nice, Momma, they didn't mean it nice. Fourteen times to the Circus without even one callback—and once—once!—Solly takes me to eat a steak at some gussied-up clipjoint and I'm a "showgirl." "Beauty" they called me.

RUBY: Well, you are.

EVELYN: If it had happened to someone else, it could make you believe. "Hope," the girls said. They said it gave them hope. It was like Cinderella, they said. Only different. Solly comes . . .

RUBY: What are you saying his name is?

EVELYN: Sol. Sol.

RUBY: I want to get it right for when I meet him.

EVELYN: Sol. Like the sun. Like Ol' Sol. Like Bam-De-Sol-Lay. Like (*Singing*) "Don't know why, there's no sun up in the sky . . .

RUBY: "Stormy weather . . ."

EVELYN: Only there is a sun up in the sky and he's my Sol.

RUBY: Ol' Sol.

EVELYN: See, Solly had been coming around for six months, maybe—and he's dropping a hundred on one girl and two hundred on another girl . . .

RUBY Where's this?

EVELYN: At the . . .

RUBY: At the "club"?

EVELYN: At the club. He was like I told you.

RUBY: He was a regular.

EVELYN: The girls called him—well, they had their pet name for him, 'cause of his difficulty.

RUBY: What was that?

EVELYN: No, Momma, it was a disrespectful name; it was . . .

RUBY: I mean his difficulty.

EVELYN: (*Pause*) Well, everything changed after me. Just imagine that with me there wasn't any difficulty any more. Old Solly was a new man.

RUBY: You made a new man of him.

EVELYN: Or, like he was like a man for the first time.

RUBY: Oh. (*Beat*) How did you manage . . .

EVELYN: So in a manner of speaking, I was his first.

RUBY: My . . .

EVELYN: It was like magic.

RUBY: It was like a fairy tale.

EVELYN: Some of the girls said something very similar to that, but they were being vindictive. It's a cut-throat business.

RUBY: It was like Cinderella.

EVELYN: Only different. That's what they said. The Grapefruit King . . .

RUBY: And Juliet.

EVELYN: (*Pause, dreamily drinks coffee*) In fifty-two years you haven't learned to make coffee.

RUBY: Thirty-seven.

(*Pause*)

EVELYN: (*Smelling the air*) What did you call that stuff?

RUBY: It's thyme. There was a bunch of different herbs, but now it's just thyme. It sort of took over. We got a favorable climate for it.

EVELYN: Can't you get rid of it?

RUBY: I would, only it reminds me. *Thymus vulgaris.* That's what they call it over in Latin.

EVELYN: Where?

RUBY: You know, like that language in church. It's name in the Latin language is *Thymus vulgaris*. I mean I didn't know . . . José told me. It just means thyme. Common thyme, like you cook with.

EVELYN: I think I'm scared to call Ed and Nora.

RUBY: Do you know their number?

EVELYN: Oh, sure. . . I remember things . . . Solly never does. He's got business worries something fierce. (*Dialing slowly*) What does it matter? When I saw you I knew what it was. It was like the whole Cinderella didn't happen. Like the whole upward mobility didn't happen . . . He wanted you to come visit with us. I told him how wonderful you was. Wouldn't that be nice? With a garden and a swimming pool and maids?

RUBY: Maids?

EVELYN: Everybody I know now has maids, Momma. Ed and Nora's got three or four. Solly's got six or eight. It's funny, you think you won't know how to act. You think all that help is just gonna get in your way, but after a few minutes it's no different than a waitress bringing you coffee. (*On the phone*) Hello? (*To Ruby*) This is one now. (*Phone*) Is Nora there? This is Evie. (*To Ruby*) See? She's going to get her. They do their thing and you do . . . (*Phone*) Hi, honey. (*To Ruby*) Hold my hand. (*Phone*) Oh, yeah—she was here, just like always. She was workin' in the herb garden. (*Beat*) He hasn't.

RUBY: He hasn't?

EVELYN: And you ain't heard?

RUBY: They ain't heard?

EVELYN: Well, we're here . . . having a cup of coffee. Why don't you jot down the number? Then you call if you hear. VAlley 6-84 . . . (*To Ruby*) What is that; is that a three or another eight?

RUBY: Let me get my glasses.

EVELYN: Well, it's your number—never mind, it's a three. (*On phone*) It's a three. Three-four. Yes, I imagine he got stuck in traffic. (*Aside*) My ass. (*On phone*) Well, we're having a nice visit. I haven't had a visit with Momma in a long time. Not in a long time, we ain't visited; that's true ain't it, Momma? Okay. Bye-bye. (*She hangs up*)

RUBY: I can't really swim anyway.

EVELYN: Neither can Sol. He's got it for his friends and business associates. That's what he's like . . . I expected you to notice something in the columns.

RUBY: I hardly had a chance to read them.

EVELYN: Well, it says, "Sol—Maidblest—Soretti"—that's the way they do it in the columns, they put the grapefruit name in the middle of his name. Maidblest is his grapefruit— and Miss Evelyn Blare . . .

RUBY: Maidblest is his grapefruit?

EVELYN: That's not what I'm trying to show you.

RUBY: I know Maidblest. They're a popular grapefruit.

EVELYN: Oh, Momma. Forty-two states. Out of a possible fifty.

RUBY: They're a good grapefruit.

EVELYN: He's very conscientious about them.

RUBY: Well, he ought to be.

EVELYN: But just look: It says "Miss Evelyn Blare."

RUBY: I thought you was usin' Chi-Chi.

EVELYN: All those other names Solly made me throw away. He said, just throw them all away.

RUBY: I thought some of them were catchy.

EVELYN: So did I, but he didn't want me catchy, he wanted me presentable.

RUBY: I always thought Evelyn was such a pretty name.

EVELYN: I wasn't gonna tell him my real name, but I fig- ured after the way we met, what was I gonna lie about.

RUBY: She used to come on the radio and play the violin. Evelyn and her magic violin.

EVELYN: We was gonna call you about the marriage, but I couldn't find your number in the book, so I wrote you a letter. Only you didn't get it.

RUBY: Well . . . (Sadly sheepish) you looked in the book under Ruby Bentley, didn't you? And when you wrote, you wrote to me under Ruby Bentley. Something addressed to the name of Bentley would not find me here no more.

EVELYN: Huh?

RUBY: Well . . . living here all by myself . . . time on my hands.

EVELYN: Momma!

RUBY: But, it wasn't no good. I was just foolin' myself. It wasn't real. I was livin' in a Cinderella world like you. But you should have seen how I fixed myself up. Every day. You wouldn't have known me.

EVELYN: What did he take?

RUBY: I didn't want to tell you, only I don't know how else to explain my heavy heart.

EVELYN: Momma, you ain't gonna ever have a heavy heart again.

RUBY: Honey, it broke this time. I'm too old for it. Promise you won't think bad if I tell you something.

EVELYN: What?

RUBY: I won't tell you if you're gonna think . . .

EVELYN: Momma, how could I think bad of you? Haven't I been to every one of your weddings and never been anywhere but on your side every time?

RUBY: He was nineteen.

EVELYN: Oh, God.

RUBY: He drove in on a motorbike and he took me by storm.

EVELYN: Oh, dear God.

RUBY: José Gonzales.

EVELYN: Oh, dear Jesus God.

RUBY.   He dreamed. He was a real dreamer. You should have heard what this place was supposed to look like. We was gonna have a fountain—not for drinking, just to look at. He was such a worker. He planted tomatoes and herbs and grapevines and all kinds of Italian things. Only they never came up, and he drove off.

EVELYN: Momma, your whole life since I've known you has just been one sad story after another.

RUBY: He liked my golden hair. Since he left, I've just not had energy to do for myself. He wore me out. He just took all my energy with him when he left. This year I've just sat around.

EVELYN: What else did he take?

RUBY: He wasn't like those others, Evelyn. Honey, he spoke English better than me. But the thyme is the only thing that reminds me.

EVELYN: Momma, as far as I'm concerned, I've come here none too soon. You don't want to let yourself go. You have to have a grip on yourself. That's the thing we've always had is a grip on ourselves.

RUBY: I have, always till now. We sent out announcements of our wedding. I didn't even do that with my first. My first and me just run off. My sailor Willy and me run off and eloped the day before he shipped out. Then he got himself killed at sea.

EVELYN: He didn't get himself killed at sea.

RUBY: Honey, even if you slip off the deck while you're swabbin' it down, it's being killed at sea. I've always thought they shouldn't have those slippery soapsuds on deck. You'd think with all the chemicals they got, they'd invent something less hazardous. After Willy I met your daddy and we didn't let anybody know.

EVELYN: I'd hope not.

RUBY: I don't want you to be bitter about your daddy, Evelyn. I've never thought he abandoned us.

EVELYN: I know you ain't.

RUBY: He used to drink so bad, and he had such trouble finding the house, I've always thought that one night he just didn't find it.

EVELYN: I know you have.

RUBY: Out of all of them, I liked José the best.

EVELYN: José Gonzales, Jesus God.

RUBY: He dreamed. And I always had a fondness for Otto.

EVELYN: I don't remember no . . .

RUBY: You know Otto. The gambler. You was just little. I had a fondness for Otto because he had a twinkle in his eye. I mean, it wasn't for me, it was for blackjack, but it was a twinkle. (*Pause*) José and me couldn't send you an announcement about the marriage because we didn't know where you was living. And I wanted you there real bad.

EVELYN: I've just been terrible to you this last two years, ain't I? We ain't had no time together in too long.

RUBY: Not since you growed up. But you was such a nice little girl. That's how I know your heart, because I know how nice you was.

EVELYN: I know. (*Comes to a decision*) Can I be perfectly honest, Momma?

RUBY: Honey, your momma isn't strong. She can't take criticism the way she used to.

EVELYN: No, this is perfectly honest about me. See, Solly didn't show up and you didn't show up and I said I'd go looking for you. Momma, I got into that air-conditioned taxicab, with the windows rolled up, and pulled away from Ed and Nora's house, and the last thing I'd expected happened to me. It was like a huge weight was being lifted off my body.

RUBY: How big a man is he?

EVELYN: It was like my whole body was just sayin': Oh, thank God, I'm not gonna have to go through with it.

RUBY: I don't think that means anything. I think that's just butterflies. I get them every time.

EVELYN: He is big, actually.

RUBY: Oh.

EVELYN: I mean, he ain't tall, but . . .

RUBY: But he's big. But he's nice, though.

EVELYN: Oh, he gets nice sometimes . . . I guess . . .

RUBY: Is it the money? Maybe you ain't used to having money.

EVELYN: Oh, no, Momma, it's never quite the money; it's more like what I gotta do to get it.

RUBY: Solly sounds like a generous person. That's important, honey.

EVELYN: Oh . . . no. I don't think really generous people make millions of dollars. They ain't like us, Momma.

(*The cop returns, rather bounding onto the platform. He has unbuttoned his shirt to the waist*)

COP: Excuse me, ladies.

RUBY: Oh, my goodness.

EVELYN: Oh, good grief.

COP: Just passing back through. See, I've been feeling pretty bad. I think I projected a misleading impression and it's been troubling me. See, I think I was kinda soft on the outside and hard on the inside.

RUBY: I don't see anything wrong with that, do you?

EVELYN: Momma.

COP: But, see, the ticket is to be kinda tough on the outside, and kinda marshmallowy on the inside, if you follow me. I think that covers a wide range. See, that's good for, say, army personnel. That's good for cowboys—now, I don't want to say that I've actually ridden a horse, but I have a natural athletic ability.

RUBY: I bet you have.

EVELYN: Momma.

RUBY: And I think he'd make a very lovely football player on the television.

COP: Now, see, there it fits again. They're tough outside and kinda puddin'y on the inside.

RUBY: I know, like when their wife has her miscarriage.

COP: I'd just fold up.

RUBY: Or when their best buddy comes down with one of those terminal things they're always havin'.

COP: Oh, lord, Miss, see, I'd just crumble. I mean, I wouldn't crack.

RUBY: I know, but you'd crumble.

EVELYN: Momma.

RUBY: Have you had any luck with trying to fulfill your appointed duty?

EVELYN: Momma!

COP: What? Oh, well, to tell you the truth, I haven't done too well on that. See nobody in this trailer park seems to know anybody else in this trailer park. And I was trying to concentrate on being kinda—soft, you know—

RUBY: On the inside.

COP: Yeah, and I'm afraid I didn't get too far. They mostly shut the door in my face.

EVELYN: Well, anytime.

COP: See, I thought I'd come on all tough, you know. Duty first.

RUBY: But that wouldn't fool nobody. They could see the real marshmallow that you was hiding.

COP: Right.

EVELYN: Momma.

COP: And they'd say: Yes, this is the Bentley trailer, and then I'd sit down and say: I bring you good tidings of great joy.

RUBY: Which shall be to all . . .

EVELYN: Hold it. Hold it. Whatta you mean? You got a message?

RUBY: Oh, my goodness, why didn't you say that?

COP: Yes, ma'm, somebody called the highway patrol with a message for a Mrs. Bentley, female, Caucasian, about sixty.

RUBY: Sixty?

EVELYN: Well, even though this isn't the Bentley uh—residence, and even though we don't know the party of whom you seek . . .

RUBY: But, honey, if it's good, then . . .

EVELYN: Foxy, Momma, I've seen it a hundred times.

RUBY: Not this sweet young . . .

EVELYN: Every step of the way.

RUBY: Such a nice honest chest.

EVELYN: Cool it, Momma.

RUBY: Breezed in on a motorcycle.

EVELYN: That's what I mean. (*To cop*) Even though we're not the party of whom you seek, should we have been such a party, what message of great joy would you have imparted?

COP: Oh. Well, ma'm, I'm sorry, but that would come under official, private police department duty and couldn't be divulged.

RUBY: You could maybe pretend . . . I'll bet you could do that.

COP: No, ma'm, I'm afraid that . . .

EVELYN: What Momma is sayin' is we wouldn't want you to blow your big scene.

COP: Oh! Oh, yeah. Oh, boy. Well, it—under the right circumstances—it would go something like . . . (*Thinks for a very long time. Finally*) I'll tell you, I'll go home and work on it and come back tomorrow.

RUBY: Come on, just whatever comes to your mind.

EVELYN: Just spit it out.

COP: I'd feel more comfortable if . . .

EVELYN: Spit while the iron's hot.

COP: See, I just wish I had a little more time, 'cause how I do on this is very important to me. I mean, I'm not gettin' any younger.

EVELYN: I've aged ten years since you come in.

COP: Well, it would go something like: Mister Solly said that we was to turn over every stone looking for this Mrs. Rose . . .

RUBY: Ruby.

EVELYN: Momma.

COP: Thank you, Mrs. Ruby Bentley, 'cause that party was his precious fiancée's mother.

EVELYN: That's lovely, isn't that lovely. That has great human warmth and hope.

RUBY: Under every stone?

COP: And to tell her if she heard from her lovely and talented daughter, that he had lost the address of his best friend in the world and couldn't find the street, and that he would be waiting at Schwab's drugstore all night, which he is sure he can find.

RUBY: Oh, honey. It's all come true. It's the answer to an unspoken prayer.

EVELYN: Did you hear? Is all right with the world? Momma, not once did I doubt. Not in my heart of hearts.

COP: Excuse me, could I run that through again?

EVELYN: Honey, it was fine . . .

COP: It's important to get it right, I'm not getting any . . .

EVELYN: We know, honey—you go home like you planned and you work on it.

COP: I'd feel much more comfortable doing that. I think the important thing is to relax.

RUBY: In almost everything you do.

COP: Is eight o'clock tomorrow morning too early?

EVELYN: I think you're going to make something really marvelous out of this.

COP: It's not big; you know, it isn't much—it shouldn't be bigger than the circumstances warrant, if you . . .

EVELYN: You work on it, we'll let you know.

COP: (*Being nudged out*) Simple, you know, but effective. (*Falls off platform*)

EVELYN: That's it; that's the ticket.

COP: Warm, you know, but simple and direct.

EVELYN: First thing tomorrow.

COP: I appreciate it, I do. Thank you. (*Exits*)

(*Ruby and Evelyn sit*)

RUBY: (*After a pause. Beaming*) My little baby. On her wedding day. I never thought I'd see it.

EVELYN: I know. He just couldn't find the house. See, usually he has a chauffeur for that, but we're going on our honeymoon today.

RUBY: Sure she is. My little baby on her honeymoon.

EVELYN: He just couldn't find the house.

RUBY: Just like your daddy. (*Pause. Evelyn is staring off. She lights a cigarette, sighs, frowning*) What's wrong, honey? (*Pause*) Are the butterflies back again? (*Pause*) Did you feel the weight again?

EVELYN: Oh . . . kinda.

RUBY: Sometimes good things when they really come are kinda a letdown, I know. But think of your future.

EVELYN: Ummm.

RUBY: Do you love him? (*Pause*) You love him, don't you?

EVELYN: Oh, it's just . . . I wouldn't want to let you down or anything. I mean the swimming pool and never having to turn your hand. But, Momma, I was beginning to feel so . . . comfortable, here with you.

RUBY: I was too. It was nice.

EVELYN: I don't know when the last time it was that I was comfortable. I mean, I can't spread out in here like I'd like and I'm really beginning to feel choked up on that weed, but in spite of that . . .

RUBY: We ain't had much time.

EVELYN: Not here.

RUBY: I know.

EVELYN: We ought to get you away from here.

RUBY: I know.

EVELYN: So maybe the two of us should go somewhere.

RUBY: That would be nice. I was kinda beginning to imagine it.

EVELYN: We ain't had no time at all, like we should.

RUBY: What do you want to do, honey?

EVELYN: Well . . . (*A wondering pause*) . . . uh . . . (*Off*) Could I have a spot? I'd like one of your pale amber spots. (*The lights fade to an amber spot on her*)

RUBY: That's just amazing.

EVELYN: Momma, I told you, carte blanche. (*To the audience*) You see, it's all a question of priorities. Like life is basically a question of priorities. Like that's a big surprise, but that kid said, "I'm not getting any younger," and that changed everything. That just went right through me. I mean, he can say that and mean one thing, but to me it hit something else. It hit like: What are those things that you're gonna wish you'd done, Evelyn? Or like—see, marrying Solly is a possible. But where am I? And what are the things that . . . (*To off*) Could we get this wide enough for Momma? (*To Ruby*) Scoot in. You okay? (*To audience*) Now, see, this is gonna come as no earth-shattering revelation, but there are two kinds of people in the world. Everything you read, anyone you talk to knows that. In Sunday school we learned there was the alive and the dead.

RUBY: Quick and the dead. Amen.

(*All these responses, quiet echoes, as in church*)

EVELYN: That's the users and the used. Or as Solly says, him being in the produce business, he thinks in food, Solly says there's the eaters and the eatens. And it doesn't take bifocals or microscopes to see that Momma and me are mainly both eatens.

RUBY: Eatens, that's right.

EVELYN: Which is alright. . .

RUBY: It's alright.

EVELYN: I mean, the eaters gotta have something to eat or everybody would be up the creek.

RUBY: Without a paddle.

EVELYN: But once in a while an eaten has gotta get away and store up. 'Cause it takes a lot of fortitude being an eaten.

RUBY: Once in a while the eatens got to take a break.

EVELYN: So what is it that I need and Momma needs? Well, really, not much. There's a little place I know on the ocean, with a breeze and the sun . . . that'd be enough.

RUBY: That'd be enough.

EVELYN: A while there, getting to re-know the things we knew. Just the two of us.

RUBY: Would you like that? I think I'd like that.

EVELYN: Just to draw a little strength.

RUBY: Take a little time off.

EVELYN: That's what I want.

RUBY: So now we know. That's gonna be nice.

EVELYN: It is.

RUBY: What's wrong, honey?

(*Pause*)

EVELYN: Oh, Jesus. I feel just rotten, 'cause I guess this is the end, and I really can't abide ends. Like they say someone was okay, but he came to a bad end. Well, I'm here to tell you as far as I'm concerned, all ends are bad. And we all come to a bad end. And of course, finding Momma here, I say: Oh, that's terrible, I'll take her out of here. And that damned kid says: I'm not getting any younger, and you know that there ain't no out of here. 'Cause past the two kinds of people, past the eaters and the eatens, it's all just meat, it's all just one kind of people and every man-jack of them comin' to a bad end.

RUBY: Oh, sure.

EVELYN: And every man-jack of 'em living here. With no real getting out of here. (*Blows her nose. To Ruby*) Did you want to say something?

RUBY: If that place is on the ocean, I hope there's a pool, 'cause I hate gettin' my hair wet.

EVELYN: You can't swim, I thought.

RUBY: Well, no, but it'd be cooling to splash around a bit. That'd be nice. But, honey, even though one man-jack might be coming to a bad end, some other man-jack might be just in the middle of a real interesting beginning, and that man-jack don't need to be reminded he'll be coming to a bad end.

EVELYN: I know.

RUBY: You think about somebody else and it kinda takes your mind off yourself.

EVELYN: You ready to go now?

RUBY: I think I'd like that. (*To off*) Could we have our theme song again?

EVELYN: (*To off*) And could we have like a slow fade out? (*The lights begin to fade*)

RUBY: Oh. That's just amazing.

EVELYN: Momma, I told you, anything you want.

(*The lights are out*)

David Edgar

BALL BOYS

David Edgar

The most spectacular event of the 1981–82 Broadway season was an eight-and-one-half-hour adaptation of Charles Dickens's *Nicholas Nickleby.* After its successful run at London's Aldwych Theatre, the production was imported to New York with thirty-nine members of Britain's Royal Shakespeare Company playing 150 characters. Under the direction of Trevor Nunn and John Caird, the company filled the Plymouth Theatre with the swirling life and social conscience of Dickens's 19th century England.

The adaptor of this theatrical extravaganza was David Edgar, who throughout his playwriting career has exhibited strong social and political interests. His short play, *Ball Boys,* is another splendid example of these concerns. (For the author's thoughts on these themes, see the *Note* at the end of the play.) As the ball boys Rupert and One-Eye plan the murder of tennis player Sven, their motives bounce between the courts of personal and social differences, philosophical and ethical rationalizations. And though they perceive themselves as deprived in comparison to the privileged Sven, the ball boys question their own morality in attempting to even the social score. This script is one of five written by Mr. Edgar under the collective title *Blood Sports*—all dealing with sports and sportsmen.

Born in Birmingham, England, in 1948, David Edgar became familiar with the performing arts at an early age, for his father was a television producer, and his mother a former radio announcer and actress. While attending Oundle public school, David began developing his own artistic expression by editing the school poetry magazine, designing for *Henry IV, Part One* and *The Fire Raisers,* and playing Miss Prism in *The Importance of Being Earnest.*

Though Mr. Edgar studied drama at Manchester University (1966–69) and wrote one play, *The Author,* during that time, his major interests were political and journalistic. He became editor of the student newspaper and chairperson of the university's Socialist Society.

From 1969–72 he worked as a journalist on the *Bradford Telegraph* and *Argus,* specializing in educational affairs and theatre. Several of his plays written during this time were exhibited in the Edinburgh Festival.

Leaving journalism in 1972 for a full-time career as a playwright, Mr. Edgar wrote numerous plays for British touring groups and worked with students at Leeds and Bingley College of Education. He was appointed Thames Television Resident playwright at Birmingham Repertory Theatre in 1974, and since 1975 he has taught playwriting at Birmingham University.

Destiny, his play concerning British fascism, presented in 1976 by the Royal Shakespeare Company at the Other Place theatre in Stratford, received the Arts Council's John Whiting award. After *Destiny* was transferred to the Aldwych Theatre in 1977, Mr. Edgar became involved in anti-fascist and anti-racist organizations. This activity ultimately led to his election to the Council of the Institute of Race Relations. *Destiny* was produced by BBC Television in 1978.

Other recent productions include *Mary Barnes* (1978), adapted from *Mary Barnes—Two Accounts of a Journey through Madness* by Mary Barnes and Dr. Joseph Berke, first presented at the Birmingham Rep and later transferred to the Royal Court; and *Jail Diary*, produced in New York at the Manhattan Theatre Club, where Mr. Edgar was Resident Writer in 1979.

Ball Boys, directed by its author, was first presented at the Birmingham Arts Lab in July 1975 and revived a year later at the Bush Theatre in London, directed by Dusty Hughes. The casts were:

	(*Birmingham*)	(*London*)
ONE-EYE	Alan Hulse	Derrick O'Connor
RUPERT	John Dowie	Stephen Bill
SVEN	Alan Hawkridge	Simon Stokes

The author dedicates his play: To Alan.

Characters:

SVEN

RUPERT

ONE-EYE

As the audience comes in, in a spot lies the hideously mangled body of a blond tennis player, Sven. He has been strangled with catgut. Two chairs lie near him. On a tape, we hear his voice. If necessary, the speech is repeated.

SVEN'S VOICE: Und I remember, dat vinter. Vid Anya. Un du beach. Und it ist cold. Und I am sayink, for our circulation, ve must haf a svim. Und Anya ist agreeing. Und so ve are takking all our clothes uff and runnink into du icy vaters. Und it is being such gud fun.

But all I am seeink, as ve are runnink and svimmink, ist du blud.

Und I remember, too, ven I am beink trapped un du mountain rescue hut vid Lotje. Und it ist ver cold. Und ve are beink trapped till mornink ven du rescuers are cummink vid du skis und snoeshoes und du dogs vid du Corvoisier. Und to tak our minds uff it ve are takking all our clothes uff und haffing lots uf fun.

Blud. Blud. All I am seeink ist du blud.

Und I am rememberink too my first time vid Helga. Ufter our first sauna. Out uf du sauna on to du ice-pack ve are runnink. Ver ver ver cold. Beatink our nakkid buddies vid du branches und du stickies vrom du black trees. Runnink across du ice-pack. Nakkid. Buildink du snowmen und trowink du snowballs on each udders nakkid buddies. O vat fun we haf.

Du blud.

Und den I see him. Du man. He ist sittink on du treestump. Vid a dark cloak und a vite face und a symbolic expression. He ist axing me to sit. Und I am sittink. Und he is axing me, do I know who he is? Und I am saying, da, I know who he ist. Und I am axing him, ven it must be. Und he is sayink, it must be ven it must be. Und he ist axink me vetter to vile avay du time I fancy a qvik rubber. Und I am sayink, bit ve haf no pack. Und he ist sayink, I haf a pack. Und I am sayink, ve cannot play because ve are only two und who ist to be dummy. Und he ist sayink, you're du dummy, dummy. So ve are playink. O, Anya.

Und he ist dealink. Und I am pickink up my hand. Und I am strung in Hearts. Bit howiffer strung I am, he ist strunger. Und I am void in Clubs. Bit howiffer void I am, he ist voider. O, Lotje Und he ist biddink. Und he ist sayink five Spades. Und I am sayink double, for I haf twenty points. Und he ist sayink redouble. Und I am realisink dat haffing twenty points ist no great comfort ven you're playink Contract Bridge vid du pale ferryman on du ice. O, Helga.

Und he ist openink into my Clubs and I am thinkink dat I am trompink, bit I am not trompink for you cunnot be trompink ven you're playink double-suspension vid du grim reaper und anythink you do he vill just lead into your veak diamonds. Und so I am givink him du trick.

Und du ice-pack. Und du black pine-trees. Und I am seeink Anya und Lotje und Helga not to mention Marja and Ingrid and Olga dancing across du ice-pack. Und dey are dancink vid du man vid du dark cloak. Und I am owink him many, many krona. Und du blud. Du blud.

Und I revoke.

Und it ist du end.

Blackout

A locker room. Enter Rupert with a chair. He is a small boy, played by an actor, wearing shorts and a two-tone shirt. He looks around, places the chair carefully. Exit. He re-enters with another chair, places it about ten feet from the other chair. He takes a roll of catgut from his pocket and ties a piece between the two chairs. He goes out and re-enters with a tennis ball. He places it on the floor, below the centre of the line. He goes and crouches by one of the chairs. A moment. Then he runs across, still at the crouch, picks up the ball, and to the other chair. We realise he is a ball-boy. Rupert sets the ball centre again, and runs across picking it up. He does this a couple of times—once he misses—before One-Eye enters. One-Eye is another, two-eyed, ball-boy. He watches Rupert. Rupert is concentrating too hard to notice One-Eye. One-Eye sits on one of the chairs and sticks his leg out. Rupert runs past and trips over. Pause.

RUPERT: Hallo, One-Eye.
ONE-EYE: Hallo, Rupert.

(*Pause*)

RUPERT: That was an unfriendly thing to do, One-Eye.

ONE-EYE: It was meant to be, Rupert.

(*Pause*)

RUPERT: Why?

ONE-EYE: I'm working out my pique, Rupert. Unable to work it out on those who caused it, they being stronger and more powerful than I, I work it out on the only available person who is weaker and less powerful. In this case, you.

RUPERT: Oh. Right.

(*Pause, Rupert stands. He goes to one of the chairs, crouches, runs through, picking up the ball. Replaces the ball. Looks at One-Eye, grins nervously*)

ONE-EYE: Oh, by the way, Rupert.

RUPERT: Yes, One-Eye?

ONE-EYE: One question I wanted to ask. Been on my mind. Ever since I came in. Employing my thoughts, in fact, before I resolved to catharcise my ire on your person. This query. I wished to put.

RUPERT: Yes, One-Eye?

ONE-EYE: What the fuck you playing at, old son?

RUPERT: I was. I was practising.

ONE-EYE: Practising.

RUPERT: That's right. The net-run.

ONE-EYE: The net-run.

RUPERT: That's right.

ONE-EYE: Why, Rupert? (*Pause. Rupert shrugs. One-Eye, pleasantly*) Why, Rupert, old chum.

RUPERT: (*Coyly*) Well, you know . . .

ONE-EYE: Yes. I think I do. (*Rupert grins sheepishly*) You were practising because it's getting close. (*Rupert grins sheepishly*) We're into the fourth round. (*Rupert grins sheepishly*) So you are practising. I understand.

RUPERT: That's good, One-Eye.

ONE-EYE: So that you, Rupert, can remove a spent half-lob from before the net so fast that blink you'd miss it.

RUPERT: That's right, One-Eye.

ONE-EYE: So that you, Rupert, can clear a volley drop-shot from the park before it hits the ground.

RUPERT: I hope so, One-Eye.

ONE-EYE: So that when, on Ladies' Semi-Final day, as is traditional, Mr. Dan Maskell has a word of praise for all the sterling labours of the ball-boys, there you'll be, in close-up, grinning vacuously into number three camera, beamed into seven million homes.

(*Pause*)

RUPERT: You've hit the spot there, One-Eye.

ONE-EYE: *Why?*

RUPERT: Why what?

ONE-EYE: Why do you wish thus to ascend fame's ladder, Rupert?

RUPERT: 'Cos it's there, One-Eye?

ONE-EYE: Not for your mother, surely. Not so she can sit before her nineteen-inch suffused with the miasma of maternal pride. (*Pause*) Her having dumped you. At two months. On the Central Line. Somewhere between Leytonstone and Ongar. (*Pause*) Before, so rumour has it, flinging herself amid the gungy waters of the Serpentine.

(*Pause*)

RUPERT: Can I please carry on now, One-Eye?

ONE-EYE: If you like. You've no chance, anyway.

RUPERT: Why not?

ONE-EYE: 'Cos we all know who it will be.

RUPERT: We do?

ONE-EYE: It will be he. The boy most likely to. He. The most handsome, and most charming, and most cute of all the ball-boys. Nicky Nightlight it will be, in tight-shot, looking as if he's got half a pound of solid butter in his cheek. He. He. He. Not you.

(*Pause*)

RUPERT: Why the aggro, One-Eye.

ONE-EYE: *I am piqued, Rupert.*

(*Pause*)

RUPERT: Why?

ONE-EYE: Didn't I tell you?

RUPERT: No.

ONE-EYE: I got sent off.

(*Pause*)

RUPERT: You can't get sent off, One-Eye. For one, people don't get sent off in tennis, and, for two, you're a ball-boy.

ONE-EYE: Then I've set a precedent. For off is the direction in which, quite incontrovertibly, I was sent.

(*Pause*)

RUPERT: Why?

ONE-EYE: Right. (*He picks up the ball on the floor, takes another from his pocket, hands both to Rupert*) You are me. This chair (*He moves one of the chairs to centre*) is the centre-line judge. This chair (*He indicates the other chair*) is Nicholas Nightlight. And I—am Sven Svensson, the flying Finn, the blond bombshell, he of the swinging service and the vicious forehand volley-drop, I am he. O.K.?

RUPERT: O.K.

ONE-EYE: Picture the scene. I—that's you—have not had a good day. For a start, on Court No. Two, I was positioned behind old Farty Frobisher, the incontinent net-cord judge. The worst position in all of Surrey, on a hot day, humid, thunderous. Knelt right behind that powerhouse of wind. And so, not good. My temper not improved by Madcap Mustovna, the bomber of Bulgaria, who, having beaten some poor sad sod in straight sets, flings wide his racket, gesturing his victory, thrilling the crowd and catching me a nasty blow on the right temple. With his Latin gesture. In round four. I ask you. So. Not good. And then, on Court No. One, my woes going up in the world, the umpire issues his umperial command.

RUPERT: New balls please, boys.

ONE-EYE: The same. So off we scurry, touching our forelocks, plunging our puddies into the refrigerated container, that to preserve the bounce, risking frostbite, tingling the fingers, all keen and in my case, despite my throbbing temple, and what then?

RUPERT: What then?

ONE-EYE: Hurry up now, boys, he says.

RUPERT: They always say that. If they're in shot. Always—

ONE-EYE: *Not at me they don't!*

RUPERT: No, not at you. (*Pause*) That's why you got sent off, then, One-Eye?

ONE-EYE: No, that is the preamble. This that follows is the action. You are me. That is Nick Nightlight. I the sainted Sven. My coming. Paint the scene in words.

(*Exit One-Eye*)

RUPERT: The Centre Court. The crowd is hushed. From face to face we pan. From dowager to dolly, matron to maiden, virago to virgin. Clutching their tea, unsipped, their strawberries untasted. All of them, waiting. Looking. Sharp with expectation. All's prepared. The seat umperial. Well stocked. The paper cups are counted, and the lemon barley water's chilled. The net, the peace-line, at its centre, hung precisely, to a millimetre. The ambulances ready. O, St. John, thou shouldst be living at this hour. The barbed-wire, slung around the gleaming greensward. Groundsmen, in their helmets, with their perspex shields, run nervous fingers up and down their truncheons. Savage hounds perambulate. And, then. Who knows, who first, the whisper. "He's coming." Whispers. "O, he's coming. Coming. Coming." Grows to a chant. "He's coming. Coming. Coming." First, but the young, the pre-pubescent. Then the older join. Spring to November. "O he's coming. Coming. Coming." Sound like rushing water, or the music of the spheres. One young Bacchante faints. Another screams. The groundsmen flex. "He's coming. Coming. Coming." Then, he comes. (*Enter One-Eye with a racket*) Stands. Holds up his racket, as if for blessing. For a moment, but a moment that's eternal, he stands, and nothing moves. And then the charge. Wild, screaming, like the horses of Diomedes that fed on human flesh, first, young and luscious virgins break across the wire, in platform heels, their imprint on the sacred turf, then others through the riot lines, young mothers, screaming, sturdy matrons, then the groupie grannies too, rush like Niagara across the turf, the sacred turf, torn flesh, blood on the sacred turf, now two millennia of civilisation, culminating, as it does, in individual combat on a Surrey afternoon, up-ended, wracked, by this outpouring of a primal energy, from the dark places, from the darkest depths, a passion uncontrolled, that men have lost the word for, the word is worship. . . . Then, destroyed. Heads beaten. Broken souls. The bodies cleared. The acolytes pressed back. The turf is naked. Once again. A whimper. Silence. Mystery. The sacrifice is over. The God has spoken. Being, and becoming, one, that moment. Sven is now the Universe. The Universe is Sven.

(*Pause*)

ONE-EYE: Right, I'm Sven, that's Nicholas, and you're me. (*He gives Rupert two balls*) My service. (*Serves, with imaginary ball. Ventriloquises*) Out! (*He serves again*) An ace. On second serve. Fifteen-love. (*He turns to Rupert, who is waiting to throw him a ball. Rupert is just about to throw, when One-Eye turns to the chair representing Nick Nightlight, and, in mime, accepts an imaginary ball from him. Serves. Ventriloquises*) Net! (*Different voice*)

First service. (*Serves again. Takes the return*) A half-lob kills the return. It's thirty-love. (*The same routine, turning to Rupert, who's about to throw, when One-Eye turns away, accepting the ball from the other ball-boy. Rupert getting tetchy, One-Eye serves, then misses the return*) I give away a point. For charity. Thirty-fifteen. (*He serves with his other ball. Ventriloquises*) OUT! (*Same routine. Rupert getting very tetchy*) Ace. Forty-fifteen. (*Same routine with Rupert, but this time, he leaves it long enough for Rupert to throw the ball. One-Eye has turned, takes a ball from the imaginary ball-boy, turns back, sees the ball on the ground in front of him*) UND VORT IST DA?

RUPERT: My God.

ONE-EYE: He says, "Und vort ist da?"

RUPERT: My Christ.

ONE-EYE: He says. To me. "Und vort, boya, vort ist da?"

RUPERT: My—mother.

ONE-EYE: "Da? Unt dur grounda, sucred turfa, da?"

(*Pause*)

RUPERT: What you do One-Eye?

ONE-EYE: We swap. (*They swap places. One-Eye giving Rupert the racket*) Go on. Again.

RUPERT: (*Nervously*) "And—wart—is—dar?"

(*One-Eye to Rupert, takes his racket, holds it up, to the crowd, and breaks it across his knee. Presenting the pieces back to Rupert*)

ONE-EYE: Da.

RUPERT: O my God.

ONE-EYE: (*Quickly, out front*) Sven Svensson. Superstar. His habits. Superstitions. Like the taking of one racket, one alone, on to the court.

RUPERT: O my Christ.

ONE-EYE: As in the famous final, Forrest Hills, he won the fifth set, twenty-seven twenty-five, with just four strings intact. The habits, superstitions of Sven Svensson.

RUPERT: O my—mother.

ONE-EYE: So I got sent off.

(*He sits, takes off his shoes and socks, twiddles his toes, during*)

RUPERT: I can understand your pique, now. Crystal clear, your ire now is.

ONE-EYE: That's good.

RUPERT: Even the taking out of it on me. Quite comprehensible.

ONE-EYE: That's fine.

RUPERT: Unable, as you said, to visit your displeasure on the guilty, you being so much smaller, weaker, yes. Quite clear, that is.

ONE-EYE: That's great.

RUPERT: Unwilling to make the leap, from individual oppression to collective strength, unable to build links, between your suffering and the suffering of others, forge a chain that's stronger than its individual parts, unhappy with the old things but unaware of the possibility of change, you find a bogeyman, a scapegoat, any but the real source of exploitation, on to whose shoulders you lay all your pain, I understand.

ONE-EYE: You what?

RUPERT: I understand.

ONE-EYE: What are you talking about?

(*Pause*)

RUPERT: Been reading.

ONE-EYE: What?

RUPERT: Marx. The theses on Feuerbach.

ONE-EYE: You who?

RUPERT: Ludwig.

ONE-EYE: Beethoven.

RUPERT: No, Feuerbach. Exponent of the classical tradition in German materialist philosophy.

ONE-EYE: I see.

RUPERT: The argument of Marx, in his *Theses on Feuerbach*, this Ludwig Feuerbach, published in eighteen-forty-five, a classic text though not in any sense traditional, his argument is this—that the chief defect of all hitherto existing materialism is that the thing, reality, is conceived only in the form of the object, or of contemplation, but not as human sensuous activity, practice, not subjectively. Or so he says.

ONE-EYE: Go on, Rupert.

RUPERT: The dispute, Marx takes the view, over the reality or nonreality of thinking which is isolated from practice is a purely scholastic question.

ONE-EYE: Continue, Rupert.

RUPERT: The materialistic doctrine, he continues, that men are products of circumstances and upbringing, and that, therefore, changed men are products of changed upbringing, forgets that it is men that change circumstances and that the educator himself needs educating.

ONE-EYE: I think I begin to get your drift, Rupert.

RUPERT: Social life is practical, he says. All mysteries which mislead theory to mysticism find their rational solution in human practice and in the comprehension of this practice.

ONE-EYE: So?

RUPERT: The philosophers have only interpreted the world, thus does the sage conclude: the point, however, is to change it.

(*Pause*)

ONE-EYE: How?

(*Pause*)

RUPERT: He doesn't say.

ONE-EYE: Oh?

RUPERT: No.

ONE-EYE: He doesn't say. (*Pause*) Sven will be still out there, Rupert. His famous grip, on which chapters have been written and from which Mr. Maskell gets a delicate frisson of delight, that grip performing yet another function, that of keeping his racket in one piece. Holding together that which is broken. Disguising contradiction. Papering the cracks. (*Pause*) He doesn't say.

RUPERT: Perhaps he does later. Other works. I haven't read.

ONE-EYE: Perhaps he does. (*Pause*) Why's your name Rupert?

RUPERT: Given me.

ONE-EYE: Of course. But with what reasoning.

RUPERT: (*Sits, enthusiastically*) Well, I suppose, fashions. Reflected, perhaps particularly, in naming orphans. Need to integrate them with the fashionable modes. To give them names, to mark their place. To follow trends. But certain trends. Trends of the ruling class. Not Putney names. Not names of the produce of a Chelsea bijou residence. Not Jude or Jason, Damian or Saul. Nor yet the firm and gritty names, the monosyllables, that grace the offspring of the West; the peasant-dressed, and civil-liberties-obsessed of Holland Park or Ladbroke Grove or Hammersmith, their names to conjure with, like Ned or Sam or Dan or Hank or Ben. Nor yet provincial names; good, north of Watford names; sound, honest, *Daily Mail*-type names, like Simon, Robin, Timothy or John. Nor yet West Country names, earth-friendly names, names of the issue of North Devon commune-makers, ethnic names, like Gethan, Jethro, Pedr, Rhys or Seth. (*Slight pause*) But upper order names. Names of the living dead. Names of the half-light, those who have outlived their usefulness but not their power, those who walk in limbo, with death's fingers in their hair. Like Charles. And St. John. Alexander. Algernon. And Rupert. Burke's peerage names. Hereditary names. And orphans' names.

(*Pause*)

ONE-EYE: Still there.

RUPERT: Who, there?

ONE-EYE: Sven. Still out there.

RUPERT: S'pose so.

ONE-EYE: Know so. Winning.

(*Pause*)

RUPERT: Why you called One-Eye, One-Eye?

ONE-EYE: Didn't I ever tell you?

RUPERT: No.

ONE-EYE: Do you know of the Weathermen?

RUPERT: You mean those nice men on the telly with the plastic charts, then, One-Eye?

ONE-EYE: No, Rupert.

RUPERT: Then I don't, no.

(*Slight pause*)

ONE-EYE: The Weathermen were an American group of urban guerillas who rejected the tactic of peaceful protest on the one hand, or the forging of links with the proletariat on the other, and instead resolved to create a revolutionary situation by individual acts of terror. They, being middle-class and of a literary bent, decided to choose their name as a reference, not to they of the isobars and V-shaped depressions over Iceland, but to a line in a song, the song in question being "Subterranean Homesick Blues" by B. Dylan, who had the advantage of being not only culturally contemporary but also art. At first they were tempted by the idea of calling themselves The Vandals, from the line, "the pump don't work, 'cos the vandals took the handle." But finally they settled on the Weathermen, taking their ref. from the line, "You don't need a weatherman to know which way the wind blows." For the irony.

(*Pause*)

RUPERT: Why you called One-Eye, One-Eye?

ONE-EYE: "The Ballad of a Thin Man." It tells the tale of a

man called Jones, who walks into the room, a pencil in his hand. At this point, he sees somebody naked, and enquires, who is that man. He tries so hard, but he can't understand, just what he will say when he gets home.

RUPERT: Why you called One-Eye, One-Eye?

ONE-EYE: A little later this gentleman, this Mr. Jones, hands in his ticket, and goes watch the geek, the precise meaning of which is obscure. This, geek, in any event, comes up to him, Mr. Jones that is, when he hears him speak, and says, how does it feel to be such a freak, whereupon he, Mr. Jones, says impossible, as he, the geek, hands him a bone.

RUPERT: Why you called One-Eye, One-Eye?

ONE-EYE: The lyric then provides us with some background on Mr. Jones. He's associated with professors, we are told, who have all liked his books. He's also been involved in criminological research, we gather, for with great lawyers he's discussed lepers and crooks. But his interests are wider, we are informed. He is a man with a keen interest in literature. He's been through, indeed, all Scott Fitzgerald's books, he's very well read, it's well known.

RUPERT: Why you called One-Eye, One-Eye?

ONE-EYE: Back at the plot, a new character, a sword-swallower, comes up to Mr. Jones, and for reasons which are not explained, kneels. He then, for whatever motive, crosses himself, and clicks his high heels. And then without further notice he asks how it feels. And says, in a ghoulish moment, here is your throat back, thanks for the loan.

RUPERT: Why you called One-Eye, One-Eye?

ONE-EYE: *You see a one-eyed midget shouting the word now. And you ask for what reason and he says how. And you say what does this mean and he screams back you're a cow. Give me some milk or else go home. And you know something is happening but you don't know what it is, do you, Mr. Jones?* (*Pause*) I do not recall my real name. For I was but a three-month old when my old man and his old dam were gallumphed by a bulldozer while resisting the demolition of their cosy old ancestral family shack. (*Slight pause*) Hence my dark thoughts and black imaginings. (*Slight pause*) Hence are you with me, Rupert.

RUPERT: With you where, One-Eye.

ONE-EYE: Are you going to do it?

RUPERT: Do what?

ONE-EYE: What we said.

RUPERT: What you said.

ONE-EYE: What I said. You going to do it?

RUPERT: What we—

ONE-EYE: Talked about.

RUPERT: I don't—

ONE-EYE: Well, Rupert?

RUPERT: Just don't know.

ONE-EYE: The point, point being, to change it.

RUPERT: Just don't know.

(*Pause*)

RUPERT: Why—quite the manner—you suggested— quite, such viciousness, quite—such a bloody way.

ONE-EYE: I saw *If* at an impressionable age.

RUPERT: *If?*

ONE-EYE: Film by Lindsay Anderson. Starring Malcolm MacDowell and Arthur Lowe. Culminated in a machine-gun massacre. The Ultimate Public School Horrorshow. Cornered the market for years. Hundreds of ex-public-school writers, wandering round, unable to write the story of their life, forced instead to make agitational propaganda chock full of unlikely ethnic references, or indulge in obscure fantasies in closed rooms in which the two plumbers who call in Act Two turn out to be the ego and the id.

(*Pause*)

RUPERT: Nick Nightlight went to public school. On a grant. The school had places for orphans, free places, to create a social mix. They're very keen on that, apparently, a social mix. A token prole he was, a token representative of the oppressed orders, an awful reminder of, what's underneath. (*Pause*) They treated him just the same, he said. Not toffee-nosed at all. Just because he came from a rotten foster-home, his foster-father beat him up, and his foster-mother beat him up, that didn't stop them treating him just like their mates. And beating him up. With all varieties of weaponry. Just like the others. (*Pause*) But forms go deep. Modes, etiquettes and rules, unwritten and unspoken. Nurtured like lawns, through generations. Know every rule, but cannot know the hidden ethos of the British ruling class. Their solidarity. Their law unto themselves. (*Pause*) Told, when he arrived, resist all sexual suggestiveness. So, when a pederastic advance was made, resisted. Strongly. Physically. (*Pause*) Head of the Fives Team. Captain of Rackets. Cock of Squash. His putative seducer. (*Pause*) Expelled. Unmiddle-class activities. Poor old Nick.

(*Pause*)

ONE-EYE: Well, that's all very interesting, Rupert, but I'm not convinced it's quite germane.

RUPERT: Germane to what?

ONE-EYE: The question. Of whether you are going to do it. (*Pause*) Let's play a game. While you decide.

RUPERT: What game?

ONE-EYE: Suggest.

RUPERT: Manual or intellectual?

ONE-EYE: Intellectual.

RUPERT: Darts?

ONE-EYE: No, not darts.

RUPERT: Not darts.

ONE-EYE: We will play Erudition.

(*Pause*)

RUPERT: Erudition.

ONE-EYE: Yes. (*To audience*) Erudition. Pure knowledge. No form, no logical construct, no maths. Just information. Know it or you don't.

RUPERT: I never liked this game.

ONE-EYE: Useful for those, as I, whose minds are like the sea, liquid, formless, facts floating like flotsam on the salty brine, unconnected with their purpose or original intent. You start.

RUPERT: Oh, architecture.

ONE-EYE: What's a spandrel?

RUPERT: Eh?

ONE-EYE: My go. Codenames.

RUPERT: What?

ONE-EYE: Codenames of operations. Military operations. As in Overlord.

RUPERT: (*Shrugs*) Overlord.

ONE-EYE: D-Day. Sealion.

RUPERT: Dunkirk?

ONE-EYE: Hitler's invasion of Britain.

RUPERT: Didn't happen!

ONE-EYE: Had a code. Three. Barbarossa.

RUPERT: What?

ONE-EYE: The same's invasion of the chilly wastes of Russia. Four. Gemstone.

RUPERT: Ah. The bugging of the Watergate Hotel.
ONE-EYE: Sod you.
RUPERT: One. My go.
ONE-EYE: Come on.
RUPERT: Um, er—
ONE-EYE: Come on.
RUPERT: Oh, assemblages.
ONE-EYE: Partridges.
RUPERT: A wing? A wing of partridges?
ONE-EYE: No, a covey. Five. Tennis.
RUPERT: What.
ONE-EYE: Tennis. Ask a question.
RUPERT: Why . . . ?
ONE-EYE: TENNIS. (*Pause*) You might ask, who. Did what. To whom. On a sunny. Afternoon. In June.
RUPERT: Don't like this game.
ONE-EYE: Darts, then.
RUPERT: You what?
ONE-EYE: Darts, then.
RUPERT: But, One-Eye—
ONE-EYE: (*Strides out*) DARTS. (*Re-enters with six darts*) Bull for start.
(*He throws, offstage. Pause. Rupert throws*)
RUPERT: I think, just slightly nearer, One-Eye.
ONE-EYE: Of course you're nearer. You got twenty-five. I missed the board. So—play.
RUPERT: You're sure?
ONE-EYE: So *PLAY*.
RUPERT: (*Nervously, as he throws*) Missed. Double-twenty, twenty, score two hundred and forty-one.
(*Gets his darts from off, returns. One-Eye throws*)
ONE-EYE: Single six. Missed the circle. Missed the board.
RUPERT: (*Throwing*) Double twenty, treble twenty, twenty, total one hundred and twenty-one.
ONE-EYE: (*Throwing*) Single ten, single six, missed the circle.
RUPERT: (*Throwing*) Double fifteen, eight—losing my touch now, One-Eye—
ONE-EYE: Play!
RUPERT: (*Throws*) Treble twenty, score left, twenty-three.
ONE-EYE: (*Throws*) Missed the circle, missed the board, missed the board.

RUPERT: Twenty. Leaving three.

ONE-EYE: One double one.

RUPERT: I never get this—

ONE-EYE: Play!

RUPERT: (*Throws*) One. Double one. I'm sorry, One-Eye, sorry—

ONE-EYE: Why?

RUPERT: I won.

ONE-EYE: Of course you won!

RUPERT: Perhaps I cheated.

ONE-EYE: Hm.

RUPERT: Perhaps you played to lose. (*Pause*) You know you're terrible at darts, One-Eye. You're worse at darts than I am at Erudition. Why d'you play it? You never play it. Whenever I suggest it, you get angry. 'Cos you know you'll lose. 'Cos you're so terrible.

ONE-EYE: It is not true, Rupert, that the revolutionary, ideally, is the man with nothing to lose. He must have something, two things, still unlost. His anger, and his self-respect. Well?

RUPERT: What?

ONE-EYE: Well? (*Pause. Shouts*) ONE DOUBLE ONE!

(*Pause*)

RUPERT: (*Gives up*) I'll do it.

ONE-EYE: Why. *Why?*

RUPERT: Why.

ONE-EYE: Because philosophers have always interpreted the world, Rupert.

RUPERT: Because philosophers have always interpreted the world, One-Eye.

ONE-EYE: But the point is to change it, Rupert.

RUPERT: But the point is to change it, One-Eye.

ONE-EYE: And you are very ugly, Rupert.

RUPERT: And I am very ugly, One-Eye.

(*In the distance, the sound of screaming girls, coming closer*)

ONE-EYE: He's coming.

RUPERT: That's Sven?

ONE-EYE: Of course it is. Who else.

RUPERT: He's won?

ONE-EYE: Of course he has. What else.

RUPERT: So, now?

ONE-EYE: Of course, now. When else? You ready?

RUPERT: Yes.

ONE-EYE: The catgut, Rupert. (*Rupert unties the catgut from the chairs. He stands, holding it*) Good.

(*Exit One-Eye. Screaming very close. Slam of a door. Enter Sven. He is breathless. He grins at Rupert. Banging on the door and screaming*)

SVEN: Gurls. (*Rupert grins weakly*) Orlvoys. Du gurls. (*Rupert nods*) Orlvoys. Du charsink. Und du runnink. Vrom du gurls. (*Rupert twines the catgut in his fingers*) Bit vort kun a poor boy do? (*One-Eye enters behind Sven. He carries before his face, a dartboard. Instead of the usual face, the poster-face of Sven, hideously torn, six darts in it. Rupert notices. Sven turns*) Vort—(*Slight pause*) Und vort—(*Slight pause*) Und vort ist da? (*One-Eye throws down the dartboard*) You!

ONE-EYE: Yes, Svensson. Me. (*He nods to Rupert, who pulls the catgut round Sven's neck. Freeze, sound out, and One-Eye out front*) For who among us, for who among you, good people all, has not at some moment, from time to time, surreptitiously, nursed the desire to dismember Robert Redford, Paul McCartney, David Soul? And who among us has not, at some stage, off and on, secretly, nurtured the urge to mutilate Brooke Shields, Bianca Jagger, and the entirety of Abba? Savagely? Those who are beautiful and know it, those who are powerful and love it, those who are fashionable and have lost even the passion to desire it. Those who will take whatsoever things are violent, whatsoever things are base, whatsoever things are revolutionary and ugly, sexual and primitive, and they will sterilise these things, and they'll pollute them with their beauty, and they will wear them and play them on their eight-track stereo and they will frame them and hang them on their white-glossed walls and they'll accomodate the anger of these things, their power, they will drain them, make them pure. Those who will look at us with no reaction, no, not even scorn. (*Pause*) There is a theory, spoken in quiet places, whispered in dark corners, that Karl Marx got it wrong. There is a concept, expressed in dirty leaflets, chalked on foggy walls, that it is not classes that divide the world. But beauty. Ugliness. (*Pause*) AND ONE DAY. ONE DAY. WE'LL RISE. And, up and down the land, the boiled and warted wreak a horrible revenge. Then shall unlovely losers liquidate the latest faces, then shall the balding massacre the hirsute, and the weaklings, roving in wild mobs, kick sand in every eye; then ageing tailors run amok in dark boutiques and obese house-wives butcher slimmers of the month. Then shall plump, acned groupies rise and slay the Bee Gees; starlets juggle with the severed limbs of stars, and stars will dance round smoking pyres of superstars; and secret wankers, formed in violent gangs, shall do destruction on the objects of their masturbation fantasies. . . . And all the maimed, deformed and corpulent; the ugly, harelipped and incontinent; shall rise and seek, destroy, and will inherit the earth. (*Pause*) So then. And there. We killed Sven Svensson. Horribly.

(*Sounds of banging and screaming back as One-Eye helps Rupert strangle Sven. Sound of the door crashing in and blackout and silence*)

RUPERT: (*Whispers*) The door's broken, One-Eye.

ONE-EYE: (*Whispers*) Yes, I know.

RUPERT: (*Whispers*) They'll come in, One-Eye.

ONE-EYE: (*Whispers*) Yes, I know.

RUPERT: (*Whispers*) They'll see us, what we done here, One-Eye.

ONE-EYE: (*Whispers*) Yes, I know.

(*Pause. Lights and screaming. One-Eye stands, one foot on Sven's mangled body, in a hero's pose. We cannot tell if the screams are in horror or worship. Cut out*)

RUPERT: I think we got it wrong, One-Eye.

(*Blackout and "The Ballad of a Thin Man," very loud*)

End of play

Author's Note

Ball Boys is an attempt, through the story of two unlovely orphans in a tennis club locker-room, to expose the essential contradictions inherent in late monopoly capitalism, to analyse the role of neo-colonialism in confirming the repressively-tolerant ideological interface between superstructure and base (while remaining not unmindful of the need to be fully cognizant of the essential dualism of the decaying bourgeois apparatus), to express implacable hostility to the running dogs of craven reformism in the labour bureaucracies, and to stress the vital need for alternative modes of leadership to pose the essential question of state power.

It is arguable that in this project the play is not totally successful.

David Edgar

Mary Gallagher

CHOCOLATE CAKE

Mary Gallagher

As one of the short plays in the 1981 Festival of New American Plays at Actors Theatre of Louisville, Mary Gallagher's *Chocolate Cake* received plaudits for its originality, characters, and humor. Sean Day-Lewis in *The Daily Telegraph* (London) praised the production: "I . . . enjoyed the originality of *Chocolate Cake* . . . a one-acter about two vastly different women stranded in a grubby motel, having both escaped briefly (or perhaps for longer) from not-too-loving husbands. They find they share a common consolation for their distresses: gourmandising. Susan Kingsley as the dynamic, over-sexed ex-showgirl and Kathy Bates as the hick-town girdle saleswoman, turn in performances of striking humanity." And William Albright, writing in *The Houston Post*, praised Ms. Gallagher's play as ". . . the most delightful play in this bunch by a country mile. Her comic dialogue cracked with fun. The poignancy . . . rang all too true," while Jack Kroll in *Newsweek* observed, "Skillfully Gallagher steers her play into a chocolate-dark farce about fear and loneliness." The play received the $1,000 Heidemann Award for one-act plays, and was one of the Festival's most popular shows. Initially produced by Actors Theatre of Louisville in their 1980 *Shorts* series, *Chocolate Cake* was also later revived in 1981 for two international theatre festivals—one in Toronto and one in Dublin.

Born in Van Nuys, California, in 1947, Mary Gallagher has enjoyed a career as an actress and director as well as writer. She began acting professionally at the Cleveland Playhouse in 1969 after receiving her B.S. from Bowling Green State University. Her acting career took her all over the country with performances in New York City as well as in regional theatres, including Stage West in Massachussetts, the Barter Theatre in Virginia, the Meadow Brook theatre in Michigan and the Alaska Repertory Theatre in Anchorage. Her directing credits include: *The Radio Show*—a cabaret spoof of radio in the forties—which opened in New York in 1976 and played at the Golden Lion Pub for four months before playing in Sitka, Alaska; and Wendy Wasserstein's *Uncommon Women and Others* for Playmakers Repertory theatre in Chapel Hill, North Carolina.

A fiction writer as well, Ms. Gallagher has published short stories in *Cosmopolitan, Playgirl,* and *Redbook.* Her first novel, *Spend It Foolishly*—a "frolic about an Ohio waif footloose and irrepressible in France and Italy"—appeared in 1978, and her second novel is nearing completion for publication in 1982.

Other produced plays include: *Fly Away Home* and *Father Dreams*, both produced as works-in-progress by the American Conservatory Theatre in San Francisco. *Father Dreams*, first developed through staged readings at New Dramatists in New York, received a production by the Ensemble Studio Theatre in March, 1981, to which Mel Gussow of the *New York Times*, responded: "This is an abrasive, unswerving portrait of a family allied against itself, with each member unable to forgive past transgressions, actual or imagined . . . *Father Dreams* attests that this is a dramatist with virtuosity as well as potential." Other productions of *Father Dreams* have been presented by The Empty Space Theatre, Seattle; the Loretto-Hilton Repertory Theatre in St. Louis; and Theatre 4, Dallas. *Little Bird*, also developed at New Dramatists, was produced at the Berkshire Theatre Festival in Stockbridge, Massachusetts; Syracuse University; and the 78th Street Theatre in New York. Ms. Gallagher has received grants for her writing from the Office for Advanced Drama Research, the National Endowment for the Humanities, and the Alaska State Council on the Arts.

Reflecting on her work, Ms. Gallagher writes: "Theatre is my first and greatest love, and the writing which most absorbs me is playwriting. . . . I tend to explore more serious themes in my plays. Writing a play is an enormous risk; it's an attempt to create an emotional structure which is strong enough to carry a whole body of people with it."

Ms. Gallagher is married to the writer Michael Swift, and they have two children, Leslie and Sarah.

Characters:

JOELLEN FITZER, *twenty-seven. She is a pretty, soft-looking, slightly overweight woman with a shy manner and a low self-concept. She thinks of herself as not right—not built right, not dressed right, not educated, with no special talent or charm.*

DELIA BARON, *early forties. She has the ageless, polished look of someone who's been fighting off age for some time and has the money and the absolute will to do it. She has a good body; what flaws there are, she has learned to hide. But she is fascinating and likable.*

Time:

6:30 p.m., February, 1980. A bitterly cold and snowy winter evening.

Scene:

The action takes place in a motel room in a dying neighborhood of an ugly, industrialized small city in Massachusetts. This week the motel is lodging thirteen women and two co-ordinators of a week-long seminar called "HORIZON '80: YOUR NEW LIFE STARTS HERE!"

The room is inhabited by Joellen Fitzer. A plywood partition divides the space into a large bedroom area and a tiny kitchen. The bedroom contains two beds and other well-worn furniture. In the kitchen, a small square icebox and a two-burner stove with an oven above it. Downstage is a small counter. The closet door is closed.

It has been snowing all day, but the snow has now stopped, leaving drifts and heavy cold.

At curtain's rise, Joellen Fitzer is propped up on the right bed. She is reading a paperback gothic novel. She wears a dress, but her feet are bare. Restless, she turns on the TV, then turns it off again.

Then she crosses to the closet, up-ends a suitcase and climbs on it to reach the closet shelf. She pulls out a bakery box, containing a cake. Then, quickly, she puts it back and shuts the door. She takes a pink nylon nightie out of the suitcase, goes into the bathroom and closes the door.

Outside the sound of a car motor is heard. The motor stops, the car door opens and slams, and Delia hurries in along the path downstage of the motel room, stomping through the snow in her boots. She glances at Joellen's door as she hurries past, then stops, returns, and knocks.

Meanwhile in the bathroom the water is running, and Joellen sings a plaintive song such as "I'm So Lonesome I Could Die."

DELIA: (*Knocking again*) Anyone in there? Patty Jo, or Ruth Ann, or whatever, hello?

(*Delia continues out to her own room. Her door opens and slams. At the same time Joellen comes out of the bathroom into the kitchenette, dressed in her nightie. In a moment there is a blast of noise from the TV in Delia's room, then the sounds of footsteps pacing restlessly*)

JOELLEN: (*Depressed, mouths*) Great!

(*Joellen starts to make dinner, singing the mournful song softly. Joellen goes to the refrigerator, takes out a plastic bowl of salad and a can of Tab. She then sits on the end of a bed in front of the TV. She turns on the TV, gets a blast of static, then voices—a newscast. She picks up the bowl and eats without enthusiasm*)

POLLY'S VOICE: (*From TV*) . . . here on the lawn in the snow, firemen and police have begun to assemble the remains of the bodies of residents of the Tuppleton Nursing Home who perished in last night's fire. Some one hundred and forty-two residents, most of them invalids, lost their lives. Identification will be difficult, authorities say, because most of the residents had not seen their relatives in many years. And as you can see, the bodies have been greatly disfigured by the fire. Ted?

(*Joellen is eating and watching, horrified*)

TED'S VOICE: (*From TV*) Thank you, Polly. Stay tuned now for live action coverage of a massacre of school children in Addis Ababa, after this word from Chunky. Chunky . . . what a chunk of chocolate!

JOELLEN: Oh, God!

(*Joellen turns off the TV. After a beat she begins to eat again. Sounds of tap dancing come from Delia's room. Joellen sets the bowl on the floor, goes to the phone and dials*)

MAN'S VOICE: (*From phone*) Hello? Hello? Hello? Joellen? Joey, is that you?

(*Joellen hangs up the phone. She starts to cry*)

JOELLEN: Oh, quit! (*The footsteps from Delia's room tap up a storm. A look of grim determination comes over Joellen's face. She marches into the bedroom, drags the suitcase to the closet, climbs up, takes down the bakery box, removes the lid, revealing a large chocolate cake, which she takes into the kitchen. She begins humming and singing "Zippity Doodah" as she sets the cake on the counter. From the cupboard Joellen takes a plate and a handful of utensils. She selects a spoon, and discarding a soup ladle, a hot dog fork, a whisk, and a corkscrew, keeps a pizza server too. Using the pizza cutter and her fingers she cuts a very large piece of cake and dumps it on the plate, licking her fingers luxuriously*) Mmmmmm . . . (*To the cake*) Hello, you little honey! (*She carries the cake plate and spoon into the bedroom, picking up her glass of Tab and a paperback book on route. She does a little Tango step, her song changing to "You Made Me Love You." Lying on the bed, she opens the book, cuts a large bite of cake, and lifts the spoon to her mouth. As she takes the first bite, Delia's door slams. Delia hurries to Joellen's door. She wears her sable coat, carries a six-pack of Tab, her purse and a brown bag. She bangs on the door*)

DELIA: Hello? Are you there? Betty Sue? Hello?

(*Joellen, mouth full, is frozen. Hastily she sets the cake plate on the bed, puts the book down, and sits, swallowing*)

JOELLEN: Yes? Who is it?

DELIA: Listen, I'm upstairs. I mean I have the room above you here in the motel, you know . . . I'm with the Conference, too. We met today. Your name's . . . it's two names, isn't it? I can't quite picture your name tag. But I'm Delia. Delia Baron. May I speak to you a moment?

(*Meanwhile Joellen runs to her suitcase, pulls out a matching pink robe with a fuzzy angora boa sewed to the neck—this is also pink— and throws it on. She sees the cake on the counter, runs to it, puts it in the icebox. She runs back toward the door, throwing clothes in the suitcase as she goes*)

JOELLEN: Oh, sure . . . um . . . just a minute . . .

DELIA: (*Knocking louder and longer*) Listen, are you all right in there?

JOELLEN: (*Rushing to door*) Oh, yes . . . I'm coming. . . . I was just putting on my robe . . .

(*She unlocks the door, opens it. They look at each other*)

DELIA: I thought it must be you in here.

JOELLEN: (*At the same time*) Oh, yes . ˙ of course . . . hello.

DELIA: You're not wearing your name tag.

JOELLEN: I'm sorry.

DELIA: Isn't it Lindy Lou or something?

JOELLEN: Joellen.

DELIA: I knew it! May I . . . ?

JOELLEN: Oh, please . . .

(*She turns away as Delia enters, and sees the cake on the bed. Horrified, she skitters over and grabs it, turns to face Delia, the cake behind her back. Meanwhile Delia has turned away to close the door. Now they look at each other, smiling*)

DELIA: You're in your nightgown.

JOELLEN: Oh, yes. Excuse me . . .

DELIA: You weren't sleeping, were you? I hope I didn't wake you . . .

JOELLEN: Oh, no, no . . . you didn't wake me. (*Inoffensive laugh*) It's pretty noisy around here, anyway. I mean . . . I didn't mean . . .

DELIA: Is it? I like other people's noise. Listen, what time is it? Maybe my clock stopped. You're ready for bed, it must be . . .

JOELLEN: No, no . . . that is, I am, but I wasn't going to *go* to bed or anything. It's only six-thirty or something.

(*She drifts downstage, cake behind her back*)

DELIA: *Six-thirty?* . . . Oh . . .

JOELLEN: I just . . . there was nothing else to do, so I got ready for bed . . . (*She laughs*)

DELIA: Mmm. Yes, this isn't eactly Caesar's Palace, is it? Have you been into the bar? The one here in the Gothic Court or whatever they call this dump. There's that charming little "intime" entrance off the parking lot, with the Christmas lights around the doorway.

(*Delia turns away, sets the brown bag on the bureau, and wrenches one Tab off the six-pack, sets the pack on the bureau. At the same time, Joellen ditches the cake in the suitcase*)

JOELLEN: Oh, no. I don't drink that much. A whiskey sour or something at a wedding, maybe. . . . I did sort of peek in as I went by. But it looked a little . . .

DELIA: All those deer heads are off-putting, aren't they? And there isn't even a pinball machine. Would you like a Tab?

JOELLEN: Oh, no thanks. I have one. (*Joellen hastily picks up Tab can; with her foot, slides the salad bowl under the bed*)

DELIA: I knew it! You're a member of my club! I picked

you out at once. Isn't it a godsend? Come upstairs if you run out. I've got cases of it.

JOELLEN: Cases?

DELIA: Literally. Looks like a loading dock up there. The trunk of my car is full of it too. Big Bill says that's why the Mercedes is riding so low. I say, "Better it's ass than mine." (*Laughs*) I'll stash this in the frige. (*Delia starts for kitchen with Tab*)

JOELLEN: (*Nods, smiles, then remembers cake*) Oh, no! I mean, please, let me! (*Takes pack, runs to kitchen*) I'd offer you some ice, but there aren't any ice trays.

DELIA: I've got all the ice trays. My room must have been the bar in its last life. And they left me a pastry brush, too. If you get desperate for a pastry brush in the middle of the night, just pound on the ceiling. I'll rush it right down.

(*Quickly, Joellen puts the pack in the frige, removes the cake, hides it in the plate cupboard. At the same time, Delia quickly opens a bureau drawer, peeks in. This finished, Joellen returns*)

JOELLEN: I'm afraid I just have one glass, too. I could wash it out . . .

DELIA: Don't bother. I'm a can person, really. What was yours wrapped in?

JOELLEN: Excuse me?

DELIA: Your glass?

JOELLEN: Oh. Newspaper. It was an old paper, too. At least, it seems like it's been a long time since Johnson was President.

DELIA: Yes . . . my bathroom glass was wrapped in Christmas paper. And it's a Christmas glass. It says, "Hallelujah, unto us a Savior."

JOELLEN: (*At nightstand, picks up glass*) Mine says, "JOLLY-OLLY ORANGE."

(*Delia sees the book on Joellen's bed, gets up, carrying Tab, goes below bed and around to side of it, picks up book*)

DELIA: You were reading. I'm interrupting you.

JOELLEN: Oh, no, really. It's just some book I found in the grocery store.

DELIA: (*Sniffs book*) Mm-hmm. Smells like chicken. (*Looks at title*) *The Torrent and the Tumult*, by Daphne Shalimar.

JOELLEN: I hardly ever read books like that. But it was all they had.

DELIA: (*Opens book at random, reads*) "Suddenly, wildly, he seized her quivering downy arms and pressed her trembling body into his. She shuddered, and her long, fawn-like lashes swept her delicately-tinted cheeks as she whispered faintly, 'Oh . . . you musn't . . .' And then wave upon wave of dizzying passion engulfed her . . ."

JOELLEN: (*Humbly*) I guess it's pretty silly.

DELIA: Where's your chocolate, dear?

JOELLEN: (*Stunned*) Excuse me?

DELIA: Don't you need a pound of M&Ms to get through this?

JOELLEN: (*Laughs, relieved, but still thrown*) Oh . . . I can manage without, I guess . . .

DELIA: Really? Talk about sex always makes me starved for chocolate. But maybe chocolate's not your vice. What is it . . . chips and dip?

JOELLEN: (*Nervous*) I don't understand . . .

DELIA: Never mind, I'm rushing things. We have lots of time. A whole week in this pit. Well, it could be worse. I could be in a Holiday Inn in Terre Haute, on Sunday afternoon. . . . I've actually done that and lived.

(*Pause. Delia smiles. Joellen indicates book*)

JOELLEN: It was just something to do.

DELIA: Yes! Desperate measures are called for. I went out and cruised a while ago. It was snowing like hell, I could barely see the road. Fortunately, there weren't any cars on it. Literally, none! I thought, where the hell *is* everybody? This is middle America, right?

JOELLEN: Well . . . Massachussetts isn't really . . .

DELIA: It's the same idea. A suburb is a suburb, wherever, right?

JOELLEN: I guess I see what you're . . .

(*Delia shrugs out of her coat, drops it on floor. Joellen picks it up*)

DELIA: So little husbands go to work and little wives stay home and shoot up Windex, or whatever it is they do . . . and then I stumbled on them. *Hundreds* of cars! You know where they were gathered? At the biggest frigging drugstore in the world! The whole population was trundling through snowdrifts with bags full of Drano and plastic flowers and copies of *Daytime Stars*.

JOELLEN: Oh, sure . . . the Sav-Mor.

DELIA: The Sav-Mor! It's the frigging Pentagon!

JOELLEN: They sell everything, just about. Groceries and appliances and tires and birds and turtles . . . and cotton candy and soft ice cream . . .

DELIA: I had to go in. It was clearly the hub of life. I wandered around there for an hour. At least it was something to do. I can blow time anywhere where there's some sound and motion. Movies, stores, Greyhound stations . . . penny arcades are the best, I adore them! And any bar that has machines. I don't drink, but I go mad for pinball. I can play for hours and hours.

JOELLEN: Alone?

DELIA: I told you, I like noise. And fool that I am, I didn't even bring a radio! I usually do, when I make an excursion into the hinterlands. Thank God for television! It's moronic, but it's company. Just like the Sav-Mor. I bought some lovely items! Industrial cleaner, a huge vat of it, pink, and it *smells* pink . . . and a bathtub brush with kittens on it. . . . and an ashtray with a little procession of plastic monks and donkeys marching around the rim . . .

JOELLEN: (*Helpful*) That sounds sort of . . . cute . . .

DELIA: Oh, my dear, it's classic . . . And! Would you believe there's a Chinese restaurant in there? . . . Though God knows what the food is like . . . the Chink at the front desk was eating a B.L.T. Maybe that passes for Chinese food in. . . . What is the name of this outpost?

JOELLEN: West Clarkson.

DELIA: Yes, right, West Clarkson. God . . . here in West Clarkson, it was Chin's Drugstore Takeout or cotton candy.

JOELLEN: There's a Dunkin' Donuts, too.

DELIA: Yes. Right next door to us. That's how I found my way back to this dump. By the great pulsing pink siren call of the Dunkin' Donuts sign. You can see it half a mile away. It's like the Christ in the hills over Rio. Ever been to Rio?

JOELLEN: No. (*A little joke*) I've been to Dunkin' Donuts.

DELIA: (*Glumly*) Haven't we all, dear. . . . Really, have you ever in your life seen such a depressing, grubby town?

JOELLEN: I haven't seen much else.

DELIA: Jesus, you don't mean . . .

JOELLEN: I'm from West Clarkson.

DELIA: I'm so sorry.

JOELLEN: Oh . . . it's not so bad . .

DELIA: But why are you locked in this convent of mold with the rest of us? We're trapped! But you . . . why don't you go out and . . . I don't know . . . *boogie* . . . if that's *feasible* . . .

JOELLEN: I didn't bring my car.

DELIA: Why ever not?

JOELLEN: (*Smiling bravely*) So I'd have to stay.

DELIA: I wouldn't let that stop me. If I knew of a movie within ten miles, I'd snowshoe out of here.

JOELLEN: There's a movie at the Mall. That's out the road the other way.

DELIA: My God, let's go! What's playing?

JOELLEN: A Disney double bill.

DELIA: Yahweh must be angry.

JOELLEN: It's like you said, there's no place much to go. Especially in the winter. The Sav-Mor or the Mall. Or Dunkin' Donuts, that's where the kids hang out. There's a bowling alley. Oh, but that's no good. It's leagues tonight.

DELIA: (*Sincere*) Oh, damn!

JOELLEN: Monday nights in any town aren't exactly hopping.

DELIA: They're hopping in New York.

JOELLEN: Do you live in New York.

DELIA: You're damn right. New York is crazy every night. That's where I belong. Big Bill wanted to buy a condo in Jersey, when he moved his operation there. I told him, listen, sweetie, it took me the first twenty years of my life to get the hell *out* of Jersey! . . . So now he's always in Jersey, and I'm always in New York. Except when I take the Mercedes and vanish into the hinterlands . . . making a getaway . . . Oh, listen, why don't we go to your place? Just for a couple of hours. Do you have any of those electric games, football or hockey or anything? Or even a ping-pong table . . .

JOELLEN: Oh, no! I'm sorry, but we can't . . .

DELIA: Excuse me. I'm so pushy when I'm bored.

JOELLEN: Oh, no, it isn't that. I mean, it was nice of you to offer. I don't have company much. But I . . . I just can't go home. Not yet.

DELIA: Ah . . . husband?

JOELLEN: (*A little joke*) So they say.

DELIA: How long?

JOELLEN: Five years. In March.

DELIA: Big Bill and I have slogged through nine. They say the first five years are the toughest.

JOELLEN: Everyone says that.

DELIA: It's crap. . . . (*Delia drains the last of her Tab*) How about another?

(*Joellen hesitates, then*)

JOELLEN: I think I will.

DELIA: What the hell! Let's live! . . . (*She takes empties into kitchen, dumps them in the trash, opens frige, gets two more cans; then very quickly and quietly opens freezer and looks in; opens lettuce bin, checks in there; meanwhile*) So you don't think your husband wants you at home? My, we're sisters under the skin.

JOELLEN: Oh no, it isn't that! He does want me at home! See . . . Robbie, my husband . . . he thinks I'm pretty crazy
. . .

DELIA: Oh, well. *That* . . .

JOELLEN: For coming to this conference, you know. And staying overnight, when we live right here in town. But I told him, this conference might be . . . I mean, it seemed like my only chance to . . . I think it's a real good thing to get off on your own sometimes, you know?

DELIA: No doubt! (*She looks in the oven; behind the counter*)

JOELLEN: And so when I saw the ad about this conference . . . "HORIZON '80: YOUR NEW LIFE STARTS HERE! A Conference on Careers For Women . . ." I thought it would open up all kinds of possibilities, you know? Like it would take me and shake me, and show me . . . give me some idea . . . so I could change myself. Take steps or something. I don't know . . .

(*Delia is about to look in the cupboards. She hears a pause, rushes into the bedroom with the Tab, gives one to Joellen*)

DELIA: Of course.

JOELLEN: You know what he said? He said, "Take the car." He said, "I don't want to have to come out in the snow and get you, just because you were too stubborn to take the car." He said, "Joey, I know you. First time they leave you alone for five minutes, you'll be on the phone. 'Robbie, come and get me.' "

DELIA: The shit.

JOELLEN: Yeah.

DELIA: Did you call him yet?

JOELLEN: Twice. But I hung up.

DELIA: Good girl.

JOELLEN: I shoulda' told them not to let me have a phone, either.

DELIA: (*Picks up snapshot leaning on lamp*) Is this Robbie?

JOELLEN: Yeah, that's him.

DELIA: Lovely teeth.

JOELLEN: Yeah, he's got a real nice smile.

DELIA: (*Touching the stuffed monkey with distaste*) Did he give you this?

JOELLEN: Sort of. It was a favor. From our senior prom.

DELIA: (*This makes her feel old*) God. . . . No children, I take it?

JOELLEN: (*Bothered by this*) No . . . you?

DELIA: God, no! I'm all the children Bill can handle. At least he used to say so.

JOELLEN: I expected to have kids by now . . . when we got married . . . but . . . nothing is any different. We live in the same place, we rent the half of a double house, it's fine . . . and Robbie has the same job, it's a pretty good job, he's a mechanic, you know . . . and I've got my same job selling girdles at Penney's-in-the-Mall. I've got my red pencil now, I can stay forever, if I want . . . like Robbie says, it's a pretty good life. But it's all the *same*. I kept thinking something would happen. Something would change things, you know?

(*Delia is poking around again, in the closet, drawers, under beds, etc., hunting*)

DELIA: Oh, yes. When I met Big Bill, I thought . . . "All that shit was just because I didn't have this man. Never again!" (*Delia laughs*)

JOELLEN: And, you know, I thought, "If I go to this conference, I want to do it right!" I thought it would be much more . . . meaningful . . . and more intense, you know . . . if I stayed all night like the other women. I thought we'd all get together in someone's room and just . . . talk all night! I . . . I've never had any real girlfriends. That's how it was in our school. If you went steady, you mostly just hung around with your guy, you know.

DELIA: Yes. I learned early to go for the man.

JOELLEN: Yeah . . . So . . . I thought I'd make a lot of friends here . . . women I could really learn from . . .

DELIA: (*Gives up the search, sits on the bed*) Um-hm . . .

(*They are both depressed*)

JOELLEN: It's not that they're not really nice . .
DELIA: Oh, *nice* . . .
JOELLEN: But they just aren't very . . .
DELIA: No.
(*Pause*)
JOELLEN: Phyllis is sort of interesting.
DELIA: Phyllis? The one who's retired from the Civil Service?
JOELLEN: The one who's an ex-nun.
DELIA: Oh . . . yes . . .
JOELLEN: She had the notebook with the contact-paper daisies on the front.
DELIA: I remember, yes. She was the first one to cry.
JOELLEN: In the very first workshop. At nine a.m.
DELIA: I didn't think it was all that cathartic myself.
JOELLEN: It was only "Grooming Tips."
DELIA: Well, perhaps for an ex-nun, that's cathartic . . . I mean, I have no right to talk. I'm an ex- . . . well. There's a lot I could tell that nun about grooming tips . . . And since I met Bill, I do nothing. I buy things. Things I hate, to kill two days . . . next day I take them back. And when Bill goes to Jersey and doesn't come back, I get in the car and go . . . somewhere . . . So this time, I came here. And I did hope . . . I have all this energy! I wish to God someone could tell me how to use it . . . or get rid of it . . . or deaden it, at least . . . besides the way I've found . . . but you know all about that . . . (*Confused, Joellen starts to speak; Delia goes on*) Doesn't it figure? A conference for women, and the whole thing's run by men? They're always at the dollar end, the little buggers, aren't they?
JOELLEN: But I bet there are plenty of things you could do. You . . . you have such a *flair* . . .
DELIA: That's a polite way to put it.
JOELLEN: Well . . . but you can tapdance, too.
DELIA: (*Darkly*) I am not going back to *that.* . . . How did you know I can tapdance?
JOELLEN: I heard you upstairs.
DELIA: Oh, yes . . . that's a measure of how crazed I am already.
JOELLEN: I bet it's fun. I always wanted to learn myself, but . . .

DELIA: I'd offer to teach you tonight, but I think it would end in suicide . . .

JOELLEN: Still, I bet your life is pretty exciting and glamorous, you know, compared to most of us here. You live in New York, you have lots of money, you can buy clothes in the fancy stores and go to the famous restaurants . . . those are real diamonds, I guess.

DELIA: You bet your ass. And this baby is sable.

JOELLEN: I guess, like you said, your husband isn't around a lot. But he must be very generous.

DELIA: He's out of his frigging mind. Listen to this. I met him, funnily enough, at Caesar's Palace. Sinatra was singing that night. Big Bill saw me across the lounge. Well, I meant for him to see me. I was tarted up to kill, tits hanging out to . . . Anyway, I knocked him on his ass. So he sent over a bottle of Dom Perignon, and could he join me. Well, I'd knocked around a lot since Jersey. Some were high rollers. But Bill . . . he had class, and he was real. A good heart, and no bullshit. Great laughs too. We've been together ever since. And don't kid yourself, whatever else I say, we're still together. That's how it is with us. Now get this. From that time on, every time Sinatra plays Caesar's Palace, Big Bill books a room. He puts his whole operation on hold. We get on a plane, and we go out to hear Sinatra. And we drink Dom Perignon.

JOELLEN: Gee . . . that's really sweet . . .

DELIA: I'll tell you the truth. It's gotten very stale. In recent years, it's been downright painful. (*She is moved, telling it*) But that's Big Bill . . . he won't quit now. He's a stubborn guy.

JOELLEN: I guess you love each other a lot.

DELIA: I guess. A lot of good it's done us.

JOELLEN: (*Timidly*) Then . . . why does he stay in Jersey . . . ?

DELIA: Let me tell you something. You can be very crazy, and a man will let it pass, if he really wants to make you. But that doesn't last, and the other thing does. The other thing gets worse. You know what I mean? (*Pause*) Listen, I'm starving. Have you eaten yet?

JOELLEN: Oh. Well. Yes. Sort of. I mean, yes.

DELIA: Because I haven't, and I'm absolutely famished,

and I have my dinner with me, it's right here in this bag. (*Gets brown bag from dresser top*) Chin's Drugstore Takeout, you know. Would you think I was godawful rude if I ate in front of you?

JOELLEN: Oh, no. Please, go ahead.

DELIA: That's why I came and knocked on your door. Partly, at least. I can't stand to eat alone. That's the greatest danger, isn't it, for people like us? Eating alone?

JOELLEN: People like us?

DELIA: Do you have a plate I can use? They gave me six plates, but I left them upstairs. You don't mind? I'll get it.

(*Delia starts for the kitchen. Joellen heads her off*)

JOELLEN: No! . . .

DELIA: No plate? Well, I guess I can eat from the carton. It won't be the first time, God knows. I've been known to cut a Sara Lee cheesecake with my car keys in midtown traffic. . . . (*Joellen is startled by this remark. Delia sees this, returns her gaze*) Cheesecake? Is that your thing?

JOELLEN: No! I mean . . . I have a plate. But I have to think where it is. I'll go and see. (*Delia lets her go. Joellen runs into the kitchen, takes the cake out of the plate cupboard, starts to put it in the oven*) Will you want to heat that up?

DELIA: No. I like it any way it comes. (*She is taking white cartons out of the brown bag, setting them on the bureau, opening them*) Where the hell did they put the extra duck sauce? I told him at least six times. I told him to charge me a dollar a tube as long as he gave it to me. Big Bill taught me that. If you've got money, you can get it just the way you like it. You're a fool if you take less. Big Bill is frequently full of shit, but he's dead on about that. (*Meanwhile Joellen takes down the plate, wipes it clean with a wetted finger, brings it in, gives it to Delia*) How about a fork? I really prefer to eat with my fingers, but not moo goo gai pan. At least, not when someone is watching. Not even you, Joanne. And I know I'm safe with you.

JOELLEN: Oh, sure. . . . That is . . . oh, well. I'll just have to rinse it off.

(*Reluctantly, as Delia watches, Joellen gets the salad bowl from under the bed, picks the fork out of it*)

DELIA: Oh darling, were you eating when I barged in? Lovely, you can join me!

JOELLEN: Oh, uh, no, I've had enough.

DELIA: Sure? That doesn't look like much to eat . . . just

that rabbit food. It's all lettuce, isn't it? Iceberg lettuce, too. I haven't eaten iceberg lettuce since I left New Jersey. But I suppose that's all they had at the Fail-Safe, or whatever they call it. You ought to sex that up. Put some cheese in it or something. Listen, I've got the most marvelous cheese. I brought it with me from New York. We buy it in wheels as big as your ass. . . . Oh dear, how crude, forgive me. That's Big Bill again. I've gotten so crude since I married him. (*Delia has taken the salad bowl, is digging in her purse*) I have to admit it, I was always crude. But before I was poor, so I had to mind my manners. Now I've got money to piss on, so I can crude it up all over town. One thing money doesn't do is improve your manners. (*Delia has taken a hunk of cheese out of her purse, is breaking it into the salad*)

JOELLEN: Really, I wish you wouldn't. I'm not hungry, really.

DELIA: It's fabulous cheese, the best. I carry it with me at all times. Something to nibble on. I know I have it right here with me, and it keeps me sane. Hunger I can live with, what I *can't* stand is being afraid I *might* be hungry. (*Joellen follows Delia to refrigerator*) Listen, if you're not hungry now, keep it, eat it later. I've got pounds of it upstairs. Literally. Don't you have any salad dressing?

JOELLEN: No. See . . . I'm supposed to be on a diet, kind of . . . I mean I sort of thought this week would be a good time . . . while I'm on my own, and I don't have to cook for my husband . . .

DELIA: Of course! My dear, you know I understand. I've been on a diet since I was thirteen years old. I turned thirteen, I got tits, and I went on a diet. Life's been like that ever since. It just keeps getting harder. That's the lousy secret they don't tell you when you're young. Now isn't that better? Even if you're dieting, you have to eat *something*. You'll need your fork for that. Just give me a tablespoon . . . anything. (*She gives Joellen the salad bowl. Joellen puts the bowl on the bed and goes to the kitchen, takes out utensils. She returns with a pancake turner and a hot dog fork. Meanwhile Delia is dumping Chinese food from three cartons all together on her plate, and squeezing duck sauce on it*) They didn't give me extra duck sauce, those little slanty-eyed bastards. I knew they wouldn't. All that bowing and smiling, it means "Up yours." I'd offer you some of this glop, but my doctor forbids me to share my food, even with Big Bill. It's part of his "Plan." He's a Nazi, my doctor, literally, he's been hiding from Zionists for years, and he bleeds Big Bill for thousands. But he's brilliant. He got me on the machine. Two hours a day. It's agony, but it saves me. With my little trick, of course.

(*Joellen gives her the pancake turner and the hot dog fork*)

JOELLEN: I'm terribly sorry. This is all I have . . .

DELIA: No, no, these are fine, they're perfect for *me*. (*With the utensils, she mixes the food together*) Big Bill says I should eat with a coal scoop . . .

JOELLEN: (*Watching, fascinated*) Robbie'd never let *me* buy a reducing machine. He thinks my dieting and all is a big joke . . . like everything else I do.

DELIA: It's wonderful how a man can make you feel like a puppet show.

JOELLEN: Well, I guess it is pretty silly how I go on all these diets.

DELIA: Tell me about it. Tell me about your diets while I eat.

(*With that, Delia begins to eat, her eyes shifting from her food to Joellen's face with equal intensity. She eats like a starved child, shovelling in huge mouthfuls with the pancake turner, using her fingers too, gobbling. Joellen is appalled and yet reassured by this. She can't take her eyes away*)

JOELLEN: Well, I . . . I put on a lot of weight . . . after I married Robbie. But I never can seem to stay on a diet more than a day or two. I mean, there's Robbie all the time, and he's a real meat-and-potatoes man, like he always says . . .

DELIA: (*With her mouth full*) What a novel way to put it.

JOELLEN: And when I have to cook pork chops and hash browns and biscuits and applesauce for him, it seems so dumb to just sit there watching him eat . . . hearing him chew . . . while I'm playing with carrot sticks . . . (*Absently, watching Delia, Joellen starts eating lettuce out of the bowl*) . . . especially when he keeps telling me how tasty everything is and what a great little cook I am. Most of the time he never says a word about my cooking. Just when I'm on a diet. At least it seems like that. So then, even if I make it through dinner and TV, which is real hard, with Robbie drinking beer and eating snacks . . . when we get in bed, every time, here comes Robbie in his P.J.s with a great big rootbeer float. He has this mug that he got in high school football that says "SPUDS," that was his nickname in high school because he loved potatoes. I even call him "Spuds" sometimes still, for fun, you know. Anyway, he always uses that great big mug when he makes a rootbeer float. So there I am in bed in my see-through nightie with my hair fluffed up and all, and he gets in right beside me and starts eating his rootbeer float and making noises . . .

DELIA: (*Eating greedily*) What noises?

JOELLEN: Like . . . "Mmmmm . . ."

DELIA: Mmmm.

JOELLEN: So I say, "Robbie, you're just mean." And Robbie says, "Come on, Joey. You know you hate this diet stuff. You're no fun when you're doing it. And you don't need it. You look good, you look like a woman. You're always beautiful to me."

DELIA: And what do you say?

JOELLEN: (*Softly*) I say, "Well you sure don't act like it . . ."

DELIA: And then what?

JOELLEN: Then he says, "Come on, Joey." And he eats his rootbear float. And then he goes to sleep.

DELIA: (*Watching her avidly*) And then . . . ?

JOELLEN: And then I lie there . . . as long as I can stand it . . . (*Her eyes on Delia's, she seems mesmerized*) . . . and then I get up and put my bathrobe on, the old one with the holes, and I go in the kitchen and make myself a great big rootbeer float. It's twice as big as Robbie's. I make it in the orange juice pitcher. And I eat the whole thing standing up, right there at the counter. And then I eat whatever Robbie left at dinner, and whatever I didn't have for lunch because it was too fattening, and whatever I skipped at breakfast . . . (*Delia is eating ravenously, their gazes locked*) . . . and every single thing that I can get my hands on that I shouldn't eat, old stale crackers and broken pretzels and Girl Scout cookies that are still all frozen from the freezer and peanutbutter sandwiches and moldy coffee cake and even Kahlua if somebody happened to give us a bottle for Christmas or something . . . everything that's bad.

DELIA: (*With enormous satisfaction*) Yes . . . yes indeed. (*She has finished what was on her plate in amazingly quick time. Now she puts the plate down on the floor*) You know, I picked you out in the first five minutes, before I'd heard your name. The fool who's in charge of this farce was giving his "Dare we meet the future" spiel, and that girl, that assistant of his, the one who was born to sharpen pencils . . .

JOELLEN: Darlette, her name is.

DELIA: Yes, good God, Darlette, she was prancing around with a coffee pot and a bucket of Dunkin' Munchkins, and she shoved it at you and I heard you say, "Oh no, I can't eat anything like that." She said, "Oh, one won't hurt you," or something inane like that. And I heard you say, "If I eat one, I won't stop there. I can't." And I knew you at once. "Aha!" I thought. "A member of my club!"

JOELLEN: You mean . . . you're like that too?

DELIA: What's the most ice cream you've ever eaten in one sitting?

JOELLEN: I hate to tell you. Probably a quart. A whole quart by myself.

DELIA: A quart! I've eaten gallons! How many pancakes can you eat?

JOELLEN: I get full on pancakes. Maybe six, I guess.

DELIA: Big Bill and I once ate at a pancake restaurant where they advertised "All You Can Eat For Three Dollars." I ate seventeen.

JOELLEN: Seventeen pancakes?

DELIA: There was sausage, too.

JOELLEN: Gosh, that's worse than me! But how can you look like you do when you eat like that?

DELIA: (*Smiles mysteriously*) Partly, its the money. Machines and shots and doctors and little stitchings here and there. But I have to work at it harder now. What the money buys does less and less. And what I do to myself in the night, in my crazy state . . . when I start and I just can't stop . . .

JOELLEN: Yes . . . in the night when I'm alone . . . I'd die if Robbie knew! I can't believe that you ate all those pancakes in front of your husband.

DELIA: He's seen worse than that.

JOELLEN: Doesn't it . . . you know . . . bother him?

DELIA: That I eat like a monster?

JOELLEN: Well . . .

DELIA: He used to think it was cute. When we were first together. He used to love it when we'd go out to dinner some chichi place and I'd devour a three-pound lobster and throw the shells all over the floor. He'd laugh like hell. He'd kid with the waiters. "Bring her everything she wants, save yourself some grief!" And he'd grab my ass under the table. . . . But he doesn't think it's funny now. He just looks tired. And old. When a man feels old around you . . . (*She lets this trail off, very depressed; then she shrugs, says with the old bravura*) Big Bill used to say to me, "I don't which I'd rather do, eat with you or screw you." But I knew which I'd rather do. Food's always been my drug. It's a damn good thing it has. Let me tell you a thing, my dear. You can count on a man for a month . . . if you get a good one, for a year. But hot fudge is for life.

JOELLEN: I guess you and your husband don't do it so much anymore?

DELIA: What about you and Spuds? Does he always dive into a rootbeer float when you put your nightie on?

(*Having finished her own dinner, Delia reaches for the salad bowl and starts eating Joellen's salad as Joellen talks. Joellen doesn't protest*)

JOELLEN: (*After a painful pause, she nods*) He used to want to do it all the time. Before we were married, I mean. We started going together in high school. I had a crush on him for months, and then at a sock hop, this girl I knew dared me to ask him to dance at a ladies' choice . . . and I did. It was the only time I ever asked a boy to dance. I remember he had on a mohair sweater, pale green with a V-neck. He was chunky even then, and with all that mohair . . . he looked like a fuzzy lima bean. They were playing "Blue Velvet," you know, that real old Bobby Vinton song? We started dancing double-clutch, and he was sweating like crazy, and he had on all this English Leather. . . . I never felt so warm and safe, you know, wrapped up in all that mohair, like in a cocoon or something. . . . Ever since, it's just been Robbie. We waited to get married till we had two thousand dollars saved. Robbie didn't want to start with debts. And so I said, okay, but we're not gonna do it until we get married. I made him wait. (*Appealing to Delia for an answer*) Maybe it's my fault, maybe I wrecked it, making him wait like that.

DELIA: What? He couldn't get it up?

JOELLEN: I don't know. I don't know what it is. We did it on our honeymoon. But, you know, I never did it with anyone else, so I didn't really know. But something wasn't right. He'd get upset, and stop . . . and I'd be afraid to say, "What is it, what's the matter?" And then he just quit trying. I waited and waited . . . and finally a couple of times I tried to start it. But I felt funny about it, you know. I probably didn't do it right. He'd say, "Cut it out, Joey." One night when he said that, I started to cry. He said, "What's the matter, honey?" And I said, "There's something wrong, isn't there? I mean, we never do it." And Robbie said, "A lot of couples never do it. That's the best-kept secret. A lot of couples don't even like each other. But we love each other. And we're best friends, too. We like doing things together and talking together and just holding each other close like this . . . so if we don't do it very often, we got a lot of other stuff going for us. We're pretty lucky, you know?" So I said, "Yeah, I guess you're right . . ."

DELIA: Ha!

JOELLEN: Yeah . . . I can't help thinking . . . maybe it's because I've gotten fat. So I try to diet, you know? I really try. But . . . it's like he doesn't want me to. I don't know what he wants. And I get to feel so lonely . . . so empty . . .

DELIA: Yes . . .

JOELLEN: I didn't want to tell a soul . . . I felt so ashamed. But . . . maybe you can tell me . . . do you think . . . I was afraid to ask Robbie about it, but . . . there must be some kind of counselors to go to. . . . I know Robbie loves me. If I tell him everything, how lonely I get, and how much it hurts me that we don't make love . . . maybe he'd go and see somebody with me . . . and everything would change . . . do you think that could work?

DELIA: You think it all comes down to that? If only your husband would screw you, your life would be perfect, huh?

JOELLEN: (*Startled*) Well . . . I don't know . . .

DELIA: Screwing doesn't do it. Nothing does! If you're like me, nothing else can fill you up or take that loneliness away, not so it lasts. Oh, eating doesn't last, of course. But while it lasts, it *works*! Look. My life was shit when I was a kid. So when I got tits, I got out. I learned how to please, and I went for the man. But I never found a damn thing I could count on, except something I could eat! But I always thought, "Wait till someone loves me! Me, the one I *really* am! I'll never be afraid again!" But is isn't true. Nothing Bill gives me can take it away . . . that pit I have inside. Nothing heals it, even for an hour, except. . . . That's why he hates to watch me gorge myself. He thinks it means he's failed me. He loves me, the poor sad son-of-a-bitch . . . and that's going to drive him away. . . . So I make my little getaways, to give him room and time. . . . I wear on people, don't I? (*Delia goes to the window, looks out*) What time is it?

JOELLEN: A little after eight.

DELIA: Oh God, and dinner's over. What are we going to do for the rest of the night? It's like an ice cave out there. Am I making this up, or is it always night in Massachusetts?

JOELLEN: It does get dark pretty early these days.

DELIA: So of course the men came up with Daylight Savings Time. What do they care if it's day or night? They're busy all the time. . . . I'd kill for a chocolate bar. A giant Hershey's chocolate bar, with almonds!

JOELLEN: The Sav-Mor's closed by now.

DELIA: I know it's closed. They shooed me out into the snow, and I heard them lock the door behind me. God, that depressed me, that sound. Why didn't I buy something when I was there? I knew I wanted chocolate! I walked up and down the aisles, looking at the wrappers, picking up boxes and packages and feeling the weight in my hands. . . . But I put them all back. And I told myself, "No. I won't do this tonight. There's someone who will talk to me. I'll go and stay with that girl until I'm tired enough to sleep." But now I've got that feeling . . . when you'd kill someone for something chocolate, rich and dark and sweet. God, I hate the night, don't you?

(*Delia is prowling, anxious, tense. Joellen watches her nervously, but with fellow feeling. She considers something, tests Delia out*)

JOELLEN: Delia . . . if you *had* bought something chocolate . . . at the Sav-Mor, you know, and you had it here . . . you'd share it with me, wouldn't you?

DELIA: (*Not picking up on this; wryly*) Do you think I'm holding out on you? So you won't ask me for it? I wish to God I were. I'd do that, too. Big Bill doesn't ask any more. He knows I won't share. If I had ten pounds of chocolates and I gave a pound to you, it would just about kill me to do it . . . and I wouldn't give you any peace, I wouldn't rest till I got it back again. . . . (*This convinces Joellen to keep her mouth shut about the cake*) Pretty, isn't it? Maybe you thought it would go away as you got older . . . or you'd get control. But it doesn't work like that. I have less and less control. I really scare myself. (*Pause. Delia looks at Joellen. Joellen, quite depressed now, is looking wistfully at the phone*) Thinking of calling Spuds again?

JOELLEN: I guess there's not much point. But . . . I really miss him, you know? This is the first night in five years that I've ever been away from him. We always sleep cuddled up together. I guess that seems strange, when we don't . . .

make love . . . but that's the best part of the whole day, when he cuddles up and holds me . . .

DELIA: Don't call him. Wait.

JOELLEN: But . . .

DELIA: If I go away, and I stay there, and wait . . . sooner or later he calls me, and he asks me to come back.

JOELLEN: He does?

DELIA: He always has before. The first time I did it, he called four times before I even got there. Four messages were waiting for me. "Please come home. Love, Bill."

JOELLEN: And now . . . ? (*Pause. Delia doesn't answer. Then gently*) This conference only lasts a week.

DELIA: What's the nearest city?

JOELLEN: Springfield.

DELIA: What's in Springfield?

JOELLEN: The Professional Basketball Hall of Fame.

DELIA: I guess I'll stay here. Or maybe I could come to your house? Just for a couple of days.

JOELLEN: (*Not sure if this is a joke*) Gee . . . I don't know . . . we only have one bedroom.

DELIA: Oh, I could sleep on the couch. I hate going into a bedroom and turning off the light. There's something so final about that. I like to keep the TV on and lie on the couch and watch it with my clothes on, even my shoes, till I fall asleep. It's like I don't really mean it, you know. I'm not really alone in the dark. And back in New York, in our building, there's a deli that's open all night. So even if there's nothing rich and heavy in the house, I can go to sleep, because I know that all I have to do is go down to the lobby and open my purse, and I can buy it all. The one thing that sends me into a panic is knowing that I can't go out and bring back what I need. Everything is locked up tight. Everyone is gone. (*Sits beside Joellen, takes her hand, pleads*) Please, I can't go back upstairs alone. I didn't think it would get this bad, I thought I could control it, but . . . . Can I sleep here with you? I won't talk or anything. I'll just sit here quietly and you can read your book. I know you're getting tired of this . . . it's depressing, listening to me . . . and you wanted help, and I didn't help you . . .

JOELLEN: No, it isn't that . . . but I don't think . . .

DELIA: I scare you a little, don't I? But that's why you can understand. You'll let me sleep here, won't you? Just once, just for tonight . . .

JOELLEN: (*Frightened, pulling away*) No. I . . . I would . . . but . . . I might not stay. I'm going to call my husband. And then I might go home. (*Pause. Rejected, Delia withdraws. Joellen watches her anxiously*) Delia . . . why don't you go home, too? You say your husband loves you . . .

DELIA: (*Driven, barely hearing this*) If I just had one small thing to get me through the night! Something sweet . . . so I know its there . . . when I'm alone upstairs . . .

(*Pause. Joellen goes to the suitcase, takes out the piece of cake, holds it out*)

JOELLEN: Here. This is all I have. (*Delia is amazed. Then she goes to Joellen and takes it, knowing that there is more, a whole cake somewhere in the room*)

DELIA: Oh, my dear. You are a friend. Are you sure you want me to take it all? Don't you want to keep half . . . in case . . . ?

JOELLEN: (*Embarrassed*) No . . . I don't need it now . . .

DELIA: (*Knowing better*) I see. Well, thank you. Thank you. (*Puts down cake, gets her coat, then stops, turns to Joellen, continues*) I want to give you something in return, because you've been so generous . . .

JOELLEN: (*Guiltily*) Oh no, no . . .

DELIA: Yes. You asked me why I don't gain weight. But I didn't tell you about my little trick. That's really all you need. If you know the trick, you can eat everything, every night, you can gorge till your heart is about to burst, till the sweat breaks out and you can hardly swallow, and there won't be a sign of it on your body.

JOELLEN: (*Mesmerized*) What do you do?

DELIA: I puke.

JOELLEN: Oh, no . . .

DELIA: Why not? Children do it.

JOELLEN: You mean you throw up every day?

DELIA: Not every day. Just when I've lost control. I let go completely, I eat like a mad thing, seventeen pancakes, a whole chocolate cake. . . . Then I go to the nearest toilet or sink . . . a wastebasket will do, or an alley . . . and I do my little trick. And I don't gain weight.

JOELLEN: It would be perfect . . . if I could eat everything I want and still be thin . . .

DELIA: For people like us, it's the only state of grace.

JOELLEN: But there's something creepy about it. Making yourself . . . besides, if I knew no matter what I ate, I could get rid of it again and nobody would know . . . there'd be nothing to stop me. I could just go crazy every night.

DELIA: Shall I show you now?

JOELLEN: Wait! I don't understand. Why didn't you buy lots and lots of chocolate at the Sav-Mor and eat it, and get rid of it?

DELIA: Because it makes me sad. . . . Shall I show you?

JOELLEN: No!

(*Pause*)

DELIA: All right, dear. But I owe it to you . . . because you gave me this. We'll both be here every night . . . I mean, if you decide to stay. If you change your mind, just come upstairs and knock on my door. I'll know who it is. Don't worry if it's late. Even later on tonight . . . if you have trouble sleeping . . . (*Takes the piece of cake and her purse*) Thank you, dear. For everything. See you soon. Enjoy.

(*Delia winks, goes out. She exits along the platform to the stairs, goes up. We hear her feet on the upstairs platform. The door upstairs opens and closes. Pause. We hear the blast of the upstairs TV. Joellen waits till she hears the TV. Then she goes and locks the door. She hesitates, thinking. Then she goes to the phone, picks it up, hesitates again. She puts it down. She goes and gets the cake. She sets it on the counter, looks at it. She looks at the phone. Then, utterly torn, she sits on the bed, thinking*)

Fade

David Henry Hwang

THE DANCE AND
THE RAILROAD

David Henry Hwang

Winner of the 1980–81 Obie for his play *FOB*, David Henry Hwang makes his debut in this series with the highly acclaimed *The Dance and the Railroad*. In its initial New York production at the Henry Street Settlement's New Federal Theatre in March, 1981, this unusual play about Chinese railway construction workers during a strike in 1867 in the Sierra Nevada Mountains was praised by Laurie Stone in the *Village Voice:* "David Henry Hwang . . . uses fantasy and poetry without coyness or inhibition, all the time dramatizing that there is no real freedom for these men—only novel forms of servitude. At 23, Hwang already knows how to take a bare stage and an hour and make something theatrical happen." Frank Rich, critic for the *New York Times*, responded: "Mr. Hwang's works have the verve of well-made American comedies and yet, with little warning, they can bubble over into the mystical rituals of Oriental stagecraft. By at once bringing West and East into conflict and unity, this playwright has found the perfect means to dramatize both the pain and humor of the immigrant experience."

Contributing to the production success of *The Dance and the Railroad* were the excellent performances of Tzi Ma as Ma and John Lone as Lone, who directed and choreographed the production, receiving an Obie for his performances in both *FOB* and *The Dance and the Railroad*. An equally successful revival of *The Dance and the Railroad* was presented in July, 1981, at New York's Public Theatre.

Mr. Hwang first came to public attention with his Obie-winning play *FOB* (which stands for "Fresh Off the Boat"), presented at the Public Theatre in New York in June, 1980. The son of Chinese immigrants—his father arrived in the United States in the late 40's, his mother in 1952—Mr. Hwang grew up in an upper-middle class family in San Gabriel, a suburb of Los Angeles; yet he identifies with the history of the Chinese in both this country and that of his grandparents, who used to tell him stories of their native country when David was a child.

After high school Mr. Hwang went to Stanford University in the fall of 1975 and soon began writing plays. During his senior year in 1978 he wrote *FOB*, which was selected for the O'Neill Playwright's Conference in Waterford, Connecticut. For a couple of years he taught writing at Menlo-Atherton High School in Menlo Park, California. Then he enrolled in

Yale School of Drama, where he first started work on *The Dance and the Railroad*, which was commissioned by the New Federal Theatre under a grant from the Ethnic Heritage Studies Division of the United States Department of Education.

His most recent work, *Family Devotions*, produced at the Public Theatre in New York in the fall of 1981, shows three generations of Chinese-Americans in a well-to-do family in Los Angeles. Mr. Hwang explains, "It's about the myths that grow up around a family history and how legends of past family members affect the lives of the living." Frank Rich, writing for the *New York Times*, describes the play as a "sassy, contemporary American comedy with the gripping, mythological stylization of Oriental theater—ending up with a work that remains true to its specific roots even as it speaks to a far wider audience."

Mr. Hwang expresses concern about creating more opportunities for Asian-Americans in the United States theatre, "I write about Asian-Americans to claim our legitimate, but often neglected, place in the American experience. . . . One very important thing for me is to give Asian-American actors a chance to work and increase our visibility."

The playwright dedicates this play: "For John and Tzi."

Characters:

LONE, *twenty years old, Chinaman railroad worker*

MA, *eighteen years old, Chinaman railroad worker*

Place

A mountain top near the transcontinental railroad.

Time:

June, 1867.

Scene One:

Afternoon. A mountain top. Lone, sitting on a rock, rotating his head so that it twirls his pigtail like a fan. He jumps to the ground, practices opera steps. Ma enters, cautiously, watches from a hidden spot. Ma approaches Lone.

LONE: So, there are insects hiding in the bushes.

MA: Hey, listen, we haven't met, but . . .

LONE: I don't spend time with insects.

(Lone whips his hair into Ma's face; Ma backs off; Lone pursues him, swiping at Ma with his hair)

MA: What the . . . ? Cut it out! *(Ma pushes Lone away)*

LONE: Don't push me.

MA: What was that for?

LONE: Don't ever push me again.

MA: You mess like that, you're gonna get pushed.

LONE: Don't push me.

MA: You started it. I just wanted to watch.

LONE: "You just wanted to watch." Did you ask my permission?

MA: What?

LONE: Did you?

MA: C'mon.

LONE: You can't expect to get in for free.

MA: Listen. I got some stuff you'll wanna hear.

LONE: You think so?

MA: Yeah. Some advice.

LONE: Advice? How old are you, anyway?

MA: Eighteen.

LONE: A child.

MA: Yeah. Right. A child. But listen . . .

LONE: A child who tries to advise a grown man   . .

MA: Listen, you got this kind of attitude.

LONE: . . . is a child who will never grow up.

MA: You know, the Chinamen down at camp, they can't stand it.

LONE: Oh?

MA: Yeah. You gotta watch yourself. You know what they say?

LONE: No. Tell me.

MA: They call you, "Prince of the Mountain." Like you're too good to spend time with them.

LONE: Perceptive of them.

MA: After all, you never sing songs, never tell stories. They say you act like your spit is too clean for them, and they got ways to fix that.

LONE: Is that so?

MA: Like they're gonna bury you in the shitbuckets, so you'll have more to clean than your nails.

LONE: But I don't shit.

MA: Or they're gonna cut out your tongue, since you never speak to them.

LONE: There's no one here worth talking to.

MA: Cut it out, Lone. Look, I'm trying to help you, all right? I got a solution.

LONE: So young yet so clever.

MA: That stuff you're doing—it's beautiful. Why don't you do it for the guys at camp? Help us celebrate?

LONE: What will "this stuff" help celebrate?

MA: C'mon. The strike, of course. Guys on a railroad gang, we gotta stick together, you know.

LONE: This is something to celebrate?

MA: Yeah. Yesterday, the weak-kneed Chinamen: they were running around like chickens without a head: "The white devils are sending their soldiers! Shoot us all!" But now,

look . . . day four, see? Still in one piece. Those soldiers . . .
we've never seen a gun or a bullet.

LONE: So you're all warrior-spirits, huh?

MA: They're scared of us, Lone . . . that's what it means.

LONE: I appreciate your advice. Tell you what . . . you go
down . . .

MA: Yeah?

LONE: Down to the camp.

MA: Okay.

LONE: To where the men are.

MA: Yeah?

LONE: Sit there . . .

MA: Yeah?

LONE: And wait for me.

MA: Okay. (*Pause*) That's it? What do you think I am?

LONE: I think you're an insect interrupting my practice.
So fly away. Go home.

MA: Look, I didn't come here to get laughed at.

LONE: No, I suppose you didn't.

MA: So just stay up here. By yourself. You deserve it.

LONE: I do.

MA: And don't expect any more help from me.

LONE: I haven't gotten any yet.

MA: If one day, you wake up and your head is buried in
the shitcan . . .

LONE: Yes?

MA: You can't find your body, your tongue is cut out . . .

LONE: Yes.

MA: Don't worry 'cuz I'll be there.

LONE: Oh.

MA: To make sure your mother's head is sitting right next
to yours. (*Ma exits*)

LONE: His head is too big for this mountain.

(*Lone returns to practicing*)

Scene Two:

*Mountain top. Afternoon, the next day. Lone is practicing. Ma
enters.*

MA: Hey.

LONE: You? Again?

MA: I forgive you.

LONE: You . . . what?

MA: For making fun of me yesterday. I forgive you.

LONE: You can't . . .

MA: No. Don't thank me.

LONE: You can't forgive me.

MA: No. Don't mention it.

LONE: You . . . I never asked for your forgiveness.

MA: I know. That's just the kinda guy I am.

LONE: This is ridiculous. Why don't you leave? Go down to your friends and play soldiers, sing songs, tell stories.

MA: Ah! See? That's just it. I got other ways I wanna spend my time. Will you teach me the opera?

LONE: What?

MA: I wanna learn it. I dreamt about it all last night.

LONE: No.

MA: The dance, the opera . . . I can do it.

LONE: You think so?

MA: Yeah. When I get outa here, I wanna go back to China and perform.

LONE: You want to become an actor?

MA: Well, I wanna perform.

LONE: Don't you remember the story about the three sons whose parents send them away to learn a trade? After three years, they return. The first one says, "I have become a coppersmith." The parents say, "Good. Second son, what have you become?" "I've become a silversmith." "Good . . . and youngest son . . . what about you?" "I have become an actor." When the parents hear that their son has become only an actor, they are very sad. The mother beats her head against the ground until the ground, out of pity, opens up and swallows her. The father is so angry, he can't even speak, and the anger builds up inside him until it blows his body to pieces—little bits of his skin are found hanging from trees days later. You don't know how you endanger your relatives by becoming an actor.

MA: Well, I don't wanna become an "actor." That sounds terrible. I just wanna perform. Look, I'll be rich by the time I get out of here, right?

LONE: Oh?

MA: Sure. By the time I go back to China, I'll ride in gold sedan chairs, with twenty wives fanning me all around.

LONE: Twenty wives? This boy is ambitious.

MA: I'll give out pigs on New Years and keep a stable of small birds to give to any woman who pleases me. And in my spare time, I'll perform.

LONE: Between your twenty wives and your birds, where will you find a free moment?

MA: I'll play Kwan Kung and tell stories of what life was like in the Gold Mountain.

LONE: Ma, just how long have you been in "America?"

MA: Huh? About four weeks.

LONE: You are a big dreamer.

MA: Well, all us Chinamen here are—right? Men with little dreams have little brains to match. They walk with their eyes down, trying to find extra grains of rice on the ground.

LONE: So, you know all about "America?" Tell me, what kind of stories will you tell?

MA: I'll say, "We laid tracks like soldiers. Mountains? We hung from cliffs in baskets and the winds blew us like birds. Snow? We lived underground like moles for days at a time. Deserts? We . . ."

LONE: Wait. Wait. How do you know these things after only four weeks?

MA: They told me—the other Chinamen on the gang. We've been telling stories ever since the strike began.

LONE: They make it sound like it's very enjoyable.

MA: They said it is.

LONE: Oh? And you believe them?

MA: They're my friends. Living underground in winter—sounds exciting, huh?

LONE: Did they say anything about the cold?

MA: Oh, I already know about that. They told me about the mild winters and the warm snow.

LONE: Warm snow?

MA: When I go home, I'll bring some back to show my brothers.

LONE: Bring some . . . On the boat?

MA: They'll be shocked . . . they never seen American snow before.

LONE: You can't. By the time you get snow to the boat, it'll have melted, evaporated, and returned as rain already.

MA: No.

LONE: No?

MA: Stupid.

LONE: Me?

MA: You been here awhile, haven't you?

LONE: Yes. Two years.

MA: Then how come you're so stupid? This is the Gold Mountain. The snow here doesn't melt. It's not wet.

LONE: That's what they told you?

MA: Yeah. It's true.

LONE: Did anyone show you any of this snow?

MA: No. It's not winter.

LONE: So where does it go?

MA: Huh?

LONE: Where does it go? If it doesn't melt, what happens to it?

MA: The snow? I dunno. I guess it just stays around.

LONE: So where is it? Do you see any?

MA: Here? Well, no, but . . . (*Pause*) This is probably one of those places where it doesn't snow—even in winter.

LONE: Oh.

MA: Anyway, what's the use of me telling you what you already know? Hey, c'mon . . . teach me some of that stuff. Look . . . I've been practicing the walk . . . how's this? (*Ma waddles awkwardly*)

LONE: You look like a duck in heat.

MA: Hey . . . it's a start, isn't it?

LONE: Tell you what—you want to play some *Die Siu?*

MA: *Die Siu?* Sure.

LONE: You know, I'm pretty good.

MA: Hey, I play with the guys at camp. You can't be any better than Lee . . . he's really got it down.

(*Lone pulls out a case with two dice*)

LONE: I used to play 'til morning.

MA: Hey, us too. We see the sun start to rise, and say, "Hey, if we go to sleep now, we'll never get up for work." So we just keep playing.

LONE: (*Holding out dice*) *Die* or *Siu?*

MA: *Siu.*

LONE: You sure?

MA: Yeah!

LONE: All right. (*He rolls*) *Die!*

MA: *Siu!* (*They see the result*) Not bad.
(*They continue taking turns rolling through the following section; Ma always loses*)
LONE: I haven't touched these in two years.
MA: I gotta practice more . . .
LONE: Have you lost much money?
MA: Huh? So what?
LONE: Oh, you have gold hidden in all your shirt linings, huh?
MA: Here in "America" . . . losing is no problem. You know . . . End of the Year Bonus?
LONE: Oh, right.
MA: After I get that, I'll laugh at what I lost.
LONE: Lee told you there was a bonus, right?
MA: How'd you know?
LONE: When I arrived here, Lee told me there was a bonus, too.
MA: Lee teach you how to play?
LONE: Him? He talked to me a lot.
MA: Look, why don't you come down and start playing with the guys again?
LONE: "The guys."
MA: Before we start playing, Lee uses a stick to write "Kill!" in the dirt.
LONE: You seem to live for your nights with "the guys."
MA: What's life without friends, huh?
LONE: Well, why do *you* think I stopped playing?
MA: Hey, maybe you were the one getting killed, huh?
LONE: What?
MA: Hey, just kidding.
LONE: Who's getting killed here?
MA: Just a joke.
LONE: That's not a joke, it's blasphemy.
MA: Look, obviously you stopped playing 'cause you wanted to practice the opera.
LONE: Do you understand that discipline?
MA: But, I mean, you don't have to overdo it either. You don't have to treat 'em like dirt. I mean, who are you trying to impress?
(*Pause; Lone throws dice into the bushes*)
LONE: Oooops. Better go see who won.
MA: Hey! C'mon! Help me look!

LONE: If you find them, they are yours.

MA: You serious?

LONE: Yes.

MA: (*Finds the dice*) Here.

LONE: Who won?

MA: I didn't check.

LONE: Well, no matter. Keep the dice. Take them, and go play with your friends.

MA: Here. (*He offers them to Lone*) A present.

LONE: A present? This isn't a present!

MA: They're mine, aren't they? You gave them to me, right?

LONE: Well, yes, but . . .

MA: So now I'm giving them to you.

LONE: You can't give me a present. I don't want them.

MA: You wanted them enough to keep them two years.

LONE: I'd forgotten I had them.

MA: See, I know, Lone. You wanna get rid of me. But you can't. I'm paying for lessons.

LONE: With my dice.

MA: Mine now. (*He offers them again*) Here.

(*Pause; Lone runs Ma's hand across his forehead*)

LONE: Feel this.

MA: Hey!

LONE: Pretty wet, huh?

MA: Big deal.

LONE: Well, it's not from playing *Die Siu*.

MA: I know how to sweat. I wouldn't be here if I didn't.

LONE: Yes, but are you willing to sweat after you've finished sweating? Are you willing to come up after you've spent the whole day chipping half an inch off a rock, and punish your body some more?

MA: Yeah. Even after work, I still . . .

LONE: No, you don't. You want to gamble, and tell dirty stories, and dress up like women to do shows.

MA: Hey, I never did that.

LONE: You've only been here a month. (*Pause*) And what about "the guys?" They're not going to treat you so well once you stop playing with them. Are you willing to work all day listening to them whisper, "That one—let's put spiders in his soup."

MA: They won't do that to me. With you, it's different.

LONE: Is it?

MA: You don't have to act that way.

LONE: What way?

MA: Like you're so much better than them.

LONE: No. You haven't even begun to understand. To practice every day, you must have a fear to force you up here.

MA: A fear? No—it's 'cause what you're doing is beautiful.

LONE: No.

MA: I've seen it.

LONE: It's ugly to practice when the mountain has turned your muscles to ice. When my body hurts too much to come here, I look at the other Chinamen and think, "They are dead. Their muscles work only because the white man forces them." I live because I can still force my muscles to work for me. Say it—"They are dead."

MA: No. They're my friends.

LONE: Well, then, take your dice down to your friends.

MA: But I want to learn . . .

LONE: This is your first lesson.

MA: Look, it shouldn't matter . . .

LONE: It does.

MA: It shouldn't matter what I think.

LONE: Attitude is everything.

MA: But as long as I come up, do the exercises . . .

LONE: I'm not going to waste time on a quitter.

MA: I'm not!

LONE: Then say it—"They are dead men."

MA: I can't.

LONE: Then you will never have the dedication.

MA: That doesn't prove anything.

LONE: I will not teach a dead man.

MA: What?

LONE: If you can't see it, then you're dead too.

MA: Don't start pinning . . .

LONE: Say it!

MA: All right.

LONE: What?

MA: All right. I'm one of them. I'm a dead man too.

(*Pause*)

LONE: I thought as much. So, go. You have your friends.

MA: But I don't have a teacher.

LONE: I don't think you need both.

MA: Are you sure?

LONE: I'm being questioned by a child.

(*Lone returns to practicing; silence*)

MA: Look, Lone, I'll come up here every night—after work . . . I'll spend my time practicing, okay? (*Pause*) But I'm not gonna say that they're dead. Look at them. They're on strike; dead men don't go on strike, Lone. The white devils— they try and stick us with a ten-hour day. We want a return to eight hours and also a fourteen-dollar-a-month raise. I learned the demon English—listen: "Eight hour a day good for white man, alla same good for Chinaman." These are the demands of live Chinamen, Lone. Dead men don't complain.

LONE: All right, this is something new. But no one can judge the Chinamen 'til after the strike.

MA: They say we'll hold out for months if we have to. The smart men will live on what we've hoarded.

LONE: A Chinaman's mouth can swallow the earth. (*He takes the dice*) While the strike is on, I'll teach you.

MA: And afterwards?

LONE: Afterwards—we'll decide then whether these are dead or live men.

MA: When can we start?

LONE: We've already begun. Give me your hand.

Scene Three:

Late afternoon, four days later. Lone and Ma are doing physical exercises.

MA: How long will it be before I can play Kwan Kung?

LONE: How long before a dog can play the violin?

MA: Old Ah Hong—have you heard him play the violin?

LONE: Yes, Now he should take his violin and give it to a dog.

MA: I think he sounds okay.

LONE: I think he caused that avalanche last winter.

MA: He used to play for weddings back home.

LONE: Ah Hong?

MA: That's what he said.

LONE: You probably heard wrong.

MA: No.

LONE: He probably said he played for funerals.

MA: He's been playing for the guys down at camp.

LONE: He should play for the white devils—that will end this stupid strike.

MA: Yang told me for sure—it'll be over by tomorrow.

LONE: Eight days already. And Yang doesn't know anything.

MA: He said they're already down to an eight-hour day and five dollars raise at the bargaining sessions.

LONE: Yang eats too much opium.

MA: That doesn't mean he's wrong about this.

LONE: You can't trust him. One time—last year—he went around camp looking in everybody's eyes and saying, "Your nails are too long. They're hurting my eyes." This went on for a week. Finally, all the men clipped their nails, made a big pile, which they wrapped in leaves and gave to him. Yang used the nails to season his food . . . he put it in his soup, sprinkled it on his rice, and never said a word about it again. Now tell me—are you going to trust a man who eats other men's fingernails?

MA: Well, all I know is we won't go back to work until they meet all our demands. Listen, teach me some Kwan Kung steps.

LONE: I should have expected this. A boy who wants to have twenty wives is the type who demands more than he can handle.

MA: Just a few.

LONE: It takes years before an actor can play Kwan Kung.

MA: I can do it. Back home I would spend a lot of time watching the opera when it came to town. Everytime I'd see Kwan Kung, I'd say, "Yeah. That's me. The God of Fighters. The God of Adventurers. We have the same kind of spirit."

LONE: I tell you, if you work very hard, when you return to China, you can perhaps be the Second Clown.

MA: Second Clown?

LONE: If you work hard.

MA: What's the Second Clown?

LONE: You can play the p'i p'a, and dance and jump all over.

MA: I'll buy them.

LONE: Excuse me?

MA: I'm going to be rich, remember? I'll buy a troupe and force them to let me play Kwan Kung.

LONE: I hope you have enough money, then, to pay audiences to sit through your show.

MA: You mean, I'm going to have to practice here every night . . . and in return, all I can play is the Second Clown?

LONE: If you work hard.

MA: Am I that bad? Maybe I shouldn't even try to do this. Maybe I should just go down.

LONE: It's not you. Everyone must earn the right to play Kwan Kung. I entered Opera school when I was ten years old. My parents decided to sell me for ten years to this Opera company. I lived with eighty other boys and we slept in bunks four beds high and hid our candy and rice cakes from each other. After eight years, I was studying to play Kwan Kung.

MA: Eight years?

LONE: I was one of the best in my class. One day, I was summoned by my master, who told me I was to go home for two days, because my mother had fallen very ill and was dying. When I arrived home, mother was standing at the door waiting, not sick at all. Her first words to me, the son away for eight years, were, "You've been playing while your village has starved. You must go to the Gold Mountain and work."

MA: And you never returned to school?

LONE: I went from a room with eighty boys to a ship with three hundred men. So, you see, it does not come easily to play Kwan Kung.

MA: Did you want to play Kwan Kung?

LONE: What a foolish question!

MA: Well, you're better off this way.

LONE: What?

MA: Actors—they don't make much money. Here, you make a bundle, then go back and be an actor again. Best of both worlds.

LONE: "Best of both worlds."

MA: Yeah!

(*Lone drops to the floor, begins imitating a duck, waddling and quacking*)

MA: Lone? What are you doing? (*Lone quacks*) You're a duck? (*Lone quacks*) I can see that. (*Lone quacks*) Is this an exercise? Am I supposed to do this? (*Lone quacks*) This is dumb. I never seen Kwan Kung waddle. (*Lone quacks*) Okay. All right I'll do it. (*Ma and Lone quack and waddle*) You know, I never realized before how uncomfortable a duck's life is. And you have to listen to yourself quacking all day. Go crazy! (*Lone stands up straight*) Now, what was that all about?

LONE: No, no. Stay down there, duck.

MA: What's the . . .

LONE: (*Prompting*) "Quack, quack, quack."

MA: I don't . . .

LONE: Act your species!

MA: I'm not a duck!

LONE: Nothing worse than a duck that doesn't know his place.

MA: All right. (*Mechanically*) Quack, quack.

LONE: More.

MA: Quack.

LONE: More!

MA: Quack, quack, quack!

(*Ma now continues quacking, as Lone gives commands*)

LONE: Louder! It's your mating call! Think of your twenty duck wives! Good! Louder! Project! More! Don't slow down! Put your tails feathers into it! They can't hear you!

(*Ma is now quacking up a storm. Lone exits, unnoticed by Ma*)

MA: Quack! Quack! Quack! Quack. Quack . . . quack. (*He looks around*) Quack . . . quack . . . Lone? . . Lone? (*He waddles around the stage looking*) Lone, where are you? Where'd you go? (*He stops, scratches his left leg with his right foot*) C'mon— stop playing around. What is this? (*Lone enters as a tiger, unseen by Ma*) Look, let's call it a day, okay? I'm getting hungry. (*Ma turns around, notices Lone right before Lone is to bite him*) Aaaaah! Quack, quack, quack! (*They face off, in character as animals. Duck-Ma is terrified*)

LONE: Grrrr!

MA: (*As a cry for help*) Quack, quack, quack!

(*Lone pounces on Ma. They struggle, in character. Ma is quacking madly, eyes tightly closed. Lone stands up straight. Ma continues to quack, his eyes still closed*)

MA: Quack, quack, quack!

LONE: (*Louder*) Stand up.

MA: (*Opening his eyes*) Oh.

LONE: What are you?

MA: Huh?

LONE: A Chinaman or a duck?

MA: Huh? Gimme a second to remember.

LONE: You like being a duck?

MA: My feet fell asleep.

LONE: You change forms so easily.

MA: You said to.

LONE: What else could you turn into?

MA: Well, you scared me—sneaking up like that.

LONE: Perhaps a rock. That would be useful. When the men need to rest, they can sit on you.

MA: I got carried away.

LONE: Let's try . . . a locust. Can you become a locust?

MA: No. Let's cut this, okay?

LONE: Here. It's easy. You just have to know how to hop.

MA: You're not gonna get me . . .

LONE: Like this. (*He demonstrates*)

MA: Forget it, Lone.

LONE: I'm a locust. (*He begins jumping towards Ma*)

MA: Hey! Get away!

LONE: I devour whole fields.

MA: Stop it.

LONE: I starve babies before they are born.

MA: Hey, look, stop it!

LONE: I cause famines and destroy villages.

MA: I'm warning you! Get away!

LONE: What are you going to do? You can't kill a locust.

MA: You're not a locust.

LONE: You kill one, and another sits on your hand.

MA: Stop following me.

LONE: Locusts always trouble people. If not, we'd feel useless. Now, if you became a locust, too . . .

MA: I'm not going to become a locust.

LONE: Just stick your teeth! Out!

MA: I'm not gonna be a bug! It's stupid!

LONE: No man who's just been a duck has the right to call anything stupid.

MA: I thought you were trying to teach me something.

LONE: I am. Go ahead.

MA: All right. There. That look right?

LONE: Your legs should be a little lower. Lower! There. That's adequate. So, how does it feel to be a locust? (*Lone gets up*)

MA: I dunno. How long do I have to do this?

LONE: Could you do it for three years?

MA: Three years? Don't be . . .

LONE: You couldn't, could you? Could you be a duck for that long?

MA: Look, I wasn't born to be either of those.

LONE: Exactly. Well, I wasn't born to work on a railroad, either. "Best of both worlds." How can you be such an insect?

(*Pause*)

MA: Lone . . .

LONE: Stay down there! Don't move! I've never told anyone my story—the story of my parents kidnapping me from school. All the time we were crossing the ocean, the last two years here—I've kept my mouth shut. To you, I finally tell it. And all you can say is, "Best of both worlds." You're a bug to me, a locust. You think you understand the dedication one must have to be in the opera? You think it's the same as working on a railroad.

MA: Lone, all I was saying is that you'll go back too, and . . .

LONE: You're no longer a student of mine.

MA: What?

LONE: You have no dedication.

MA: Lone, I'm sorry.

LONE: Get up.

MA: I'm honored that you told me that.

LONE: Get up.

MA: No.

LONE: No?

MA: I don't want to. I want to talk.

LONE: Well, I've learned from the past. You're stubborn. You don't go. All right. Stay there. If you want to prove to me that you're dedicated, be a locust 'til morning. I'll go.

MA: Lone, I'm really honored that you told me.

LONE: I'll return in the morning. (*Lone exits*)

MA: Lone? Lone—that's ridiculous. You think I'm gonna stay like this? If you do, you're crazy. Lone? Come back here.

Scene Four:

Night. Ma, alone, as a locust.

MA: Locusts travel in huge swarms, so large that when they cross the sky, they block out the sun, like a storm. Second

Uncle—back home—when he was a young man, his whole crop got wiped out by locusts one year. In the famine that followed, Second Uncle lost his eldest son and his second wife—the one he married for love. Even to this day, we look around before saying the word "locust"—to make sure Second Uncle is out of hearing range. About eight years ago, my brother and I discovered Second Uncle's cave in back of the stream near our house. We saw him come out of it one day around noon. Later, just before the sun went down, we sneaked in. We only looked once. Inside, there must have been hundreds—maybe five hundred or more—grasshoppers in huge bamboo cages—and around them—stacks of grasshopper legs, grasshopper heads, grasshopper antennae, grasshoppers with one leg still trying to hop but toppling like trees coughing, grasshoppers wrapped around sharp branches rolling from side to side, grasshopper legs cut off grasshopper bodies then tied around grasshoppers and tightened 'til grasshoppers died. Every conceivable kind of grasshopper in every conceivable stage of life and death, subject to every conceivable grasshopper torture. We ran out quickly, my brother and I—we knew an evil place by the thickness of the air. Now, I think of Second Uncle. How sad that the locusts forced him to take out his agony on innocent grasshoppers. What if Second Uncle could see me now? Would he cut off my legs? He might as well. I can barely feel them. But then again, Second Uncle never tortured actual locusts, just weak grasshoppers.

Scene Five:

Night. Ma still as a locust. Chinese gongs, drums, in the distance, then getting closer. It is just before dawn.
    LONE: (*Off, singing*)
"Hit your hardest,
Pound out your tears.
The more you try,
The more you'll cry
At how little I've moved
And how large I loom
By the time the sun goes down."

MA: You look rested.

LONE: Me?

MA: Well, you sound rested.

LONE: No, not at all.

MA: Maybe I'm just comparing you to me.

LONE: I didn't even close my eyes all last night.

MA: Aw, Lone, you didn't have to stay up for me. You coulda' just come up here and . . .

LONE: For you?

MA: . . . apologized and everything woulda' been . . .

LONE: I didn't stay up for you.

MA: Huh? You didn't?

LONE: No.

MA: Oh. (*Beat*) You sure?

LONE: Positive. I was thinking, that's all.

MA: About me?

LONE: Well . . .

MA: Even a little?

LONE: I was thinking about the Chinamen . . . and you. Get up, Ma.

MA: Aw, do I have to? I've gotten to know these grasshoppers real well.

LONE: Get up. I have a lot to tell you.

MA: What'll they think? They take me in even though I'm a little large, then they find out I'm a human being. I stepped on their kids. No trust. Gimme a hand, will you? (*Lone helps Ma up, but Ma's legs can't support him*) Aw, shit. My legs are coming off. (*He lies down and tries to straighten them out*)

LONE: I have many surprises. First, you will play Kwan Kung.

MA: My legs will be sent home without me. What'll my family think? Come to port to meet me, and all they get is two legs.

LONE: Did you hear me?

MA: Hold on. I can't be in agony and listen to Chinese at the same time.

LONE: Did you hear my first surprise?

MA: No. I'm too busy screaming.

LONE: I said, you'll play Kwan Kung.

MA: Kwan Kung?

LONE: Yes.

MA: Me?

LONE: Yes.

MA: Without legs?

LONE: What?

MA: That might be good.

LONE: Stop that!

MA: I'll become a legend. Like the blind man who defended Amoy.

LONE: Didn't you hear?

MA: "The legless man who played Kwan Kung."

LONE: Isn't that what you want? To play Kwan Kung?

MA: No, I just wanna sleep.

LONE: No, you don't. Look. Here. I brought you something.

MA: Food?

LONE: Here. Some rice.

MA: Thanks, Lone. And duck?

LONE: Just a little.

MA: Where'd you get the duck?

LONE: Just bones and skin.

MA: We don't have duck. And the white devils have been blockading the food.

LONE: Sing—he had some left over.

MA: Sing? That thief?

LONE: And something to go with it.

MA: What? (*Lone reveals a bottle*) Lone, where did you find whiskey?

LONE: You know, Sing—he has almost anything.

MA: Yeah. For a price.

LONE: Once, even some thousand-day-old eggs.

MA: He's a thief. That's what they told me.

LONE: Not if you're his friend.

MA: Sing don't have any real friends. Everyone talks about him bein' tied in to the head of the Klan in San Francisco. Lone, you didn't have to do this. Here. Have some.

LONE: I had plenty.

MA: Don't gimme that. This cost you plenty, Lone.

LONE: Well, I thought if we were going to celebrate, we should do it as well as we would at home.

MA: Celebrate? What for? Wait.

LONE: Ma, the strike is over.

MA: Shit, I knew it. And we won, right?

LONE: Yes, the Chinamen have won. They can do more than just talk.

MA: I told you. Didn't I tell you?

LONE: Yes. Yes, you did.

MA: Yang told me it was gonna be done. He said

LONE: Yes, I remember.

MA: Didn't I tell you? Huh?

LONE: Ma, eat your duck.

MA: Nine days. In nine days, we civilized the white devils. I knew it, I knew we'd hold out 'til their ears started twitching. So that's where you got the duck, right? At the celebration?

LONE: No, there wasn't a celebration.

MA: Huh? You sure? The Chinamen—they look for any excuse to party.

LONE: But I thought we should celebrate.

MA: Well, that's for sure.

LONE: So you will play Kwan Kung.

MA: God, nine days. Shit, it's finally done. Well, we'll show them how to party. Make noise. Jump off rocks. Make the mountain shake.

LONE: We'll wash your body, to prepare you for the role.

MA: What role?

LONE: Kwan Kung. I've been telling you.

MA: I don't wanna play Kwan Kung.

LONE: You've shown the dedication required to become my student, so . . .

MA: Lone, you think I stayed up last night 'cause I wanted to play Kwan Kung?

LONE: You said you were like him.

MA: I am. Kwan Kung stayed up all night once to prove his loyalty. Well, now I have too. Lone, I'm honored that you told me your story.

LONE: Yes. . . . That is like Kwan Kung.

MA: Good. So let's do an opera about me.

LONE: What?

MA: You wanna party or what?

LONE: About you?

MA: You said I was like Kwan Kung, didn't you?

LONE: Yes, but . . .

MA: Well, look at the operas he's got. I ain't even got one.

LONE: Still, you can't . . .

MA: You tell, me, is that fair?

LONE: You can't do an opera about yourself.

MA: I just won a victory, didn't I? I deserve an opera in my honor.

LONE: But, it's not traditional.

MA: Traditional? Lone, you gotta figure any way I could do Kwan Kung wasn't gonna be traditional anyway. I may be as good a guy as him, but he's a better dancer. (*He sings*)
"Old Kwan Kung, just sits about
'Til the dime store fighters have had it out.
Then he pitches his peach pit,
Combs his beard,
Draws his sword,
And they scatter in fear."

LONE: What are you talking about?

MA: I just won a great victory. I get—what'cha call it?—poetic license. C'mon. Hit the gong. I'll immortalize my story.

LONE: I refuse. This goes against all my training. I try and give you your wish and . . .

MA: Do it. Gimme my wish. Hit the gongs.

LONE: I never . . . I can't.

MA: Can't what? Don't think I'm worth an opera? (*Beat*) No. I guess not. I forgot—you think I'm just one of those dead men.

(*Silence. Lone pulls out a gong. Ma gets into position. Lone hits the gong. They do the following in a mock Chinese opera style*)

MA: I am Ma. Yesterday, I was kicked out of my house by my three elder brothers, calling me the lazy dreamer of the family. I am sitting here in front of the temple trying to decide how I will avenge this indignity. Here comes the poorest beggar in this village. (*He cues Lone*) He is called Fleaman because his body is the most popular meeting place for fleas from around the province.

LONE: (*Singing*)
"Fleas in love,
Find your happiness
In the gray scraps of my suit."

MA: Hello, Flea . .

LONE: (*Continuing*)
"Fleas in need,

Shield your families
In the gray hairs of my beard."

MA: Hello, Flea . . .

(*Lone cuts Ma off, continues an extended improvised aria*)

MA: Hello, Fleaman.

LONE: Hello, Ma. Are you interested in providing a home for these fleas?

MA: No!

LONE: This couple here—seeking to start a new home. Housing today is so hard to find. How about your left arm?

MA: I may have plenty of my own fleas in time. I have been thrown out by my elder brothers.

LONE: Are you seeking revenge? A flea epidemic on your house? (*To a flea*) Get back there. You should be asleep. Your mother will worry.

MA: Nothing would make my brothers angrier than seeing me rich.

LONE: Rich? After the bad crops of the last three years, even the fleas are thinking of moving north.

MA: I heard a white devil talk yesterday.

LONE: Oh—with hair the color of a sick chicken and eyes round as eggs? The fleas and I call him Chicken-Laying-an-Egg.

MA: He said we can make our fortunes on the Gold Mountain, where work is play and the sun scares off snow.

LONE: Don't listen to chicken-brains.

MA: Why not? He said gold grows like weeds.

LONE: I have heard that it is slavery.

MA: Slavery? What do you know, Fleaman? Who told you? The fleas? Yes, I will go to Gold Mountain.

(*They pick up fighting sticks and do a water-crossing dance. When the dance ends, they stoop next to each other and rock*)

MA: I have been in the bottom of this boat for thirty-six days now. Tang, how many have died?

LONE: Not me. I'll live through this ride.

MA: I didn't ask how you are.

LONE: But why's the Gold Mountain so far?

MA: We left with three hundred and three.

LONE: My family's depending on me.

MA: So tell me how many have died?

LONE: I'll be the last one alive.

MA: That's not what I wanted to know.

LONE: I'll find some fresh air in this hole.
MA: I asked, how many have died.
LONE: Is that a crack in the side?
MA: Are you listening to me?
LONE: If I had some air . . .
MA: I asked, don't you see . . . ?
LONE: The crack—over there.
MA: Will you answer me please?
LONE: I need to get out.
MA: The rest here agree . . .
LONE: I can't stand the smell.
MA: That a hundred eighty . . .
LONE: I can't see the air.
MA: Of us will not see . . .
LONE: And I can't die.
MA: Our Gold Mountain dream.

(*Lone/Tang dies; Ma throws his body off board. The boat docks. Ma exits, walks through the streets. He picks up one of the fighting sticks, while Lone becomes the mountain*)

MA: I have been given my pickaxe. Now, I will attack the mountain.

(*Ma does a dance of labor. Lone sings*)

LONE:
"Hit your hardest,
Pound out your tears.
The more you try,
The more you'll cry
At how little I've moved
And how large I loom
By the time the sun goes down."

(*Dance stops*)

MA: This Mountain is clever. But why shouldn't it be? It's fighting for its life, like we fight for ours.

(*The Mountain [Lone] picks up a stick. Ma and the Mountain do a battle dance. The dance ends*)

MA: This mountain not only defends itself—it also attacks. It turns our strength against us. (*Lone does Ma's labor dance, while Ma plants explosives in mid-air. Dance ends*) The mountain has survived for millions of years. Its wisdom is immense.

(*Lone and Ma begin a second battle dance. This one ends with them working the battle sticks together. Lone breaks away, does a warrior strut*)

LONE: I am a white devil! Listen to my stupid language: "Wha Che Doo Doo Blah Blah." Look at my wide eyes—like I have drunk seventy-two pots of tea. Look at my funny hair—twisting, turning, like a snake telling lies. (*To Ma*) Bla Bla Doo Doo Tee Tee.

MA: We don't understand English.

LONE: (*Angry*) Bla Bla Doo Doo Tee Tee!

MA: (*With Chinese accent*) Please you-ah speak-ah Chinee?

LONE: Oh. Work—uh—one—two—more—work—two—

MA: Two hours more? Stupid demons. As confused as your hair. We will strike!

(*Ma is on strike*)

MA: (*In broken English*) Eight hours day good for white man, alla same good for Chinaman.

LONE: The strike is over! We've won!

MA: I knew we would.

LONE: We forced the white devil to act civilized.

MA: Tamed the barbarians!

LONE: Did you think . . .

MA: Who woulda' thought?

LONE: . . . it could be done?

MA: Who?

LONE: But who?

MA: Who could tame them?

MA AND LONE: Only a Chinaman? (*They laugh*)

LONE: Well, c'mon.

MA: Let's celebrate!

LONE: We have.

MA: Oh.

LONE: Back to work.

MA: But we've won the strike.

LONE: I know. Congratulations! And now . . .

MA: . . . back to work?

LONE: Right.

MA: No.

LONE: But the strike is over.

(*Lone tosses Ma a stick; they resume their stick battle as before, but Ma is heard over Lone's singing*)

LONE: "Hit your hardest,   MA: Wait.
          Pound out your   I'm tired of this!
              tears.   How do we end it?

The more you try,
The more you'll cry
At how little I've
  moved
And how large I
  loom
By the time the sun
  goes down."

Let's stop now, all
  right?
Look, I said enough!

(*Ma tosses his stick away, but Lone is already aiming a blow towards it, so that Lone hits Ma instead and knocks him down*)

MA: Oh! Shit . . .

LONE: I'm sorry! Are you all right?

MA: Yeah. I guess.

LONE: Why'd you let go? You can't just do that.

MA: I'm bleeding.

LONE: That was stupid . . . Where?

MA: Here.

LONE: No.

MA: Ow!

LONE: There will probably be a bump.

MA: I dunno.

LONE: What?

MA: I dunno why I let go.

LONE: It was stupid.

MA: But how were we going to end the opera?

LONE: Here. (*He applies whiskey to Ma's bruise*) I don't know.

MA: Why didn't we just end it with the celebration? Ow! Careful.

LONE: Sorry. But Ma, the celebration's not the end. We're returning to work. Today. At dawn.

MA: What?

LONE: We've already lost nine days of work. But we got eight hours.

MA: Today? That's terrible.

LONE: What do you think we're here for? But they listened to our demands. We're getting a raise.

MA: Right. Fourteen dollars.

LONE: No. Eight.

MA: What?

LONE: We had to compromise. We got an eight dollar raise.

MA: But we wanted fourteen! Why didn't we get fourteen?

LONE: It was the best deal they could get. Congratulations.

MA: Congratulations? Look, Lone, I'm sick of you making fun of the Chinamen.

LONE: Ma, I'm not. For the first time. I was wrong. We got eight dollars.

MA: We wanted fourteen.

LONE: But we got eight hours.

MA: We'll go back on strike.

LONE: Why?

MA: We could hold out for months.

LONE: And lose all that work?

MA: But we just gave in.

LONE: You're being ridiculous. We got eight hours. Besides, it's already been decided.

MA: I didn't decide. I wasn't there. You made me stay up here.

LONE: The heads of the gangs decide.

MA: And that's it?

LONE: It's done.

MA: Back to work? That's what they decided? Lone, I don't want to go back to work.

LONE: Who does?

MA: I forgot what it's like.

LONE: You'll pick up the technique again soon enough.

MA: I mean, what it's like to have them telling you what to do all the time. Using up your strength.

LONE: I thought you said even after work, you still feel good.

MA: Some days. But others . . . (*Pause*) I get so frustrated sometimes. At the rock. The rock doesn't give in. It's not human. I wanna claw it with my fingers, but that would just rip them up. I wanna throw myself head first onto it, but it'd just knock my skull open. The rock would knock my skull open, then just sit there, smiling, still, like nothing had happened like a faceless Buddha. (*Pause*) Lone, when do I get out of here?

LONE: Well, the railroad may get finished .

MA: It'll never get finished.

LONE: . . . or you may get rich.

MA: Rich. Right. This is the Gold Mountain. (*Pause*) Lone, has anyone ever gone home rich from here?

LONE: Yes. Some.

MA: But most?

LONE: Most . . . do go home.

(*Beat*)

MA: Do you still have the fear?

LONE: The fear?

MA: That you'll become like them—dead men?

LONE: Maybe I was wrong about them.

MA: Well, I do. You wanted me to say it before, I can say it now: "They are dead men." Their greatest accomplishment was to win a strike that's gotten us nothing.

LONE: They're sending money home.

MA: No.

LONE: It's not much, I know, but it's something.

MA: Lone, I'm not even doing that. If I don't get rich here, I might as well die here. Let my brothers laugh in peace.

LONE: Ma, you're too soft to get rich here, naïve—you believed the snow was warm.

MA: I've got to change myself. Toughen up. Take no shit. Count my change. Learn to gamble. Learn to win. Learn to stare. Learn to deny. Learn to look at men with opaque eyes.

LONE: You want to do that?

MA: I will. 'Cause I've got the fear. You've given it to me. (*Pause*)

LONE: Will I see you here tonight?

MA: Tonight?

LONE: I just thought I'd ask.

MA: I'm sorry, Lone. I haven't got time to be the Second Clown.

LONE: I thought you might not.

MA: Sorry.

LONE: You could have been a . . . fair actor.

MA: You coming down? I gotta get ready for work. This is gonna be a terrible day. My legs are sore and my arms are outa' practice.

LONE: You go first. I'm going to practice some before work. There's still time.

MA: Practice? But you said you lost your fear. And you said that's what brings you up here.

LONE: I guess I was wrong about that, too. Today, I am dancing for no reason at all.

MA: Do whatever you want. See you down at camp.

LONE: Could you do me a favor?

MA: A favor?

LONE: Could you take this down so I don't have to take it all?

MA: Well, okay. (*Pause*) But this is the last time.

LONE: Of course, Ma. (*Ma exits*) See you soon. The last time. I suppose so.

(*Lone resumes practicing. The sun begins to rise. Lone jumps up on a rock, twirls his long pigtail as in the first scene. The sun continues rising until Lone is seen only in shadow*)

Curtain

Percy Granger

VIVIEN

Percy Granger

Percy Granger's *Vivien* was selected by Edward Albee along with John Guare's *In Fireworks Lie Secret Codes* (elsewhere in this volume) and Jeffrey Sweet's *Stops Along the Way* (in *Best Short Plays 1981*) for an evening of one-act plays to run for six weeks starting in March, 1981, at the Mitzi E. Newhouse Theatre of New York's Lincoln Center. *Variety's* critic praised *Vivien* as "an engrossing study of a mentally disturbed man's reunion with an anxiety-ridden son, written with sensitivity and offbeat humor." And Michael Feingold in the *Village Voice* observed that playwright Percy "has a fix on his subject that clearly comes from need, not casual observation, and he has learned to use both humor and structure to heighten, rather than evade, the pain: The father's non-sequential talk is notated with Joycean care . . ." First presented in New York at the Ensemble Studio Theatre in May, 1979, *Vivien* was subsequently produced with another Granger one-act, *Solitude Forty*, under the billing *Unheard Songs* at the Peterborough Playhouse in New Hampshire in 1980.

Mr. Granger has revealed that the idea for *Vivien* came to him full-blown: "I was jogging in Central Park, and it just came. That night I had to go to the Bronx, and I wrote it on the forty-minute [subway] ride out there and back. Believe me, it doesn't happen that often."

The success of *Vivien* followed closely on the heels of a highly praised production of Mr. Granger's *Eminent Domain*, produced at Princeton's McCarter Theatre in February of 1981. *Eminent Domain* is the story of a college professor who has been teaching in a Midwest school for twenty-two years and is waiting to hear if he has been appointed to a prestigious chair in an eastern college. He is thrown into conflict with his wife when she refuses to go east with him. Bruce Chadwick of the *Daily News* (New York) found this to be "a play that creates an evening of warmth and happiness that you never want to end." The play had first been presented at the Eugene O'Neill Center in Connecticut in 1977.

Originally from the Midwest himself, Percy Granger was born in 1945 and raised in the environment of the University of Oklahoma, where his father is still a Professor of English and his mother, a painter. Granger pursued a degree at Harvard, where he studied pre-law, but he soon started acting and writing, and upon graduation began an acting career at the Provincetown Playhouse, where his roles included Yank in *The Hairy Ape,* Kilroy in *Camino Real,* and Bottom in *A Midsummer Night's Dream.* As soon as he entered the acting profession, he discovered to his dismay that he had been drafted. In a battle with his draft board that extended over several years, Mr. Granger first attempted to obtain classification as a Conscientious Objector. Rejected on his appeal, he took a job teaching physical education at the Towne School in Manhattan to get a teaching deferment. His patience with "prematurely wealthy" students worn thin, he joined other draft protesters in Canada, where he spent four years acting and writing TV and film scripts, and surreptitiously crossing the border during summers to act under assumed names. Eventually, he moved to Manhattan, where he now resides with his wife Helen and their two young sons.

Reflecting on his art, Granger exhibits a keen feeling for character, language and a strong affirmation of human relationships: "Plays that don't deal with character aren't terribly interesting to me. The whole following for cold, unemotional drama, for cynicism, nihilism, super-sophistication—these are things I hate."

Readers of this collection will note that *Vivien* and Samuel Shem's *Napoleon's Dinner,* which follows, share a number of common concerns—father-son relationships, insanity, success, among others. The editor has placed these plays in juxtaposition so that the reader may more easily compare very different textures and treatments of similar topics. (The pair would also make an interesting double bill in the theatre.)

Characters:

PAUL HOWARD
VIVIEN HOWARD

Lights up.
A man sits on a bench. His mouth is slack and his eyes are glazed.
There is a trace of a deep anger nestled in his brow, the impression
is that of a slumbering violence. He is a large man with massive
shoulders. He wears a white shirt, yellowed with age; grey work
pants held up by suspenders and a garrison belt outside and below
the belt loops; and a shabby car coat. His black work shoes are
scuffed and his thin white socks are bunched down below his ankles.
An old tie protrudes from one pocket. No movement.
After a long moment he rocks slightly. He stops. No movement.
A younger man enters. He is fashionably dressed in sports
jacket, tie, slacks and a smart new raincoat with belt and epaulets.
He carries a set of car keys. He stops and peers at the seated figure.

PAUL: Dad? (*No response; the man does not look at him*) Dad?
It's Paul. (*No response*) Dad. . . . Mr. Howard . . . . . Viv-
ien? (*Vivien looks at him*) Hi. (*No response*) You been waiting
long? (*No response*) I'm sorry about the rain.
VIVIEN: (*Looking away*) Weather doesn't bother me.
PAUL: Are you all set to go? (*No response. Paul takes a step*
forward) Can I give you a hand?
VIVIEN: Keep your distance.
PAUL: What's the matter?
VIVIEN: I'm not going with you.
PAUL: What?
VIVIEN: You're not Paul.
PAUL: Yes I am. It's Paul. (*Vivien begins to tremble slightly*)
Are you cold? Should we get in the car?
VIVIEN: I'm not getting in your car.
PAUL: Why not?
VIVIEN: You're not Paul.
PAUL: Sure I'm Paul. Of course I'm Paul. It's me. Who else
would I be?
VIVIEN: That's your problem.
PAUL: Are you Vivien Howard?
VIVIEN: Yes.

PAUL: I'm Paul Howard, I'm your son. (*No response*) I know it's been a long time; I'm just grown up now. It's still me. (*No response*) Norristown, you remember? It was just like today, it was raining. We sat in the parking lot. Mom went in and got you. You sat in the back seat. You stared at me, do you remember that? It was 1955, I was ten. I was just ten.

VIVIEN: Everyone I know is dead.

PAUL: I spoke to—Miss Tendesco is it?

VIVIEN: Yes.

PAUL: She said you were very excited.

VIVIEN: I'm all right.

PAUL: I mean we made all the arrangements. She said you wanted to go out. (*No response*) You want me to get her?

VIVIEN: You can get her if you want.

PAUL: What should I tell her 's the matter?

VIVIEN: You're not Paul.

PAUL: What are you doing out here then?

VIVIEN: Waiting for Paul.

PAUL: (*Gestures*) You got 'im. (*Beat*) Look, it's starting to rain again, let's get in the car, okay?

VIVIEN: No.

PAUL: It's right over there—

VIVIEN: No.

PAUL: Dad, it's after twelve, we've got to go.

VIVIEN: You go on.

PAUL: What about you?

VIVIEN: I'm sorry you drove all this way for nothing.

PAUL: (*Taking out his wallet*) I can prove I'm Paul. There's my driver's license, there's my picture and my name. (*Vivien won't look*) Look—I've got credit cards, union cards—I've got identification coming out of my ears!

VIVIEN: Don't show me your private property.

PAUL: Look for yourself.

VIVIEN: Don't show me your private property!

(*Pause*)

PAUL: Can I sit down?

VIVIEN: It's a free country.

(*Paul sits next to him*)

PAUL: Paulie? Po? Pooh? I don't remember, what did you call me? (*No response*) How are you?

VIVIEN: I can't complain.

PAUL: You look terrific.

VIVIEN: You're not Paul.

PAUL: I am Paul! Why else would I be here?

VIVIEN: I'm supposed to meet Paul here.

PAUL: Okay—here, right? At the bus stop?

VIVIEN: Yes.

PAUL: In front of the buildings?

VIVIEN: Yes.

PAUL: On the bench?

VIVIEN: Yes.

PAUL: Okay, so here we are.

VIVIEN: Here we are.

PAUL: I'm your son.

VIVIEN: Go away.

PAUL: Didn't Miss Tendesco tell you who I was?

VIVIEN: You don't know her.

PAUL: Do you want to go talk to her?

VIVIEN: No.

PAUL: Why don't we go see her?

VIVIEN: No.

PAUL: All right, we won't. Look, could we start over?

VIVIEN: He's late.

PAUL: It's only twelve-fifteen.

VIVIEN: Late! There's going to be hell to pay. You stick around if you want to see some fireworks, mister. When he sees this son of his, there's going to be hell to pay! He won't stand for it—he doesn't have to. He's got other recourses. He knows the score. There's a worm of truth there; you don't think so by your expression? You think he's just free?

PAUL: I didn't know where you were, all right? I had to fight with Mom to get her to tell me. I told her I had a right to know.

VIVIEN: I'm sure you're very busy.

PAUL: (*In a frenzy*) I rented a car, you want to see the papers? Here—see?—that's my signature! That's my handwriting! And look here, I got a letter from my wife, see? It's addressed to me! What else do you want? I know I'm Paul Howard, I paid a lot of money to an analyst to establish that fact!

(*Vivien looks at him*)

VIVIEN: You ever make a basket?

(*Pause*)

PAUL: No. So what I hear you saying is, you don't want to come with me.

VIVIEN: I'm going to wait for Paul.

PAUL: Well, he won't come, because that's me!

VIVIEN: Go away.

PAUL: We were supposed to spend the day together!

VIVIEN: (*Rising, advancing on Paul*) Go away! Scat!

PAUL: Dad—

VIVIEN: Shoo!

PAUL: (*Backing up, frightened*) Hey Dad, come on, okay?

VIVIEN: Ssssss!

PAUL: Take it easy—

VIVIEN: (*Makes a large gesture with his arms, roars*) Aaaaaah! (*He turns and walks off with a jerky, stiff-legged stride*)

PAUL: (*Angry*) Why'd you say yes then, if you didn't want to come? Why'd you make me rent a car and drive all the way down here? Why'd you make me come?! (*Beat*) I thought you'd enjoy this!

Lights change:

The light on the bench crossfades with a harsher fluorescent light. Paul steps into this light, lights a cigarette and waits impatiently. He glances at his watch.

Sound:

A soft bell dings three times and a soft voice comes over a loud-speaker: "Dr. Craig. Dr. Craig."
Miss Tendesco enters pushing a cart filled with files, medicine bottles and small paper cups. She stops and begins to put pills in the cups, making a mark in each file as she does so. She is any age over forty and wears a nurse's uniform. Paul waits for her to see him. When she does not, he speaks:

PAUL: Miss Tendesco?

TENDESCO: Ah! Mr. Nystrum.

PAUL: I'm Paul Howard.

TENDESCO: Who?

PAUL: (*Beginning to think he's in Neverland*) I'm Paul Howard. I'm Vivien Howard's son.

TENDESCO: Oh yes, yes, of course—from New York.

PAUL: Yes.

TENDESCO: We spoke over the phone.

PAUL: Yes.

TENDESCO: Yes. (*She glances at her watch*) But you shouldn't be here. Vivien wanted you to meet him at the bus stop.

PAUL: I know—

TENDESCO: He was very definite about that.

PAUL: We met. I'm going back to Seattle without him.

TENDESCO: (*Concerned*) Oh? What happened?

PAUL: It seems he doesn't want to come with me.

TENDESCO: But I know he was looking forward to it.

PAUL: He was extremely hostile. He refused to recognize me.

TENDESCO: Perhaps he was embarrassed.

PAUL: By me?

TENDESCO: By himself.

PAUL: Oh. Then maybe it's just as well then, huh? Don't you think so?

TENDESCO: Shall we go find him?

PAUL: No, skip it; I'm taking off. I just wanted to let you know he got away from me.

TENDESCO: You were only interested in taking him out for the day?

PAUL: I thought I made that clear over the phone.

TENDESCO: (*Smiles*) Well, no harm in trying. I'm sure he'll be sorry.

(*She goes back to her work. Paul hesitates; he seems unable to leave*)

PAUL: I mean there's no inherent reason why he'd want to come with me, is there.

TENDESCO: You haven't seen him in quite a while.

PAUL: Hey, look I'm here, okay? Whatever happened, happened a long time before I was any part of it. I'm just here. My mother wouldn't tell me where he was. She got remarried. I never even saw a picture, for Christ's sake. I mean it was kind of a shock for me too.

TENDESCO: It usually is.

PAUL: (*Calmer*) It's just—you see my wife and I just had a kid ourselves. It's started me thinking—I just thought it might be important to see him.

TENDESCO: (*Smiles, but without looking up from her work*) That was a nice thought; it's too bad it didn't work out.

(*Pause. Paul glances at his watch, paces*)

PAUL: Did he remember who I was when you told him I'd called?

TENDESCO: Oh yes.

PAUL: What did he say?

TENDESCO: Oh, I don't remember.

PAUL: Could you try?

TENDESCO: He said, "Paul can come if he wants to."

PAUL: He remembered my name?

TENDESCO: I'd said it first.

PAUL: So what—he just changed his mind; is that what happened?

TENDESCO: I don't know. (*She goes back to work*)

PAUL: I don't know how the hell I thought I could squeeze this in anyway. We have our final preview this afternoon, and we open tonight and I'm flying out first thing in the morning.

TENDESCO: You were going to take him to a play?

PAUL: Yeah. He'd have been bored stiff, huh.

TENDESCO: You never know. (*She gives Paul an ambiguous smile*) What play was it?

PAUL: *The Seagull.*

TENDESCO: You wrote it?

PAUL: No. Anton Chekhov. I directed it; I'm a director. I only took the job in the first place so I could come see him. I mean it's not helping my career any to direct the three millionth production of *The Seagull* in some second-rate regional—(*Tendesco bursts out laughing*) What's so funny?

TENDESCO: I just got it. (*Her laughter increases*)

PAUL: Got what?

TENDESCO: (*She puts a notepad on the counter*) It's a memo pad. It says Chekhov, like the playwright and Liszt, like the composer. "Check-off list." (*More laughter as Paul stares at her*) One of the social workers gave it to me.

PAUL: I thought I'd anticipated all the possible scenerios for today, y'know? But I never thought he just wouldn't recognize me.

TENDESCO: Well, they're full of surprises, this crew. (*A final burst of laughter*)

PAUL: I don't understand why I do this to myself. I deliberately create stress situations and put myself right in the middle of them. It's an obsession; I'm sure it's a pattern. Why do you suppose I do that?

TENDESCO: Would you like to wait and try again?

PAUL: No, it's too depressing.

TENDESCO: I know. Well you'd better be off if you're going to make your show.

PAUL: What are you going to do?

TENDESCO: About what?

PAUL: Finding him.

TENDESCO: Where is he?

PAUL: I don't know. I told you he got away from me.

TENDESCO: Oh, they never go far. Excuse me, I have to go look for Mr. Nystrum.

PAUL: What's Nystrum, a patient?

TENDESCO: Yes.

PAUL: You thought I was a patient?

TENDESCO: I'm sorry, I didn't really look.

PAUL: Did you try to force him to go with me? Is that why he wouldn't come?

TENDESCO: No.

PAUL: Well, I wish you'd told me this might happen. It cost a small fortune to rent a car. I have critics coming.

TENDESCO: We had no way of knowing this is how he'd react.

PAUL: But he's in your care!

TENDESCO: (*Promptly and pleasantly amending her statement*) We had no way of knowing for certain this is how he'd react. Believe me, Mr. Howard, we're as sorry as you are. This was going to be a trial run for Vivien.

PAUL: What do you mean?

TENDESCO: We hoped he might be ready for removal from maximum security.

PAUL: Maximum . . . ! And I was going to be the guinea pig?

TENDESCO: It was perfectly safe.

PAUL: But we'd have been gone all day!

TENDESCO: So long as you had him back by curfew.

PAUL: I'm a layman!

TENDESCO: He's medicated.

PAUL: What if it wore off? What if he'd gotten violent? He looked damn angry to me.

TENDESCO: That's a very misleading look.

PAUL: We had a fifty mile drive ahead of us! Just how was I supposed to act with him?

TENDESCO: Normally. Excuse me. (*She starts out*)

PAUL: Wait, please, I'm sorry. I'm going. I'm sorry if I

upset him by coming here. It was just an impulse; I didn't stop to think, I just thought . . . Damnit! (*Pause*) Anyway thanks. Better to find out now than out on the highway at sixty miles an hour, huh. Thank you. Thanks.

(*She exits. Paul lingers as:*)

Lights change:

Hospital light cross fades with lights that illuminate yet another area on the stage and reveal the front seat of a car. Vivien enters and lingers near the car. Paul circles out of the hospital area and approaches the car. As he starts to get in . . .

VIVIEN: Hello.

(*Paul looks up. Pause*)

PAUL: (*Sullenly*) I'm going.

VIVIEN: Okay.

PAUL: I'm sorry it didn't work out.

VIVIEN: You were right about the rain. I'm soaked to the marrow. You look dank too.

PAUL: (*Grudgingly*) Do you want a lift back to your building?

(*Beat*)

VIVIEN: That should be all right.

(*They get in the car. Vivien first dusts off the seat with great energy; Paul watches this uneasily. Paul takes out a small ornate pill box and pops a pill. Vivien watches this with great interest*)

VIVIEN: What do you take?

PAUL: Just Valium.

VIVIEN: What's that?

PAUL: A tranquilizer.

VIVIEN: (*Grins*) Ah. (*Paul starts to pocket the box, Vivien takes it from him*) It's a nice box.

(*Paul watches nervously as Vivien opens it*)

PAUL: It's a present from my wife.

VIVIEN: What else have you got here?

PAUL: Just some B-12, aspirin, Dexidrine . . .

(*Vivien inspects the contents with great interest before handing it back. He watches closely to see which pocket Paul puts it in. Paul mimes starting the engine and putting the car in gear. He puts his arm on the back of Vivien's seat and looks over his shoulder to back out*)

VIVIEN: I've changed my mind.

PAUL: (*Looks at him. Freezes*) About?

VIVIEN: I've decided it will be all right to go with you.

PAUL: You have? Do you think you should?

VIVIEN: I think I can trust you.

PAUL: It's a long drive.

VIVIEN: (*Taking a pass from his pocket*) Here's my pass. We need to show it to the guard at the gate. They have dogs running wild here. Discretion is the better part of valor.

PAUL: This rain's going to make it tough.

VIVIEN: So much the better.

(*Paul, not knowing what else to do, takes the pass and puts the car in motion. After a few awkward moments of silence he nods out the window*)

PAUL: (*In a forced conversational tone*) Ah. You've got a lake here. That's something we miss in the city.

VIVIEN: There's killer whales in there'll bite your cock off.

PAUL: . . . Well, it's a trade-off I guess.

VIVIEN: (*To himself*) The Indians put them there to outlive them. . . . Nothing as fast as an Indian. . . . fleet of foot, ate berries. . . . The poisoned ones killed the weaker ones . . .

PAUL: You interested in Indians? (*No response*) They treating you okay here?

VIVIEN: Not the way they think I'd like to be treated if they had the money.

(*A beat*)

PAUL: (*Trying again*) Do they ever take you out?

VIVIEN: They took us to a county fair last year. The Pierce County Fair. In Puyallup. The Daffodil Capital of the World.

PAUL: Fun?

VIVIEN: What?

PAUL: Fun? (*Vivien doesn't seem to understand the word*) Was it fun?

VIVIEN: Oh. No, too many people. They stare at you. I managed to have a productive time, but it was a lot of trouble. I was just as glad they didn't make us go again. I'm wanted back in Pennsylvania by an institution, so I have to be careful about my movements.

PAUL: Look, are you sure you feel up to this?

VIVIEN: (*Excitedly*) There's the gate! (*In a conspiratorial tone*) Act normal. Don't worry about me, I'll sit still so they can't see me. I'm still pretty good at that. (*Paul, more nervous*

*than ever, brings the car to a halt by the gate, rolls down the window
and shows the pass. Vivien sits rigidly but his face is fairly bursting
with excitement; out of the side of his mouth to Paul)* Go! Go!
*(Startled, Paul accelerates. Vivien clenches his fists and rocks
slightly)* You see? As long as they don't catch my smell. I used
to smell of semen, but that's all over since I contracted syphi-
lis.

(Paul rolls up the window)
PAUL: It's just that I'm a little nervous. The critics are
coming tonight. They don't count for much out here but
still—

*(He breaks off because Vivien has taken the pass and is slowly,
triumphantly, tearing it up)*
VIVIEN: Paul will sure be surprised when he shows up and
I'm not there. *(Paul stops the car abruptly)* What's the matter?
PAUL: Who am I?
VIVIEN: We met at the bus stop.
PAUL: What's my name?
VIVIEN: We had a long talk.
PAUL: We're not going anywhere until you admit who I
am.
VIVIEN: You want me to get out?
PAUL: No! Who am I?
VIVIEN: The little lost sheep.
PAUL: Dad—
VIVIEN: *(Fiercely)* Let's make tracks, mister!
*(Pause. Vivien begins to tremble violently and just as violently
struggles to keep it under control. Paul, angry, takes scant notice.
He glances back towards the hospital and then at his watch. Vivien
presses his knees together and cups his hand over his mouth. He
drools. Paul impatiently puts the car in gear and drives on)*
PAUL: *(Muttered)* God damn rain, can't see a thing.
(Vivien's trembling gradually subsides)
VIVIEN: *(Apologetically)* They put stuff in your food and
make you eat it.
*(Paul takes out his handkerchief, bunches it, and wipes the fog
from the windshield)*
PAUL: Look at this, we're never going to make it on time.
(He puts the handkerchief in his lap. Vivien reaches over and takes it)
What are you doing?
VIVIEN: I'll help you.
PAUL: It's okay—

(*Vivien spreads the cloth in his lap and carefully folds it*)

VIVIEN: I had a shop instructor at Norristown, Mr. Adolphus McPherson. He said always make a pad . . . make a pad . . . (*He suddenly lunges across Paul and wipes the windshield with broad energetic strokes*)

PAUL: (*Swerving*) Watch out! Really it's—

VIVIEN: (*Raising his voice*) How's that? Can you see better?

PAUL: Yes, thank you. Just—

VIVIEN: I'll keep it wiped for you.

PAUL: That's okay, really you don't have to . . .

VIVIEN: A nice view is very restful.

PAUL: Just sit there, okay? Just relax, don't do anything. I'll get us there.

(*They drive in silence*)

VIVIEN: We're going to a play, is that right?

PAUL: Yes.

VIVIEN: Good. I'll need my tie then. (*He takes the tie from his pocket and turns the rear view mirror towards himself. He clumsily puts it on*)

PAUL: (*Finally*) I need the mirror.

VIVIEN: Just a minute. It needs to be straight.

(*After another moment Paul reaches for the mirror*)

PAUL: Okay?

VIVIEN: Is it straight?

PAUL: (*Without looking*) Yeah. (*He readjusts the mirror*)

VIVIEN: (*He continues to fret with the tie*) It doesn't feel straight.

PAUL: It's straight.

VIVIEN: It doesn't feel right.

PAUL: It's fine, leave it alone.

VIVIEN: No. (*He takes the mirror back*)

PAUL: I need the mirror.

VIVIEN: (*Frustrated*) Just a minute!

(*They struggle for the mirror*)

PAUL: Stop it! Stop! Relax!

(*Paul breaks Vivien's grip on the mirror then lets go of him. Pause. Paul readjusts the mirror. Pause. Vivien removes the tie*)

VIVIEN: There. That's better. (*They drive in silence*) I've been to a play before. They did a lopped-off Shakespeare for our benefit once.

PAUL: You want me to tell you about it?

VIVIEN: I remember it pretty well.

PAUL: I mean the one we're going to now.

VIVIEN: Oh. Just a little bit.

PAUL: It's called . . .

VIVIEN: But not the ending.

PAUL: It's called *The Seagull*. It's about a group of people living in a summer house in Russia about 1890.

VIVIEN: You've lost me.

PAUL: (*After a beat*) Well—there's a mother; she's a famous actress, and she's in love with a successful hack writer—not hack really, just second rate—and she has a son who is older than she cares to admit. (*Relaxing a bit*) And the plot thickens. The son is in love . . .

VIVIEN: Are there any animals in the play?

PAUL: There's some animal imagery, hence the title . . .

VIVIEN: Last night, two of the regular patients and I had a very happy little evening. The grounds crew said they had seen a fox on the road to the fishing dock, so we went down to try to trap a glimpse of it. On the way we saw the broken sewer drain it uses as an escape route, but no fox. So we sat on the benches on the dock and watched the boats and the water skiers. Their bathing suits were very colorful. So were the boat hulls for that matter. We waved to each one and they waved back. It made for a long to be remembered picture. When the sun was to the tops of the trees we had to start back. We walked very stealthily to increase our chance of success. We passed the sewer hole. Nothing. So we relaxed all caution and kicked the rocks on the road in disappointment. About a hundred yards up the road there was a garter snake. Its head was crushed but its tail was still moving. We gathered around to watch. Then I looked back down the road and there was the fox we'd been stalking. It was trotting after us like a little dog. When it saw us looking, it stopped and sat down in the middle of the road and scratched its ear with its hindpaw just like a dog. Then it disappeared into the bushes.

(*Silence*)

PAUL: The son is in love with a young girl who wants to be an actress. But the hack—the successful—writer is also in love with her.

VIVIEN: (*Angrily, perhaps because his story got no response*) I have to go to the bathroom.

PAUL: What? (*No response; Vivien's face contorts*) You do? (*No response*) Badly?

VIVIEN: I don't know yet.
PAUL: Can you hold it? If we stop we'll be late.
VIVIEN: I think I can do something with it. (*He lifts off the seat slightly and grunts ambiguously. Then he sits back. Pause*)
PAUL: Wha—ah, what'd you do?
VIVIEN: I got it, don't worry.
PAUL: What do you mean?
VIVIEN: (*To himself*) I'm not going to drop my trousers on an Interstate.
(*Paul glances at his watch*)
PAUL: Look if you really want me to pull off, I can.
VIVIEN: (*No longer concerned, glances out the window*) There's a motel.
PAUL: How am I on that side—any cars?
VIVIEN: No. . . . Big semi, though.
PAUL: (*Jerking the wheel back*) Jesus! Look, why don't I just turn on the radio okay? You can listen to some music; would you like that?
VIVIEN: If you think it would help. (*Paul, chagrined, does not turn it on. They drive in silence several moments*) There's another motel. Are we going to check into a motel tonight?
PAUL: No.
VIVIEN: I want to get some fresh food. I'll be better then.
PAUL: We'll have a quick bite after the show if you want, before I take you back.
VIVIEN: I'm not going back.
PAUL: What?
VIVIEN: I'm not going back.
PAUL: Of course you are.
VIVIEN: Who told you I was going back?
PAUL: You have to be back by . . .
VIVIEN: I don't have to do anything, you got that, mister?
PAUL: But I promised I'd bring you back, that was the deal.
VIVIEN: You can't. There'd be reprisals.
PAUL: Reprisals?
VIVIEN: Yes.
PAUL: What do you mean?
VIVIEN: There would.
PAUL: Against whom?
VIVIEN: Me.
PAUL: Why?

VIVIEN: I was trying to change doctors; they don't like that. My current doctor is old and cynical; he doesn't have anything to lose any more. I'd written three letters to a new Jamacian doctor named Sohkey. He acts like he hasn't received them. If he's been forced to show them to the authorities, it's curtains.

PAUL: Can't you talk to Miss Tendesco?

VIVIEN: No.

PAUL: She seems reasonable.

VIVIEN: She puts on a good show for the outsiders because we're her bread and butter, but in her heart of hearts she's a leopard.

PAUL: How would you live?

VIVIEN: I'll forage.

PAUL: What about your medication?

VIVIEN: I don't need it. I'm always okay once I get away from that place.

PAUL: Where would you go?

VIVIEN: Back to veterinary school. I'll get some clothing to improve my appearance. Professor Milton Dornhoffer said there'd always be a place for me.

PAUL: Have you written to him?

(*Beat*)

VIVIEN: I don't want to talk about it with you. (*He begins to rock back and forth violently; Paul clutches the steering wheel with both hands*) I'm tired of being in this car with you. I don't have enough room. Stop.

PAUL: I can't.

VIVIEN: I want to get out.

PAUL: It's raining.

VIVIEN: I'll be all right.

PAUL: We're going too fast.

VIVIEN: I want to get out.

PAUL: No. This is our day together.

VIVIEN: I don't make deals, mister.

PAUL: I'm not letting you out of this car.

VIVIEN: Just drop me at a clothing store.

PAUL: I'm not letting you out of this car! You're my father, and I've got you in here and you're not getting out! We're going to Seattle, you got that? So just sit there!

(*Vivien looks at him*)

VIVIEN: Are you all right?

PAUL: We can talk about it later, okay? We can talk about it at dinner.
(*Pause. Vivien looks away. Pause*)
VIVIEN: If you love me, you won't take me back.
(*Pause*)

Blackout

Sound: *Applause. Out.*

Lights up on a restaurant table: dessert plate and beer bottle and glass at Vivien's place; coffee cup and credit card slip at Paul's. Paul is smoking a cigarette. He watches his father busily finishing up his dessert. His mood is subdued, as if the final line of the previous scene still rings in his ears. Vivien stops eating, looks up
VIVIEN: Tasty, wholesome food, it makes a difference. It's nice to have things arrive on your plate hermetically sealed.
PAUL: You almost done?
VIVIEN: Um. (*He takes the last bite of his pie*) There.
(*He wipes off his silverware as Paul takes out a pen to total the bill and figure the tip*)
PAUL: It's just the opening's in two hours. (*Vivien pockets the silverware*) What're you doing?
VIVIEN: I'll need 'em for the open road.
PAUL: You can't do that.
VIVIEN: You take too many pills.
PAUL: Only when I'm under stress.
VIVIEN: Oh, here's your program back.
PAUL: Don't you want to keep it?
VIVIEN: You take it. You can use it again.
PAUL: You didn't enjoy it?
VIVIEN: I enjoyed it, but I didn't like it. Everyone was so miserable. Of course that's Communism for you.
PAUL: It happened before the Communists took over.
VIVIEN: Can I have another beer?
PAUL: I don't think you should, do you?
VIVIEN: Okay. We can go to a bar later and watch T.V. You need a stronger plot. It was too hard to keep tabs on so many people at once. That wasn't a real dead bird, was it? I didn't like that part.

PAUL: No.

VIVIEN: Why did that one fellow kill himself at the end just before he took his bow?

PAUL: He was—he didn't have his medication.

VIVIEN: (*Surprised*) He was sick? He didn't look very sick to me, just long-winded.

PAUL: He was sick in his soul. His mother had no time for him and the girl he loved didn't love him back. He was an artist without an audience . . .

VIVIEN: My mother had no use for me either, but you'd never catch me drinking two ounces of gin and a half bottle of Carbona, even if I knew it no longer contained carbon tet.

PAUL: That isn't what he did, Dad, he—

(*In the midst of writing in the tip, he stops and looks up, realizing the implication of what Vivien has said*)

VIVIEN: After a while you realize suicide hasn't taken care of anything either. The best thing is just to let them help you. (*Brief pause*) Are you all right? Aren't the critics going to like your play?

PAUL: I just don't feel so good I guess.

VIVIEN: (*Grins*) There are times when I don't feel so good myself.

PAUL: (*Rousing himself*) Look, if we're finished, we should—

VIVIEN: You'd better reconsider your decision to make a career of the theater.

PAUL: What?

VIVIEN: There isn't much future in it. This play for example, it looked like it was written a long time ago.

PAUL: Yes?

VIVIEN: So its frosting of attractiveness has rubbed off. I don't think it will be much in demand.

PAUL: But that's the beauty of it, it is in demand. It—

VIVIEN: Besides there are so many classical play productions given in secret—at the Walnut Street Theater for example. Yours won't be able to stand the competition.

PAUL: Chekhov will always be in demand because he's timeless.

VIVIEN: (*Frowning*) You have to be careful of that.

PAUL: I mean good art creates its own necessity.

VIVIEN: So does the medical profession.

PAUL: Yes, but art creates value and nothing else does

that. A doctor can save your life, but he can't make it worth living.

VIVIEN: Yes, I know.

(*Brief pause*)

PAUL: I'm happy in the theater, Dad. It's my whole life. You don't have to worry about me.

VIVIEN: Are you a success?

(*For a long moment, Paul does not respond. Finally he shrugs*)

PAUL: I'm going to Hollywood.

VIVIEN: That's a nice place.

PAUL: No, it isn't, but anyway, there it is. I directed a soap last year, and a lot of people are beginning to know who I am. (*He smiles wryly*) The nice thing about fame is they return your phone calls.

VIVIEN: (*Frowns*) Who does?

PAUL: Anyone. So I'm doing okay, I guess. I'm screwed up in other ways, but who isn't. It's a trade-off.

VIVIEN: Just remember, fame and fortune are short-lived. Phyllis Diller is living right over in Tacoma now and nobody likes her very much. And you look like you're past the age to stand the sexual stress the theater puts on one.

PAUL: Well I'm married, so that's not really a problem any more.

VIVIEN: Is your wife a woman?

PAUL: Yes.

VIVIEN: Heterosexual marriage in the theater isn't very stable, is it?

PAUL: Harriet's not an actress. She has a degree in English and another in Sociology. She's an interior decorator with a side interest in art placement.

VIVIEN: So she's got a lot of options.

PAUL: Well, not anymore; we just had a baby. I don't know how it happened—I mean, we'd made a decision against having children because we have our careers to think of. And there's a lot of different things we want to do. We knew we'd resent the responsibility. Harriet was afraid she would put too much pressure on a kid because she's such an achiever herself, and I figured it would be tough to relate to someone so much younger than I. Anyway, now that he's here, we're both trying to regard it as a positive event. If you have a kid, you're just going to miss out on some things, but if you don't have 'em you miss something too. So it's a trade-off. One thing's for certain, we're going to have to change our lifestyle.

VIVIEN: You must be happy about that.

PAUL: Well, in fact we are thinking about a separation. I'll be making enough money now to support them, so—for the first time in our marriage, divorce is a possibility. But I feel guilty about it too, so I guess I'm not completely lost. (*Pause*) Oh—Harriet just sent me some pictures of the kid this morning. You want to see them?

(*He digs the envelope out of his pocket. Vivien regards the pictures for a long moment, then drops them*)

VIVIEN: People oughtn't to take pictures of babies.

(*Paul picks the pictures up, gazes at them*)

PAUL: He is kind of cute. He looks like . . . (*He breaks off*) His name is Dougal. (*The mood reverts; he puts the pictures away*) I don't know, sometimes I get so depressed. I mean it's okay. I just used to think—I had this idea once. Oh, not really, I just thought I did, without really thinking about it. I've decided I don't have any creativity at all. I thought if I started drinking it would help. I know what I should be doing, but it doesn't work. And now I'm going to Hollywood? I'm fine. (*Beat. A final protest*) But I know I'm *good.*

VIVIEN: You ever try to commit suicide?

PAUL: I don't know, it's hard to tell; everything's so relative. (*He looks up*) Why'd you ask that?

VIVIEN: That's the first thing the doctors want to know. (*Brief pause*) If you've got a family to support, you should go into horseshoeing. It's a good money-making trade and it's well respected. Get in touch with Philip Ewing at 1016 South 45th Street in Philadelphia. He doesn't have a zip code.

PAUL: All right, I'll look into it.

VIVIEN: I'll send you some fresh fruit.

PAUL: (*Deeply moved; smiles*) Thanks. I'll eat it. (*Pause*) We have to go, Dad.

VIVIEN: Okay. Can we go to a clothing store now?

PAUL: It's late. I think everything's closed.

VIVIEN: . . . Tomorrow?

PAUL: Let's just go for a ride, okay?

VIVIEN: Where?

PAUL: We'll just drive around, digest our food.

(*Long pause. They look at each other*)

Lights change:

Down on restaurant and seconds later up on car. Paul and Vivien seated there as before, Paul driving. They drive in silence for several moments, then Vivien becomes aware of the direction they are taking.

VIVIEN: Where are we going?

PAUL: I have to take you back. I'm sorry. . . .

(*Pause*)

VIVIEN: You can turn on the radio if you want.

PAUL: (*Smiles*) You got your pad? My window could use a good wipe. (*Vivien obliges in the same energetic manner as before, then sits back*) Thanks.

VIVIEN: It's stopped raining. (*Paul nods. Vivien leans forward and gazes up at the sky*) I bet you don't see stars in the city.

PAUL: No.

VIVIEN: This is a good place to be for rainbows too. (*Brief pause; Vivien indicates the pad and the windshield*) I used to do that for my father. He let me sit beside him in the front seat and keep the windshield clean.

PAUL: Were you close to him?

VIVIEN: (*Grins*) "Cheek by jowl". He used to take me on long trips. We went to the Chicago World's Fair—"The Century of Progress" they were still calling it then—and Florida, and Michigan. Ocean Boulevard . . . Once we drove all the way to New Mexico. My mother had to sit in the back seat.

PAUL: What did he do for a living?

VIVIEN: He operated a steam shovel, dredged the Mississippi.

PAUL: Yeah?

VIVIEN: Oh yeah. We were river rats. Played poker, ate ice cream and drank whiskey and rented rooms. He took us everywhere.

PAUL: What was his name?

VIVIEN: Edgar.

PAUL: What was your mother's name?

(*Pause. Vivien's brow furrows*)

VIVIEN: Dougal.

(*Beat*)

PAUL: It's just that Mom never told me anything about you. The only thing I ever remember her saying once was that you liked the out of doors.

VIVIEN: That's right. I could disappear for days into the

mountains and no one would know where I was. Bang! I'm gone.

PAUL: Yeah?

VIVIEN: I was alone on a mountain one day when I made a discovery. If I stared long enough at the landscape and sat very still, I could blend in with it. I could disappear. The forest animals would go on about their business as if I wasn't there. And the birds would sing different songs, not the ones they sang when people were around. I was no one, and that made me special.

PAUL: . . . That sounds wonderful.

VIVIEN: The trouble was when I started doing it around the house. (*Pause*) I don't do it anymore. You get more conservative with age.

PAUL: Were you really studying to be a veterinarian? (*No response*) How—how did you and Mom meet?

VIVIEN: . . I was in charge of the pets at the college. There weren't supposed to be any. She had a cat. (*Pause. A look of pain crosses his face*) The confiscated animals were sent to the labs. (*Pause*) She never told you even that?

PAUL: (*Shakes his head; inaudibly*) No.

VIVIEN: She's very strong-minded, isn't she? (*Paul, unable to speak, just nods*) Well, I let her keep that cat, I'll tell you. The next thing you know, she invited me home to meet her father. He was pretty imposing too, ate good food. She hoped he wouldn't approve, but he took a shine to me because of my prospects which weren't bad. So I went along with it. (*Pause*) Recently I've been interested in suspended animation, freezing people until you can find a cure for them. I think that's a good idea.

(*Pause*)

PAUL: Was it Mom—was she the one who took you to Norristown?

VIVIEN: (*With great difficulty*) . . . No. I went of my own free will.

PAUL: Why? (*Vivien tries to respond; cannot*) I wish you'd tried, you know? I wish you'd tried harder. (*Long silence. Finally, Vivien looks out the window*)

VIVIEN: We're here.

(*Paul brings the car to a stop, turns to Vivien*)

PAUL: There was a lot more I wanted to ask you.

VIVIEN: I had a good time.

PAUL: Is there anything I can send you?

VIVIEN: (*Getting out of the car*) Don't bother.

PAUL: (*Getting out quickly to stop him*) Do you want me to buy you some clothes?

VIVIEN: What I have fits well enough.

PAUL: I could send you some food, some fruits or nuts, something that's fresh.

VIVIEN: They feed us very well.

PAUL: Isn't there anything I can . . .

VIVIEN: I'd better go in.

PAUL: That doctor you said you wanted, Dr. Sohkey, you want me to arrange that?

VIVIEN: You're going to miss your opening night.

PAUL: It doesn't matter. Dad—it doesn't matter.

VIVIEN: I've got everything I need.

PAUL: They want me to come back next year and direct another show. I'll bring Harriet and our son. I want them to meet you.

(*Pause*)

VIVIEN: I won't be disappointed if you don't.

(*A moment, then Miss Tendesco enters, wearing an overcoat and carrying her purse, just going off duty*)

TENDESCO: Good evening! (*To Vivien*) So you went after all.

VIVIEN: Yes, ma'am.

TENDESCO: Good for you. And did you have a nice time?

VIVIEN: Very nice. This is Paul. He's my son. He's a general theatrical director.

TENDESCO: (*With a smile, to Paul*) Oh. (*Back to Vivien*) Did you let them know at the office that you're back?

(*Vivien immediately goes off in a direction different from the one in which he was headed*)

TENDESCO: So, he recognized you after all.

PAUL: (*Impulsively*) I—I want to do something to help him. He told me he wanted to change doctors. I'd like to see that's taken care of.

TENDESCO: He and Dr. Braden get along famously.

PAUL: If it would make him happy, I'd like to see it done.

TENDESCO: Did he say who he wanted?

PAUL: Yes, a Dr. Sohkey.

TENDESCO: Dr. Sohkey?

PAUL: If there's any expense or legal problem involved, I'll pay for it; money's no object.

TENDESCO: (*Smiling*) Mr. Howard, Jimmi Sohkey is a ward attendant.

PAUL: He's not a doctor?

TENDESCO: He's a student at the local junior college.

PAUL: Oh. Well, I guess there's no problem then.

TENDESCO: No, no problem at all.

PAUL: But he seemed to get better as the day went on.

TENDESCO: Because he was enjoying himself. I've always believed that if every patient had one person who would devote himself exclusively to him, this kind of illness would melt into the shadows.

PAUL: You think Dad could get better?

TENDESCO: No.

PAUL: But you just said—

TENDESCO: I know.

(*She smiles at him and goes. After a moment Vivien re-enters and crosses towards his ward without looking at Paul and without slowing his stride. Paul makes a movement as if to speak, but something in Vivien's manner tells him not to. Vivien disappears*)
End

Author's Production Notes

Vivien has been performed with both modular units and realistic set pieces. A definitive stage design has yet to be found, thus future designers are hereby granted some latitude.

As to the style of performance, it should be almost, but not quite completely, realistic. Vivien in reality has been on Thorazine and other drugs for thirty years. Clearly the actor can not play this with total verisimilitude nor can he ignore it. A style must be found that balances reality with theatrical necessity.

Paul is high-strung, self-centered, and obsessed by time—at least at the outset of the play. As written, his reaction to his father's refusal to recognize and accept him is an over-reaction. There are moments of absurdity, leaps of logic, particularly in the first two scenes. These are intentional; go with them. Later he settles down.

There is also something slightly askew in Miss Tendesco. At first she seems merely affable and competent, but gradually we begin to suspect one of her buttons might be missing. She responds to Paul's growing frustration and anger with a consistent pleasantness that leaves him wondering if he is dreaming. Perhaps this is her way of surviving the irrationality of mental patients and their families, or perhaps she is a closet rhapsodic, as her final speech seems to indicate. Whatever cause one assigns, the important thing is for the actress to find the special and private place the character inhabits. Her "un-Ratchette-like" strangeness might be signalled by some small abberation in her appearance: perhaps a uniform that is too short or tight, a hairstyle that is too youthful, or bobby sox, or a spray of flowers on her breast. Whatever it is, it should not be flagrant; she is not a clown.

Samuel Shem

NAPOLEON'S DINNER

Samuel Shem

Samuel Shem's *Napoleon's Dinner*, a comedy for three men, was written as a companion to *Room For One Woman*, a play for three women, which was first published in *The Best Short Plays 1979*. Both plays grew out of Shem's experiences as a Rhodes scholar at Oxford, England, where Shem received a Ph.D. in Neurophysiology. When studies became tedious, Shem reports, "I found myself easing out of academics and rushing full-tilt into the life of the Cotswolds, the pubs and villages near Stratford-upon-Avon. I began to write plays."

Both *Napoleon's Dinner* and *Room For One Woman* were premiered at the Impossible Ragtime Theatre in New York in 1979 under the billing *The Shem Plays* with Peter Waldren as Denis, Hugh Byrnes as Rawls, and John Mawson as Sammy. Both plays were directed by Ted Story.

Like the preceding play in this volume (*Vivien* by Percy Granger), *Napoleon's Dinner* explores a strained father-son relationship, which Thomas Lask in the *New York Times* described as "a hectic, high-spirited romp that involves a priggish son and a down-to-earth father. . . . The twists in the plot . . . will suggest a short story by O. Henry, but the reconciliation of father and son is a genuinely moving moment."

Samuel Shem was born in 1944 and grew up in upper New York State. At Harvard College his pre-med studies precluded any playwriting, though Shem did find some moments to act in several plays. During the summers he was a toll collector on a bridge, working the midnight-to-eight shift, so that he could read on the job.

After his degree at Oxford, he returned to Harvard Medical School, where he completed his M.D. degree. He then spent a year as a medical intern, did a three-year residence in psychiatry, and is now in the private practice of psychiatry in Boston and a Clinical Instructor of Psychiatry at Harvard.

Dr. Shem is also the Playwright-in-Residence at The Boston Shakespeare Company, where his latest work, a full-length comedy entitled *The Hollywood Messiah*, is scheduled for production in 1982, as is his full-length drama, *Sisters*. Two other full-length comedies—*George and Martha* and *Freudian Lovesong*—are ready for production.

The House of God (1978), Dr. Shem's first novel—the hilarious story of interns in a big city hospital—has sold over one-half million copies, and was reviewed in *Medical Self-Care* as "the best novel ever written about internship." A major motion picture based on the novel has been completed by United Artists. His second novel, *Follies*—which Dr. Shem describes as "a big and funny love story about a short, red-haired psychiatrist married to a wise and beautiful woman who's becoming a stand-up comic, and their former best pal, a Harvard-educated, South Boston Irishman who tinkles a piano"—is scheduled for publication this year.

In his spare time, Dr. Shem serves as co-chairman of P.E.N./New England, a regional branch of the international writers' organization.

Characters:

DENIS, *a scholar of forty-five*
RAWLS, *his manservant, or "scout," thirty-five*
SAMMY, *his father, seventy*

Setting:

A Grand Room.
Early Evening.
A grandly-furnished gentleman's dressing room in the topmost tower of an Oxford College, in England. A full-length mirror is stage front. On a wooden valet is laid out a replica of Napoleon's dress uniform, complete with hat. Windows look out over "the city of dreaming spires." Steep winding stairs lead up to the room from below.

Denis stands before the mirror in his boxer shorts, studying himself. He shows his nervousness by idiosyncratic snorts and tics. He hums "The 1812 Overture," complete with mimicked cannon blasts.

Rawls enters, carrying a tray upon which is a bottle of champagne and a single glass.

RAWLS: I heard a story about you in the covered market today, sir.

DENIS: I wasn't in the covered market today, Rawls.

RAWLS: It was about your . . . your nastiness, sir.

DENIS: My nastiness?

RAWLS: Yes, sir, about your icy coldness and nasty demeanor, sir. You must have a listen to it.

DENIS: Go on.

RAWLS: Well sir, one of the other scouts overheard his master and another master chatting. The other master said that talking to you was like talking to someone covered over by a sheet of ice. Well, then the first master—my mate's master—turns to him and says "Exactly. And what you have to do, my good man, is break through that ice. Break through that ice, and you'll find—(*Cheerfully*) lots of ice-cold water underneath."

DENIS: Delicious. Better than the one about the dentist.

RAWLS: The dentist, sir?

DENIS: When my College—students and Fellows alike—voted me the man who, if one were on one's way to the dentist on a dull Monday morning in February, one would *least* wish to meet.

RAWLS: Yes, I thought you'd enjoy my story, sir. I do know just how much you do enjoy these *essentric* stories about yourself.

DENIS: Open the champagne. Bring two glasses.

RAWLS: Two glasses, sir?

DENIS: (*Calmly*) Yes. This is a special evening. The most special evening of my life.

RAWLS: (*Taking a second glass from his apron*) Yes, sir. I've never seen you more excited, sir.

DENIS: It is true that if people talk about me at all, they do so with irritation.

RAWLS: True, sir, too too true. The irritation of an aching tooth.

DENIS: Nastiness is the essence of achievement. And what is man, Rawls, what is man, if not achievement? Look at me: what do you see before you?

RAWLS: (*Working the cork*) A man, sir. A handsome man in his fancy underpants.

DENIS: Exactly. And what do these fancy underpants conceal? Nothing of any note.

RAWLS: Nothing of any note? Why sir!

DENIS: Yes, you see before you a life stripped down, distilled to essence. A perfect shape: a hedron spinning weightlessly, cleverly and clearly in the subzero of interstellar intellectual space. In less than one hour, when, at my invitation, the Royal Society sits down to dine, the perfection will be complete. (*Rawls pops cork*) A wife? At last left. A son? At last loose with her. A career? The science of history. The dovetailing of the human and the technocratic. Linear thought, Rawls, linear thought. Male thought. Let us toast male thought. (*Raising glass*) To male thought.

RAWLS: Here, here. Male thought. (*They drink*) Begging your pardon, sir, and just what *is* male thought?

DENIS: Clear, crisp, sharp. Not the sloppy ooze and weepy mess of the female.

RAWLS: Ah yes, now I've got you. *Male* thought!

DENIS: Do you realize, Rawls, that on any given day

4/28ths, or 1/7th of all the fertile women of the world are menstruating? 2/7ths billion females, three hundred million females, menstruating every day.

RAWLS: Staggering, sir, staggering. They say it's that sort of thing what makes them puffs, vegetarians.

DENIS: Puffs vegetarians?

RAWLS: Aye, sir. They say it's things like that what puts them fags off their meat.

DENIS: My ex-wife and I once went walking on Addison's Walk, round the back of College near the Cherwell. Dusk. Perfect dusk light. The perfume of the earth lay perfect in the perfectly heavy air. And do you know what my ex-wife did? She took off all her clothes, and walked round the river naked.

RAWLS: And why, sir? And why would she do that?

DENIS: Precisely. We could have been seen. Too loose, Rawls, too loose.

RAWLS: For what, sir?

DENIS: For what? Why for civilization. For mankind itself.

RAWLS: Oh yes, sir, civilization. Why my own missus went to doctor to find us some contraception you know and doctor gave her one of these rubber diaphragm cups, and he says to her, "Now luv, you take this cup and you put it in your front passage." "In me front passage?" asks the wife. "Right,, your front passage," says doctor. "And what good would that do?" asks the wife, "me front passage is where I keeps the baby's pram."

DENIS: Women. With their animals, their flowers. By the time of my divorce: thirty-eight hamsters, two mongrel dogs, a horse, a pony by the horse—out of some other horse, three cats pissing, and a rat. A rat, Rawls, a rat! We might have been exterminated, by that silly rat!

RAWLS: Oh they do loves their animals, sir, I shall give you that.

DENIS: Not to mention the sex.

RAWLS: The sex, sir?

DENIS: I grew up seeing sex as something one did just before a nice hot bath. She grew up seeing it as something one did just after. I grew up expecting that a woman would only spread her thighs reluctantly—you know—"close your eyes, spread your thighs, grit your teeth, and do it for England!"— and what did I get?

RAWLS: Too much, sir, a good bit too much, it sounds like to me.

DENIS: Exactly. And she—she said she got too little.

RAWLS: It does have its moments, though, sir, the odd bit 'a fluff.

DENIS: Moments, yes, but is it worth that horrible moaning, and, in these dog days, the sweat?

RAWLS: Well you've come to the right man to talk about sweat, sir. My missus is horribly fat and very sweaty, and I cannot deny her ugliness as well. Still, it does have its moments.

DENIS: Well then how do you do it?

RAWLS: How do I do it? Oh sir, you're having me on. A man of your learning asking that of a man of mine?

DENIS: No, no, not the mechanics, the aesthetics.

RAWLS: Aesthetics? (*Appalled*) You don't mean the leather thongs and the whips—

DENIS: No, no, I mean with her fat and ugly, how can you bring yourself to do it at all?

RAWLS: Well sir, you know what the old ones say—(*Demonstrating, crudely*) "When you're stoking the fire, you're not looking at the knick-knacks on the mantlepiece!"

DENIS: Still, the greatness of this nation is its history. Even now, with the sleazy, greasy, lazy Arabs buying up massive great chunks of London, Oxford goes on. No sheik can buy it, for it is outside of time or price. Ah history, my love. When you step from the College courtyard through the gate, Rawls, upon what does your foot rest?

RAWLS: Upon *history*, sir. By God, on history, just as you said.

DENIS: It does no such thing. It rests upon a hollow in the stone. Where did that hollow come from? From seven centuries of scholars stepping from the courtyard through the gate, into the hollow of the stone, the hollow of our past.

RAWLS: Right you are, sir, why just the other day I was saying to me missus there's nothing I look forward to more than our past, our great hollow British past.

DENIS: When I was a boy, my family sent me for a summer exchange program to France, they getting a French boy my age in return. From that first embarkation, as I watched the shoreline of England dissolve, my life changed. France! It was as if I had seen the sun for the first time! My premiere feeling of perfection was when I saw the hot slabs of sunlight slapped against the white walls of the farmhouse. Red stucco roofs the essence of red. Oiled oaken floors the essence of oak. Cool prehistoric caves where blind fish slithered in smooth, dark, limestone pools, marvelous!

RAWLS: Bloody marvelous, sir.

DENIS: Curious—my French family thought I was a musician. They led me to pianos, and placed violins and horns—of which they had many—in my room. They urged me to play.

RAWLS: Why sir, you never mentioned your musical ability—

DENIS: I have none. They soon stopped, and I got on with it.

RAWLS: With what, sir?

DENIS: With falling in love for the first time in my life.

RAWLS: Sir! You didn't!

DENIS: I did. With Napoleon Bonaparte. And finally, now, I've come full circle. My life is at its apex, balanced on its fulcrum. Tonight I have created an exact replica of the original dinner of the Royal Historical Society. Its success will assure my place. My life is about to change. An event, a slight twist—*presto!*—like magic, a life takes a dramatically different shape. Can you understand, Rawls? Have you ever experienced anything like that?

RAWLS: (*Seriously, touched deeply*) Yes . . . yes, sir, I have. The shape of a life *can* suddenly—

DENIS: (*Not listening, not sensing the seriousness*) Yes, a slight twist—*presto!*—like magic everything is changed. It is time, Rawls. Would you help me dress now?

RAWLS: (*Startled by his own seriousness*) Oh I didn't mean— (*Snapping out of it*) Yes, sir. It will be a grand evening for you, sir. (*As they talk, he dresses Denis*)

DENIS: Last month, when I was given the Queen's Medal by the Duke, I knew that this perfection was quite at hand.

RAWLS: Yes, sir, we knew it would be all *uphill* from there, sir—

DENIS: The fifth historian to receive the Queen's Medal, ever—

RAWLS: Grand, sir, just grand. My missus and I were so proud. Imagine—there we were, in Buckingham Palace itself!

DENIS: One hundred and seventy-five years ago today, on

the fourteenth of June, Napoleon defeats the Austrians at the Battle of Marengo. He orders his chef, the great Dunand, to cook him a celebratory dinner on the battlefield—

RAWLS: And the most amazing part was when the Duke gave the Medal to the rhino cage cleaner of the Regents Park Zoo, on his retirement after fifty-odd years service! Amazing, that—

DENIS: (*Not hearing him*)—Dunand could find but a hen, three eggs, four tomatoes, six crayfish, and the brandy from Napoleon's flask. And out of this, he creates a masterpiece, Poulet Marengo—

RAWLS: (*Not hearing him*)—I mean who would have thought that the rhino cage cleaner would be given the Medal on the very same day as my very same master—

DENIS: (*Not hearing him*)—and that very same year, the Royal Historical Society is founded. Tonight we twelve officers, each dressed as Napoleon, sitting in the oldest chamber of the oldest university of the world, will be served the same dish, Poulet Marengo. Grand, Rawls, grand!

RAWLS: Grand, sir, just grand! And when the Duchess goes up to the rhino cage cleaner and kisses that thin hairy bugger on the cheek, why I think to meself: me missus will faint dead away!

DENIS: Rhino cleaner?

RAWLS: Oh, no, sir, not rhino cleaner, rhino *cage* cleaner. Rhinos themselves are quite tidy. Their *cages*, sir, their *cages*. Made all the papers: DUCHESS KISSES RHINO CAGE CLEANER—BEAUTY AND THE BEAST!

DENIS: (*Incredulous*) What in bloody hell are you talking about?

RAWLS: The Medal, sir, the Queen's Medal, same as what you got yourself. All *uphill* from there, sir, and not only for you, but for the rhino cage cleaner as well. Why he's become one of the best-known faces in all of Britain. You see everyone wants to know what it's like to clean up after rhinos for fifty-some odd years. "Well," says he, "it's not the rhinos, really, rhinos are quite tidy, really, but the *hippos*, with their great mouths, their great barrels of muck—"

DENIS: How can you talk about a rhino cleaner at a time like this?

RAWLS: Rhino *cage* cleaner, sir, rhinos themselves are quite tidy—

DENIS: I don't want to hear anymore about it—

RAWLS: Not exactly rhino cage cleaner, either, really. True he *specializes* in rhinos, but he does hippos and the odd elephant or marsupial as well. But right you are, sir— (*Staunchly, loyally*) being given the Medal at the same time as the rhino cage cleaner has made you quite a great celebrity in your very own right—

DENIS: STOP IT!

RAWLS: Sorry sir, sorry. I'd best be getting your coat and hat.

DENIS: Yes, do that, Rawls, do that. (*Pause*) I can hardly wait: the moment when the Poulet Marengo is placed before us: a plump hen, ringed with tomatoes and crayfish, with an egg on top. Gently, each Napoleon punctures the yolk, it oozes down the breast of the hen, and with the perfection of historical repetition, it melds with the sauce just perfectly enough to make it . . . (*Slowly, savouring every syllable*) co-ag-u-late.

RAWLS: It sounds almost sexual, sir.

DENIS: Sensual. The sensuality of the eternal; the music of the spheres, the coagulation of a life! It will bring the Royal Historical Society to it's feet, and then— (*Forcefully*) to its knees. It will be the greatest triumph of any modern historian's lifetime.

RAWLS: No question of it, sir, no question at all! After this dinner tonight, you'll be laughing!

DENIS: And not alone. You'll be with me still.

RAWLS: To be sure I will, sir.

DENIS: Where were you when I first found you, Rawls?

RAWLS: Nowhere, sir, nowhere at all.

DENIS: Were you happy?

RAWLS: Oh no sir, I was unhappy. Most unhappy.

DENIS: And what are you now?

RAWLS: Happy, sir, most happy.

DENIS: You're grown happier, with me?

RAWLS: Oh most definitely, sir. Yes, I can honestly say that I feel a good bit more like I do now than I ever did before! There you are, sir, all ready, but for the hat. (*Gets the hat*) There, sir, there you are.

DENIS: (*Fully dressed as Napoleon, admiring himself*) Rawls? Who am I?

RAWLS: Who are you? Why Napoleon, sir, just as you said, Napoleon Bonaparte.

DENIS: Of course I am not. I am a man, as other men are. However, I am a man about to win.

RAWLS: You're a man laughin', sir, a man laugh—

SAMMY: (*Offstage, from bottom of stair, coming up, singing, the song getting louder and louder; Denis and Rawls are shocked*)
"Monday night me hand was on her ankle,
Tuesday night me hand was on her knee,
Wednesday night success in that I lifted up her dress,
Thursday night I got inside her pink che-mee-eeeeze,
Friday night I had me hand upon it,
Saturday night she gives me balls a squeeze—"
(*He trips and falls as he enters, curses. Sammy, Denis' father, aged seventy; a robust man, he too is dressed as Napoleon Bonaparte, although cheaply and sloppily. In doorway, he resumes his song*)
"I don't want to join the army, I don't want to go to warrr,
I'd much rather hang around, Picadilly Underground,
(*Sweetly*)
Livin' off the earnins of a . . . high-born laydeee—"

DENIS: JESUS CHRIST!

SAMMY: No, lad, Napoleon Bonaparte. Jesus had a previous engagement, and I've placed him on a bus to Calvary. (*Moving toward Denis to embrace him*) Grand, just grand!

DENIS: Get away, Sammy, don't you touch me—

SAMMY: A good and grand good evening to you both! (*Emptying the glasses*) More bubbly, please—

DENIS: NO! Rawls, don't give him a drop—

SAMMY: I always miss the last step, on any bloody flight of stairs. Must be the weather. Like the old ones say: it's the kind of weather you don't know whether to be pawnin' your overcoat or your good straw hat. The fruit'll be banjaxed altogether.

DENIS: What the hell are you ʊoing here?

SAMMY: Me? Bejesus, have I got the wrong station? Beggin' your pardons, sirs, but isn't this Waterloo? HA! Grand, just grand!

DENIS: You—you don't imagine that you're coming to this dinner?

SAMMY: Dinner? Oh no, not dinner. I've gone all soft in me head, I think I'm Napoleon Bonaparte; I got to feeling lonesome and I heard there were twelve more nuts dressed like Napoleon over here, so I thought I'd just drop by—

DENIS: You're drunk, you're roaring drunk!

SAMMY: Drunk on happiness, boy, on happiness. I'm a proud father, come to share the greatest moment of his only son's only life.

DENIS: If you think for one moment that you're sitting down to dinner with the Royal—

SAMMY: (*Ignoring him, starting to woo Rawls*) The lad's so modest do you know? Last month there I am up pub, morning paper on me lap, and page one there's a photo of the Duchess kissing a good old boy on the cheek: DUCHESS KISSES RHINO CAGE CLEANER—BEAUTY AND THE BEAST! Imagine my surprise when, turning inside for the details, I see that me very own son has got a medal that day, as well. And so, when I hears of this dinner, I says Sammy, hang the expense, chance of a lifetime, he *needs* you by his side, and here I am, lad, here I bloody well am!

DENIS: There's only one place you'll get dinner for free dressed like that—the Asylum in Headington—which is where you're living anyway, for all I know—

SAMMY: I'm not, lad, I'm not. I've moved in with your wife, now, and with your luvly young son.

DENIS: What!? You've moved in with my ex-wife and my boy?

SAMMY: Aye. Not a bad bivouac, really, except for the animals and the flowery plants. I stopped at the old-age pensioners home for awhile, but the peace and quiet made me nervous and made me think I was dying. And do you know we were still on the bloody bucket? No flush toilets at all! Sammy, says I, you're too old for these pensioners. So I moves in with your wife.

DENIS: How out of character, for you to move *in*. What you're best at is moving *out*.

SAMMY: Three cats, your wife has now, three of the goddamn noggins, pissin'. I hates them fuckin' furry fuckin' things. Not to mention the flowers—flowers here, flowers there—a bloody menagerie, your wife has got.

DENIS: *Ex*-wife. You've come for money, Sammy, is that correct?

SAMMY: Not the money, no. I've come for the pride of a father for a son.

DENIS: Rawls, show this proud man the door.

SAMMY: (*Sliding away from Rawls*) Oh lad, I've had such a bloody awful day: all morning and afternoon in the hot sun, alone in a boat on Great Blenheim Lake, fishing. Lonely it were. I kept wishin' there was some lad on the bank, to take out in the boat with me. All day long, and the only thing I caught was one little piece of weed.

DENIS: A weed? And what did you do with your weed? Eat it?

SAMMY: Eat it? Hell lad, I fucked it! HA! So then I comes in to shore, and there I am on the bank, and I looks down, and I sees this great tench there, moving his fins back and forth, tantalizin' me. So I puts in me hook, and moves closer to the edge and all of a sudden— (*To Rawls*) do you know what?

RAWLS: What?

SAMMY: WHOOPS! the bank gives way and there *I* am swimming about, next to that old tench, moving me arms back and forth, as cool and as peaceful as you please.

DENIS: What a fascinating story. Now get out.

SAMMY: (*Sitting down, to Rawls*) Ah but the beer isn't what it was before, is it? Do you know what I mean?

RAWLS: Oh it isn't anything near what it used to be, no.

SAMMY: It's not like what it used to be before you was born.

RAWLS: Oh, no, it most definitely is not.

DENIS: How would *he* know what it was like before he was born?

SAMMY: His mother drank it, didn't she? No, that beer we drink now don't get us drunk, it just makes us piss. Two pints, you get a great pain in your leaker, and out back and piss like a horse. Back in, two pints more, and back out for another massive ur-eye-na-tion. Not like that stuff they used to make, in wooden barrels, coming through wooden taps and spouts. That stuff—two pints and the smell off the landlord's apron and you'd be on your knees! Ah, it doesn't get you drunk, now does it?

RAWLS: No, it surely does not, no.

SAMMY: Two pints more and where are you? Right, like a great Clydesdale horse. That other stuff, that stuff before, two pints, a whiff off the shirtapron, and you'd be *on your knees!* Not to mention the soothing effect on your leaker itself.

RAWLS: You've a problem there, with the plumbing, have you?

DENIS: Sammy, leave my scout alone. Rawls—he's trying to charm you—

SAMMY: No need, lad, no need. Him and me are of the

same class: the grand old working class, same as what *you yourself* was, once't. Ah, but the taste was there, too, with the old beer. What do you taste now? It tastes like it looks: tastes like ur-eye-ne. My own theory is that some smart bastard has got the message with the way it runs right on through you and he's switched the taps.

RAWLS: What! Switched the taps?

SAMMY: Aye. See he's got the boghole connected straight up to the beerkeg itself.

RAWLS: Go on! You mean it just runs in from the boghole—

SAMMY: —and out through the spout, into your belly, out through your leaker, and sloshes into the boghole again. Have you ever noticed how sour it is?

DENIS: RAWLS!

RAWLS: Why yes, sir, but the beer *is* sour, sir, I *have* noticed that.

SAMMY: Sour? Why man, it's not even *beer!* They've hooked the pisshole drain to the taphead spout, it's no wonder the stuff don't make you drunk—

DENIS: That's enough. (*Taking his elbow*) You're leaving Sammy—I'll call you a ride—

SAMMY: (*Evading him, plopping down on his back on a sofa*) Ah, the ride, the ride! You know that's just what I was thinking out there on Great Blenheim Lake, sitting there, floating—as we old-age pensioners are wont to do—and a seagull flies past, and he looks down on me and with this silly grin on his face he goes SKRAAWK! SKRAAWK! and I says to meself Sammy, see that gull? That gull is happy. And do you know why? Because he's either just got it, is getting it, or is about to get it. I mean that's what it's all about, in't? The ride?

RAWLS: The ride?

SAMMY: The ride! Take today: I finally gets back to me home pub, The Malt Shovel up past Charlbury, and the window-woman what tends bar there—a woman with big titties from Chadlington and a heart of purest gold—

RAWLS: (*Joining in, despite Denis; enjoying the joke*) Titties from Chadlington? And where's her ass from? Stoke City?

SAMMY: HA! She asks me where I been to get soaking wet, and I says fishing and I'm not done fishing yet. Not done yet? says she. No, luv, for I'm about to take me hook out again, and put it in your gorgeous fishtank! HA! Ah, I knew me day would end like that, for I woke up this morning and looked out over me belly and saw me member standing up so stiff it'd lift a tractor, and so straight it reminded me of the steeple of a Cotswold church rising up over the turning down of a Cotswold hill.

DENIS: Aren't you too old to be talking about women like that?

SAMMY: And what's the matter with women like that?

DENIS: I mean your talking about women in that manner. Aren't you too old?

SAMMY: That's what they wants, now, them girls, they wants them old. (*To Rawls*) Don't they?

RAWLS: They wants them old, not ancient.

SAMMY: They wants someone who'll give them something that'll last. Someone who knows what he's on about, when he gets on 'em.

DENIS: You're becoming the dirtiest old man in Oxfordshire.

SAMMY: Don't you give up so easy, lad, there's still hope for you. You wife is still a picture, and if I'm not too old for it, you can't be neither. And so here I am. A bloody horrible day, what with the hot sun, the tench wise as Solomon tantalizin' me, the great pain in me leaker from the pisspoor technocratic beer, and all frustrated by the refusal of the barmaid with the big titties—and the ass from Stoke City—to let me put me horny hook in her gorgeous hairy tank, and the only thing that got me through it at all was the thought of dressing up and coming down to share your finest hour.

DENIS: You cannot come to dinner. You were not invited.

SAMMY: I'll be good, on me best behavior. I'm so proud of you, lad, let me stay. For what is man, if not the friendship and the pride?

DENIS: Proud? Come off it, Sammy. You're not proud, you're jealous.

SAMMY: Me? No, boy, no, not me. Your mother. She's the one: sending you off from Clapham Junction in short pants and a grey flannel blazer and shirt and tie and little faggoty cap. Put you on the train to Westminster School every day to mix with your uppers, all because we found out you were so clever and quick. It wasn't me, lad, it was her.

DENIS: If it weren't for her, I'd never be where I am tonight.

SAMMY: (*Standing next to him, demonstrating his point*) Right, boy, right! Look at the horrible effect that sturdy woman's had: ten years since I've laid eyes on her, she's got the both of us parading around like bleeding lunatics!

DENIS: Look, Sammy, you wouldn't *want* to come to this dinner. It's the Royal Historical Society. You wouldn't understand.

SAMMY: Not understand history? Why I *am* history. I grew up knowing every inch of the Cotswolds, every wrinkle and ridge. I fought in the war, on that old mine sweeper, and then, after, wasn't I a historical boilerman on those historical steam trains, making the historical run from historical Bristol to historical London and back in a day? Ah, bloody beautiful machines they were, too.

RAWLS: My lad Malcolm loved those old steam engines, he did.

SAMMY: All the lads loved 'em. And then, when the diesels came in what happened? No boiler. Boilerman redundant. History? Na! Nothing like redundancy to make a man feel historic. And I remember the historical King George the Fifth Golden Jubilee: silver and brass band, I was on cornet, me old man on bass, and he's swilling down the beer and I says, "I can't wait 'til I can drink beer," and he says, "No better time than now and no better man to start with than your father," and I starts glug glugging that fine *old* beer, and before you know it there was six different colored notes coming out of that cornet, all at once. Ah that old beer—two pints and the niff of the shirtapron and where were you?

RAWLS: On your KNEES!

SAMMY: YOU WERE NEARLY PARALYTIC WITH THE WOBBLES!

DENIS: *Golden* Jubilee? Nonsense. It was Silver—George was only in—

SAMMY: Yes, yes, Golden Jubilee, and the Coronation Coach tall as a double-decker bus—

DENIS: You've distorted the whole damn thing: it wasn't Gold, it was Silver; there was no Coronation Coach because no one was getting crowned; and the first time you were dead drunk was at least twenty years before—

SAMMY: (*To Rawls*) Now you take Churchill, *Winston* Churchill. I knew Winston Churchill. Wonderful man. You know all that flowery grand talk about "Nevah, in the field of human?" Think he talked like that in person? Not on your life! He'd never look you directly in the eye, true enough, but he didn't use that pissy talk on you, neither. Wonderful, firm handshake—

DENIS: Good. And what, pray, does all that mean?

SAMMY: It means that I am history, living history, the kind what's of persons, and not of books, and I don't mind sharing meself with the Royal Society, no.

DENIS: I take your point: you've lived. Goodbye, and goodnight.

SAMMY: What do you know about livin' history, about people? You with your homogenized accent and all? (*To Rawls*) You know, he used to sound like me? Before his mother ripped him from me, slapped him into a flannel blazer, shortypants, shirt and tie and little faggoty cap, stuck him in the train at Clapham and shot him off to Westminster. He comes back two days later sounding like the bloody BBC 2! He's even worse, now. He's homogenized, he sounds American, to me. He sound just like Kojak!

DENIS: It there something you want to say to *me*?

SAMMY: (*Sincerely*) There is. Denny, I miss you.

DENIS: You what?

SAMMY: I miss you. I'm old. I got nothing much to do. I'm lonely. I can't come back to your mother for she won't have me, but I'm coming back to your own wife and to your own little son, and I'm looking, now, to be coming back to you.

DENIS: (*Startled; touched by Sammy's tenderness*) Coming back to me? You?

SAMMY: Aye, lad, that's why I've come here tonight, all dressed like this—

DENIS: (*Catching himself; cooler*) You haven't. You've come here to spoil it. You can't stand my success and you know it. Well you'll not ruin this—never!

SAMMY: Give us a chance, lad, take a risk. Let me celebrate with you tonight. I'm so proud of you, boy, I—

DENIS: And I'm ashamed of you.

SAMMY: Ashamed of me?

DENIS: Ashamed of you. You should be ashamed of yourself. Now I've got to go and greet my guests—

SAMMY: (*Angrily*) Aye, go do that, go ooze the lolly and sound like the fuckin' BBC. History? You don't have a clue. You're all head, Denis, you've got no bloody heart!

DENIS: How sad. I can't ask barmaids with hearts of gold and titties from Stoke City if I can put me fishook in their gorgeous hairy tanks. You're disgusting, with your filthy habits—rolling your false teeth around in your mouth. It's a disgusting habit, that. It puts people off.

SAMMY: You'd begrudge your own father the infirmities of age? You act as if you expect me still to be young.

DENIS: I expect you to be able to control your false teeth.

SAMMY: It's me fears, son, I only does it when I'm afraid.

DENIS: You do it all the time. Not to mention what you do with your testes. What about them, then?

SAMMY: Me what?

DENIS: Your testes.

SAMMY: Me testes?

RAWLS: He means your privates, Sammy, your balls.

SAMMY: What *about* me balls?

DENIS: The way you roll them about is disgusting as well. Hands in your pockets, rolling them about. My earliest memories of my father are him rattling his teeth and fingering his balls!

SAMMY: That's me nerves, that is.

DENIS: That's not your nerves, that's your balls!

SAMMY: But it's me nerves what makes me play with me balls.

DENIS: And I suppose it's your nerves that makes you rattle your teeth as well?

SAMMY: No, that's me fears, when I'm afraid—

DENIS: Disgusting filthy pornographic habit—

SAMMY: I'M AFRAID, I TELL YOU, AFRAID!

DENIS: WELL WHAT ARE YOU AFRAID *OF?*

SAMMY: I don't know. (*Pause; noticing Denis' nervous tic*) But you'd rather I had one of your Oxford tics or snorts, would you? (*To Rawls*) You know they won't let you into this great university unless you can demonstrate a snort or a tic or a wheeze or a sneeze or a stutter or a stammer to the satisfaction of three examiners—

DENIS: The way you roll those teeth around—for years I feared they were going to fly out of your nose and hit me in the eye! Rolling your teeth and fingering your balls and all the time talking about your genito-urinary system as if it were the boiler and pipes of a steam locomotive. GOD! you make me sick!

SAMMY: (*To Rawls*) Their examiners asks them at matriculation: what's yours, mate? A snort? A slithery lisp? A plugged sinus or a rattling ossicle so you has to use one of them Master's Voice earhorns to hear? It's a bloody zoo! I thought I raised a son. I didn't raise a son. I raised an animal at a bloody zoo!

DENIS: (*Snorting, barely in control*) You're too loose, Sammy, too loose. You've got no control over yourself, no control at all.

SAMMY: *Me* too loose? HA! What about you? I heard a story about you the other day: they said you was best man at one of them posh weddin's held in College Chapel, between one of your prize students and a very proper lady. You stood up and proposed the toast: "It's fitting that I propose this toast," says you, "for I'm the only one here who has slept with both the bride *and* the groom."

DENIS: WHAT! I NEVER—

SAMMY: How do you think I feel, hearing that? Wherever I go in these Cotswolds, they don't talk about *me,* they talk *to* me about *you!* If you think it's easy being the father of an Oxford *essentric,* think again, Denny, think again—

DENIS: I never said any such thing. Who told you that—

SAMMY: (*To Rawls*) I mean is he, I mean is he a fag?

RAWLS: (*Shocked*) A FAG?!

SAMMY: I mean a fag, a homosexual—I knows Oxford: "Pass the port and bend on over." Ever since she put him in shorty pants, faggoty cap, rammed him into the train at Clapham, I knew he'd get tighter and tighter until—

DENIS: Get out. Get out and don't ever come back again.

SAMMY: I tried to teach him magic. I thought there might be magic in his soul, but he wouldn't learn from me then, and he's not about to learn from me now—

DENIS: What I learned from you was how to abandon a son. When I grew up being different from you, you couldn't stand it, and you left—

SAMMY: And now you've left your own little son as well.

DENIS: (*Deeply wounded*) Shut up and get out. Now!

SAMMY: I'll be at your elbow for dinner tonight, because you're not man enough to stop me.

DENIS: You know what you are? You're a dosshouse wreck, an old bum crying to barmaids. You've dug your grave, now lie in it.

SAMMY: (*Rushing at him; Rawls holds him back from Denis*) See this fist? This fist is calloused, not smooth, this fist has worked a day in its life. It's laid out more men than you ever had as mates. How many fights have you been in? Answer me! HOW MANY FIGHTS? HOW MANY FUCKIN' WORLD WARS?

DENIS: You're old enough to die, Sammy. It's about time you gave some serious thought to dying.

SAMMY: (*Rawls, shocked, steps back; Sammy grabs Denis*) STAND UP AND FIGHT LIKE A MAN!

DENIS: (*Goes limp; passive; pause*) Marvelous. I'll go get some of the others, the ones like you, full of fists, and when I come back, if you're still here, I assure you they'll throw you out. (*From doorway; upset; choking on the power of what he says, yet managing to say it*) It's about time you were dead, Sammy. Yes . . . yes it's time you were dead. (*Exits; long pause*)

SAMMY: Well, if I'm to be thrown out, I'll bloody well be thrown out drunk. Here, have some, will you?

RAWLS: I'd better not. He'll be back soon. Dinner's about to begin.

SAMMY: Time I was dead? Ah, I'm not afraid of dying.

RAWLS: You're not?

SAMMY: Nah. You comes back, you know.

RAWLS: You don't. There's no future in dying, there's not.

SAMMY: You do. You comes back, as a fly, or a frog, or something like that, that's always what they're telling us, they do.

RAWLS: There's nothing, and when I'm dead they can chop me up and make compost out of me, for when you're dead you're dead, that's all, just dead.

SAMMY: Ripe ones like us'n would make good manure, fair do. My homogenized son wouldn't grow a weed. But you do comes back—take you, for instance: you were once, before you were born, something different like—like a fly, or a frog. You were or will be, a little fly, flying about, or a frog. Not so bad, really, that. I mean a fellow like you would have friends and relations as a fly, or as a frog. Even as a little fly, you'd have friends, among flies. Not among frogs, though, not if you was a fly. But if you was a frog, you'd have friends, among frogs. It all depends on what you are. The biggest bastard in the earth—my own stuck-up son there—if he came back as a fly, or a frog, he'd not have a single friend among flies or frogs, not a one!

RAWLS: You really believe you come back?

SAMMY: They tells us so. When I comes back I wants to come back as a woman. I wants to come back as Princess Anne.

RAWLS: Princess Anne? Why would you want to be her?

SAMMY: So I could make some money.

RAWLS: How could you make money as Princess Anne?

SAMMY: How? Why on me back, lad, on me royal back!

RAWLS: You shouldn't have bothered him tonight. He's tense. He says this is the most special night of his life.

SAMMY: Ah, I know. He's not a bad lad, really. Laughs? We had . . . well, we had one or two. Brains? Brains! Never dreamed though, said he couldn't see nothin' in it. (*Pause*) Well, I tried, and I failed again. Imagine—he used to sound just like you or me, and now, he sounds like . . . (*Brightening up*) Now that's a queer thing, you being his servant. I'd have thought he'd got someone much more highsounding than you. You sound just like *me!* Curious. Queer. How'd he get you? .

RAWLS: No one else would stay with him.

SAMMY: And why did you?

RAWLS: Why? Because he never wanted to know anything about me.

SAMMY: And just why would you be looking for a situation like that?

RAWLS: Leave off asking, friend, it's nothing worth tellin' tonight.

SAMMY: (*Sensing the importance, sharply*) It is. Surely it is. Tell us, then, hey?

RAWLS: (*Tense, with increasing feeling*) It's nothing, just an event, a . . . a twist in a life, before I came into service with your son. Let it lie peaceful, at rest?

SAMMY: Lie peaceful? It's not lyin' peaceful on your heart, son—

RAWLS: It's not important anymore—

SAMMY: You think I was born under a rock? I've lived, and am livin' still. I've seen as much as you. If I can take what's happenin' to me this evening, with my son and me, I can take what's happenin' to you. I've an ear, and a heart, too. Tell us, mate, tell us . . . Tell us.

RAWLS: It's about my own son, Malcolm. (*Pause*) I keep thinking of a certain day we had, just him and me: he was six, him and me out on the Ridgeway to see the Great White

Horse in the Vale of Uffington. I shall never forget his eyes when he saw that great chalk horse, carved into the hill, seeming as big as the sky. He had ever so many questions: who made it, how and why and how it lasted from that day to this. He'd run from the tail to the head, and make me stand with him and wish on the White Horse's eye. He asked me about the ridge of hills above it, stretching on and on, and I told him how it was a prehistoric roadway for the men of old Britain to drive their herds along, and he took my hand and said, "We must walk it, dad, top to bottom." And even though I knew we couldn't walk it top to bottom, I said, "Yes, we shall," and we walked and walked, with the sun hot and the breeze blowin' and the clouds threatenin', always threatenin', but never bringin' down the rain. We came upon some horses eatin' hay, and that hay smelled so crisp and sweet and the sound the horses made eatin' it was so—what?—*enthusiastic!*— Malcolm and I wished *we* were horses so we could eat that hay as well. The crest of the hill joined other crests of other hills, and ran together in this Ridgeway. We walked it until the sun was barely dead on our left, and until the moon was barely born on our right, and then the excitement of the day caught up with my little laddie, and he drooped, and dropped down, tired—not cryin'—just tired, asleep. (*Pause; full of passion*) And I gathered him up in my arms, and carried him through the moonlight, back. (*Pause; eyes full of tears*) I was so happy, I cried. The tears streamin' down me cheeks, I carried this love of my life through the thickenin' moonlight, snuggled into the crook 'a my neck, asleep, home . . .

(*Denis enters, alone, obviously shaken, tense*)

DENIS: I should have thought you'd be gone by now.

SAMMY: Hush, lad, we're having a serious talk.

DENIS: Rawls, the first guests are arriving. See to—

SAMMY: Hush. He's tellin me about his boy.

DENIS: Rawls—you must go to—

RAWLS: I shall go directly as I finish my story, sir.

DENIS: What? I said the first guests are—

RAWLS: (*Angrily, almost shouting*) Someone else will have to tend them. I've started, and I'll not move off until I've finished.

DENIS: Why this is extraordinary! I can do without you, Rawls, but I cannot do without you tonight.

RAWLS: Do without me? Oh, I doubt that, sir. There aren't many like me, who'd stick with many like you.

SAMMY: Dammit, Denis, sit down and listen to someone else for once in your life.

DENIS: (*Weakly*) And why should I listen to him?

RAWLS: Because I'm telling about the love between father and son.

DENIS: (*Falsely, almost a plea*) What do I care about that?

RAWLS: Oh you do, sir, I know you do. If you didn't care, you'd have come back with cook, and thrown your father out. No one can stand wishing his own father dead, sir, not even you can stand that. Sit down, I shan't be long—

DENIS: Don't you tell me what to—

SAMMY: (*Firmly, kindly*) Sit down, son, sit you down. (*Denis sits; pause*)

RAWLS: My Malcolm loved trains. Those great steam trains were his favorite. Growing up in Gloucestershire, he'd heard in school about the London Underground, and he wanted to see it and ride it for himself. He was only six—you know how excited a lad of six can get about something as grand as a train? (*Pause*) I took him to London. You should have seen the look in his eyes when he first saw Paddington Station. He stood there with me, looking up at the girders and the sun streaming through the glass roof and the clouds racing across. Dad, it's like Heaven! Well then we went into the Underground, and got down to the tracks just after a train pulled out. Did I say how excited he was? (*Pause*) The platform was almost deserted. We chattered about trains, and how they ran on electricity, and all the rest. There was a rumble in the tunnel. Malcolm asks me if he can get a bit closer. I'll come with you, says I. We walk up near the edge. He's frightened, at the booming of the incoming train, at the beginning rush and suck of air. I has me hand on his little shoulder, and I feel him trembling with excitement and with fear. And then he takes me hand, and looks up, and . . . smiles this luvly smile at me. (*Pause*) And just as the train is upon us, some . . . someone rushes past on his side of me, and *grabs* him! and tears him from me and barrels him over and tumbles with him over the edge down onto the tracks and the first car *hits* him and then *hits* him again! and he disappears under the wheels!

SAMMY: GOOD CHRIST NO!

DENIS: WHAT?! A lunatic! It must have been a lunatic!

RAWLS: (*Pause; in shock at the memory, staring, twitching*) They said not. Ordinary man. Broker. Lost everyone. Lived alone. Model citizen. Temporary insanity. (*Pause; coming back out of it*) It must have been too much to bear, for him.

DENIS: What was too much?

RAWLS: My happiness. How my son smiled at me. (*Pause*) All I wanted from life was that my son might live to be as happy as my father had been. Now I've lost them both. They're gone, and— (*To Sammy, bitterly*) and they'll *not* be coming back. (*Pause*) It bent my life and the life of my missus all out of shape. I left my people and I came here. I wanted to forget. I wanted no one who knew me to know me. But I couldn't forget, not even the tiniest part. I won't recover, no; I've changed. It's the first time I've talked about it, these two years.

DENIS: Why . . . why did you never tell me?

RAWLS: You didn't want to hear. That's why I stuck with you—my secret would be safe. It's all right, 'til I saw what was happenin' here tonight.

DENIS: What do you mean?

RAWLS: I mean hatred, the same hatred that murdered my son, the hatred bred of love. You two bein' at each other's throats, and all the time both of you wishin' you could find a way to love each other, like father and son do love. (*Pause*) And one more thing, before I'm done and get to seein' to your guests: there was a word that came out, over and over again, by those few what had known the man who murdered himself and my son. Do you know what that word was? (*Pause; like nails driven into a coffin*) Ice. Ice, sir, ice. Cold as ice, is what they said, sir, about him. Ice. (*Pause*) Well then, I'll be seein' to your guests.

DENIS: (*Deeply moved, shaken, in a turmoil*) Yes . . . yes by all means . . . but . . .

RAWLS: Sir?

DENIS: Make them comfortable, yes, but tell them . . . that I'm seeing to something— (*Looking at Sammy, their eyes meet*) something quite *special* here and that I'll be with them directly and then . . . and then you make sure to come back here, do you see?

RAWLS: Yes, sir, I shall, sir. I shall be happy, sir, to do that.

(*Rawls exits; long pause; embarrassment; tension*)

SAMMY: Lunatics? We're the goddamn lunatics. Runs in the family, bein' lunatic. Did you know that, eh?

DENIS: (*Softly; distant*) No.

SAMMY: My father—your grandfather—now there was a certified lunatic. They said the sound of water running over a waterfall was what first drove him batty. When he was my age, he found himself in Littlemore Hospital, stuffing confetti into fluffy dogs. He soon tired of that. Do you know what he did then?

DENIS: No. (*Pause; with great effort bringing himself to ask*) What . . . what did he do then?

SAMMY: (*Sensing Denis' struggle; warmly*) Well, he got himself two donkeys, a cart, a load of animals, became a one-man circus, "The Donkey Man." From then to his death he went up and down the country, a great curiosity he were. The last I saw him was the last he passed through Oxfordshire, out at Coombe. Pitiful he were; scruffy beard, dirty fingers, soggy hat on his head, shell-shocked look in his eye, cradling a sick puppy in his arms. And he didn't know me, didn't have a clue. As he left, walking along in front of his wagon, his dogs sitting on the seat yappin', the rain wettin' his face, all he said to me was "Nice to be young, eh, nice to be young. Cheerio, my friend, cheerio, cheerio!" (*Pause*) "Friend"? I was his son. (*Pause*) I promised meself, when he left us for good, that I'd never do the same. Amazin'—the thing I feared the most of doing and being, is just what I did, and just what I am. I was so afraid of losing you, I tried to give you everything.

DENIS: What . . . what did you try to give me?

SAMMY: Sent you to France for the summer. Your mother didn't want you to go, but me wishin' you to have adventures in life, I says Ethel, it'll do the lad good. Oh I missed you, Denny! Like a great chunk of me heart had been ripped out! And something changed in you, then, for when you came back you were different.

DENIS: How was I different?

SAMMY: More serious, didn't smile as much. But so excited about Napoleon! And you said you had a grand time there in France.

DENIS: I said what? I said I had a grand time? Are you certain?

SAMMY: Aye, son, you did. Why?

DENIS: (*Confessing it for the first time; passionately*) It was awful! Bloody awful!

SAMMY: Awful?!

DENIS: The worst! I was so homesick, every night I'd cry myself to sleep. The days seemed endless. I tried running away, back to you, but I couldn't speak French well enough to find my way. Oh, God, I missed you both so much! (*Angrily*) It was a terrible mistake, sending me away, alone, so young. How could I ever trust you again?

SAMMY: (*Flustered; touched*) But I—we—well why didn't you *tell* us? We'd never have sent you away the next summer—you kept so quiet—

DENIS: Tell you? With you being so proud of me? I was ashamed of myself for missing you so much.

SAMMY: (*Pause; tenderly*) I wish you had told us, Denis.

DENIS: Yes, I wish I had. And *if* I had? What then? (*Pause; sensing the "magic" of the moment*) How bizarre, this, and how perfect: the shape of tonight, that after all this time, I *am* telling you that I missed you—

(*Rawls enters; Denis stops himself; pause*)

RAWLS: The guests are comfortable, sir. If I may say so, it's quite a sight, seeing *eleven* Napoleon Bonapartes all at once!

SAMMY: (*Cheerily; understanding Denis' embarrassment*) And it was all so bloody peculiar anyways, that summer exchange. This little French lad who came to us—you both put down for "Hobbies: magician." Well I keeps tryin to teach the French laddie the magic tricks, and he'll have none of it. Curious, that—not interested in magic at all!

DENIS: What *was* he interested in?

SAMMY: Music. "Je soo-ee musiss-ee-an." Wanted to know where the "pianer" were. "Pianer?" Bloody hell!

DENIS: Musician? And when *his* family kept shoving musical instruments at me, I'd try to say that *my* hobby was magic, being a magician—

SAMMY: Magician!

DENIS: Musician!

SAMMY: They bolloxed up the bloody hobbies! Them stupid bastards!

DENIS: Unbelievable! Marvelous!

SAMMY: Now isn't that the cat's balls—

RAWLS: I didn't know you were a magician, sir.

SAMMY: He never told you that? Why as a lad he had magic in his soul. Remember Coronation Day, Denny?

DENIS: Coronation Day! Yes! I'd set up on a corner, do my tricks, the Queen would pass by, and then I'd pack up and run to the next corner and set up again. Thirteen pounds I made! A fortune!

SAMMY: You should have seen him: so serious, trying to make his tricks perfect, and all of London so drunk it didn't matter a damn! Grand! Just grand!

DENIS: It was. I haven't thought of that for years.

SAMMY: And the magic in the family hasn't stopped, Denis—your son has it in him as well. He's one of them lads what can bend spoons by concentratin' his mind on 'em—

RAWLS: He's one of them, is he? Amazin', that—

DENIS: Go on—spoonbending is impossible—

SAMMY: It's not. These two eyes have seen it. A great lad, him. He's clever, you know, like you. (*Pause; sincerely*) You were right about my bein' jealous. Your mother knew how your cleverness was like a knife in me guts, how she had to get you away from me. Did she drive me out? Nah, I drove meself out, I did. You know she used to come with me, early on, to the pubs. And there'd be all sorts of people there—politicians, students, actors even—and we'd talk, do magic, sing—yes, we'd even sing! Ah, sometimes she's so gentle on me mind, and sometimes she leans so heavy I do wish I was dead, but I've left her, and come this far without her, and I'll keep on, keep on. (*Pause; solidly*) We need them, we do. We men are always explodin' and them women are always endurin', and that's that, in't? And it's a sad thing to lose them, it is.

DENIS: As sad as losing the magic we have in us as children. It's so far back, so foreign, I've forgotten so much—

SAMMY: (*Eagerly*) Your own son will remind you. He's just waitin' for his chance. He don't want some old boy like me to bring him up, do he? Some old ancient boy like me with these rattlin' clackers in me mouth and these slitherin' twisters in me pants.

RAWLS: Sir—the guests are waiting. What shall I tell them?

DENIS: Yes. Tell them? (*To Sammy, sincerely; trying to be "warm"*) Would you . . . Father . . . Come to this dinner. Join me, will you?

SAMMY: Me? Join the likes of you? You must be jokin'. I never intended to come to dinner.

DENIS: WHAT? You didn't?

SAMMY: Me? A sort of man as me go to dinner with twelve genuine pedigree Napoleon Bonapartes? They'd be much too aristocratic for a poor historical Cotswold man like me.

DENIS: Then why the hell did you dress up and come here tonight?

SAMMY: Why? Because it was time. I was afraid I'd lost you, that you'd never come back to me. I've lost too much to lose you as well. I'd do anything—even dress up all green and warty like a toad—to try and do what I did tonight.

DENIS: Well then, I must to dinner. Is there anything I can get you?

SAMMY: A few more bottles of this fizzy stuff, and the company of your fine servant here, to pass away the time.

DENIS: Done. (*Puts his hand in his coat, like Napoleon*) How do I look?

RAWLS: Your jacket, sir. Your jacket needs straightening.

SAMMY: (*Going up to him*) Right. Some coarse old buggar mussed up your cute little French uniform, mate. Here. How often do I get a chance to straighten the jacket of Napoleon Bonaparte, and him being my only son to boot? (*Sincerely; close to tears*) Lad, you're comin' back to me. I'm sorry. But I never stopped loving you, all these horrible years. (*Overwhelmed, embracing him*) I loves you, boy, I loves you.

DENIS: (*Stiffly, trying to respond*) Yes, well . . . I love you too, you . . . you old fox.

SAMMY: Fly high, boy, fly high! Find that magic in your soul!

DENIS: You say . . . you say my son can bend spoons?

SAMMY: That he can. He concentrates his mental powers and—*presto!*—like magic, a spoon bent nearly double under the strain.

DENIS: Well then, since I'm a cold and ruthless Oxford skeptic, it behooves me to investigate this spoonbending phenomenon for myself.

SAMMY: (*With a touch of ridicule for what Denis is*) Aye, bring that cold *essentric* mind to bear—

DENIS: (*Fighting back; appraising Sammy*) You know, father, you really have gone to the bleedin' dogs.

SAMMY: (*Surprised at the truth in it*) I've *what*?! Why you better watch what you—

DENIS: (*Standing up to him, firmly*) You heard me, mate,

you've gone to the bleedin' dogs—

SAMMY: Buggar off! Buggar off you too-clever runty little cock—

DENIS: The dogs and the donkeys, just like your nutty father before you, hey? (*Pause; in the doorway*) Good evening. Good evening to you both. (*Exits*)

RAWLS: (*Popping cork, sitting down with Sammy, drinking*) *Twelve* Napoleon Bonapartes down there, all of 'em standin' around with their fingers in their bellybuttons. Bloody silly, in't?

SAMMY: No more bloody silly than us.

RAWLS: True, too true, no more bloody silly than us.

SAMMY: He's not a bad lad, really.

RAWLS: I reckon he'll be a bit better than he were.

SAMMY: Aye, he'll be coming back a bit to me, and to his own little laddie as well. He needed a jolt. A historical jolt.

RAWLS: Aye. He'll soon feel a good bit more like he does now than he ever did before.

SAMMY: Aye—what?

RAWLS: I said he'll soon feel a good bit more like he does now than he ever did before.

SAMMY: Yes, well that's what I thought you said, yes. (*Drinking; settling in*) Ah, they're not so bad, these women, really, are they? With their moon-rhythms and their cryin' and all?

RAWLS: No, they're not. They're quite soft, really.

SAMMY: They are not soft.

RAWLS: They are.

SAMMY: They're not.

RAWLS: Well we think they are, we do.

SAMMY: We do not.

RAWLS: We don't?

SAMMY: Not on your life, man, not on your life. *They* think they are.

RAWLS: They do not.

SAMMY: Don't they?

RAWLS: Never, man, never. They think that *we* think they're soft.

SAMMY: You're tellin' me they think that *we* think they're soft?

RAWLS: That's it, yes. Now you've got it.

SAMMY: And do we think that?

RAWLS: Of course we don't. We just let them *think* we do.

SAMMY: Oh aye: that's it, for sure: we don't think they're soft, we just let them *think* we think they're soft. Now I've got you, and I couldn't agree with you the more.

RAWLS: And *why* do we let them think that?

SAMMY: (*Puzzled; resigned*) Who knows, mate, who knows.

RAWLS: All I know is that my missus has hands like sledgehammers and an arm that could break a man's neck.

SAMMY: A hard woman, your missus sounds.

RAWLS: Very hard, and, in this heat, quite sweaty as well. And do you know, for me the most amazin' part of it all is still the matter of the rhino cleaner—

SAMMY: You mean the rhino *cage* cleaner, I do believe.

RAWLS: Right. Rhino *cage* cleaner. I mean fifty-odd years in rhino droppin's and hippo shittin's and the odd great chunk of elephant turd to boot, and his collar is filthy and he hasn't shaved and the Duke shakes his dirty hand and the Duchess, on national telly with the BBC boyos right there for the closeups, goes over to your man and plants, in all that dirt, a great dollop of a kiss on the little pervert's cheek! Amazin', that, amazin'—

SAMMY: Now let's see, where was I? Ah yes, Sunday! (*Resumes his song*)

"Annnd Sunday after supper, I shoved the damn thing up'er,

And now I'm payin forty bob a week, gor blimey . . ."

RAWLS: (*A bit drunk*) He didn't enjoy bein' made famous through the rhino cleaner-outer, your son did not. Oh, but you should have seen how cross your son got, seein' the newspaper photo with him in the back and the rhinocleaner-outerwithRoyalty in front!

SAMMY: (*Singing*)

"I don't want to join the army, I don't want to go to warr,
I'd much rather hangaround Picadilly Underground,
(*Joined by Rawls*)
Livin' off the earnins of a high-born laydee . . .
I don't want a bullet up me arsehole, I don't want me gonads shot awaiy.
I'd rather live in England, in jolly jolly England,
And fornicate me bleedin' life awaiy, gor blimey . . ."

RAWLS: (*Grabbing Sammy, playfully*)

"Monday night me hand was on her ankle—

SAMMY: (*Grabbing him back*)
"Tuesday night me hand was on her knee—
(*They continue to alternate verses as the light dims to:*)
Blackout

Beverley Byers Pevitts

REFLECTIONS IN A WINDOW

Beverley Byers Pevitts

Beverley Byers Pevitts makes her debut as a published play-wright with *Reflections In a Window,* a poignant play which explores the meaning of family relationships as they relate to the problems of the elderly. With a surrealistic chorus of elderly women, Dr. Byers Pevitts provides a counterpoint to the conflict between one hundred year old Bertie Goodall and her family. First produced in A Festival of New Plays at Southern Illinois University at Carbondale in 1979, the script was presented in August, 1980, for the Playwrights' Workshop at the American Theatre Association National Convention in San Diego, where this editor was script judge and respondent. Since then the play has been produced at a number of universities and by professional groups, including the National Conference Committee for Women and the INTERART Theatre in New York, with the production directed by Broadway director Kay Carney.

During the summer of 1981 Dr. Byers Pevitts was Playwright-in-Residence at Horse Cave Theatre, Kentucky, where her script *Time and the Rock*—co-authored with Warren Hammack—was produced. The play tells the story of Floyd Collins's entrapment in Sand Cave, Kentucky in 1925, which took media focus of the Western world for over two weeks. Dr. Byers Pevitts's husband, Dr. Robert R. Pevitts, was Resident Designer.

Earlier scripts by Dr. Byers Pevitts include: *Dreams and Other Phases: By and About Women,* which the playwright directed at the Calipre Stage at Southern Illinois University in 1979; *Take Courage, Stand Beside Us,* commissioned by the Louisville, Kentucky Area NOW (National Organization for Women) in 1977; *A Strange and Beautiful Light,* commissioned by the United Methodist Church and presented throughout Kentucky; and *Epilogue to Glory,* which she co-authored, produced by the Department of Theatre at Southern Illinois University in 1966.

A native of Beaver Dam, Kentucky, Beverley Byers Pevitts completed her B.A. at Kentucky Wesleyan College, Owensboro, in 1961; received an M.A. in 1967 at Southern Illinois University at Carbondale; and in June of 1980, was awarded a Ph.D. from the same institution, completing her dissertation entitled *Feminist Thematic Trends in Plays Written by Women for the American Theatre: 1970–79.* She is presently working on two books that grew out of this study: one, an anthology of plays by contemporary American playwrights, and the other, a critical study of plays by women in the New York theatre.

Additionally, Dr. Byers Pevitts has contributed bibliographies and essays on women in the theatre to *Chrysalis,* the *Dictionary of Literary Biography,* and *American Women in Drama,* the latter edited by Helen Krich Chinoy and Linda Walsh Jenkins.

Dr. Byers Pevitts's career in educational theatre includes teaching positions at Young Harris College, Georgia; Western Carolina University; Pfeiffer College, North Carolina; and Kentucky Wesleyan College, where she is presently Associate Professor and Director of Theatre.

Active in professional organizations, Dr. Byers Pevitts has been President of the Kentucky Theatre Association, and Chairperson and on the Board of Directors of the Southeastern Theatre Conference. In the American Theatre Association she has served on the Program Committee, on the University and College Theatre Association Board of Directors, as the Project Director for the Ford Foundation Grant for the National Conference for Women in Theatre, and on the Executive Committee and as Vice President of the Women's Program. Presently, she serves on the Literary Advisory Committee on the Kentucky Arts Commission. She has been honored with a grant from the National Endowment for the Humanities to study "Avant-Garde Theatre in Europe and the United States" and received recognition as a Distinguished Woman of the American Theatre Association.

Characters:

Chorus of Old Women:
    MARTHA, *eighty-eight*
    MARGARET, *seventy-five*
    ESTHER, *eighty-three*
    RUTH, *seventy-two*
    REBECCA, *sixty-eight*
The Staff:
    FEMALE ORDERLY, *dressed in white pants uniform*
The Family:
    BERTIE GOODALL, *one hundred years old*
    ALICE, *her daughter, late sixties*
    ALFRED, *her son, mid-sixties*
    BETTY, *her granddaughter, early thirties*

Scene:

A nursing home in the Midwest. An overcast day in early summer.

The front parlor of an old Victorian house is the day room of "FAMILY HAVEN"—the name seen in reverse from the inside of stained glass panels in a large bay window located upstage. In front of the window the Chorus of Old Women sit in chairs and wheelchairs.

The Family, which rarely interacts with the Chorus, is an embodiment of all the families of the old women.

Garish plastic materialism imposed on elegant old art creates an almost surreal effect. One gets the impression of not really being in the room, an impression shared by the characters.

At rise, Ruth sits in her chair in front of the window. She is crippled with arthritis but tries to walk erect. She does not want to be confined to one of the wheelchairs and will fight it with her strong will even after her body is too weak.

RUTH: (*To herself*) I had always hoped not to come to one of these homes. (*Adjusts book in lap, muses*) Mmmm, I live here . . .

(*The orderly pushes Esther in her wheelchair from the hall that leads to the patients' rooms. There are trays secured to the fronts of the wheelchairs. Esther is an old Jewish woman with a raspy voice.*

She wears lots of jewelry with her fancy dressing gown)

RUTH: (*As she sees Esther enter room*) Good day, Esther. Where's the sunshine?

ESTHER: Good morning. How's your arthritis?

RUTH: I can't write today—it's bad in my hands.

ESTHER: They can only slow the aging process.

(*They both laugh*)

RUTH: (*A joke, sort of*) The idea is to get worse as soon or as slowly as possible.

(*Orderly brings in Rebecca, an enormous hulk of a woman; she is too large to walk, and she pours over every open area of the wheelchair. She moves out of her wheelchair into a large overstuffed chair at an angle to the rest of the chairs. Her chair is placed away from Esther and Ruth. She has a Bible*)

RUTH: There are luxury homes that cost $2,000 or $5,000 a month.

ESTHER: They get a lot more care.

RUTH: No, just the furniture and the paintings are nicer. That's the only difference.

ESTHER: There you can get up in the morning and fix your own breakfast if you want.

RUTH: I lived in one of those for six months in Chicago before I came here. They are *private*. The high-rises you can afford—but you can't afford these. You have your kitchenette—and there is a restaurant downstairs if you don't want to fix your own meals.

ESTHER: You were happy there?

RUTH: Yes.

ESTHER: You were depressed there?

RUTH: Yes.

ESTHER: You lived there for a while?

RUTH: For six months. Seemed like years. Thank goodness I just took a six month lease. They tried to get me to take a year's lease.

ESTHER: You didn't enjoy it?

RUTH: No, I didn't.

ESTHER: Were there other people there like to play cards? bridge?

RUTH: Very few and very—well, if you went with one group, the other group didn't speak with you. Such enmity. I've never seen kids that were as vicious.

ESTHER: Like children . . .

RUTH: Yes, it shocks you.

ESTHER: People are vicious.

RUTH: I don't think they are.

(*Margaret rolls herself in her wheelchair and takes her place by Rebecca, orderly follows her*)

ESTHER: They are. I always lived in a motel until I came here. I don't mind living here.

(*The front door opens. Alice, Betty enter followed by Alfred. Betty carries a small basket of fruit. Alice carries a small box of soft chocolates. Alice is a quiet, smiling, friendly, conservative, loving woman. Betty, her daughter, is outgoing, stylishly casual, very pretty, very in charge of herself, her mother, and her uncle without them knowing it. Alfred is expansive and jovial. When the Family enters, the Chorus turns three-fourths in their chairs to face the windows. When the dual conversations go on with the Chorus and the Family, the overcast day becomes sunny enough to see the reflections of the Chorus mirrored in the windows*)

ALFRED: (*To the orderly*) Hello there. Good morning, I'm Alfred Goodall. I'll check us in the desk. Will you be bringing Mrs. Goodall out soon? (*He gestures to Alice and himself*) She's our mother.

BETTY: And grandmother.

ORDERLY: She's still in whirlpool.

ALICE: As soon as she gets out?

RUTH: (*Overlapping Alice and orderly*) I lived in a trailer after that six months in the upper crusts luxury home where I definitely did not belong.

ORDERLY: (*Overlapping Ruth*) It won't be long. She'll be so happy to see you. She does love company.

RUTH: (*Overlapping*) Two of my sons—one went to Harvard and one to MIT—thought it was a hoot! Their mama couldn't stand the bejeweled bridge players!

ALICE: (*Overlapping*) Thank you.

ESTHER: Watch who you're talking about! I could possibly fit in!

ORDERLY: (*Still overlapping*) Have a seat.

REBECCA: (*Overlapping both Esther and orderly*) I lived in an apartment . . . (*Rebecca talks only to herself and responds to others without acknowledging visual contact*)

ALFRED: (*Overlapping and overbearing*) Sure, we can sit over here. I'll be right back.

(*Alfred exits. Orderly exits. The following Chorus and Family dialogues overlap*)

ESTHER: What did they call those apartments?

REBECCA: (*Answering without visual contact*) Bayside Manor.

ESTHER: (*Abruptly*) They're low rentals.

BETTY: (*To Alice and speaking above the Chorus*) Mom, I drove by the farm last night. Did Aunt Louise tell you that Cousin Freddie and his new wife and her kids are living there?

MARGARET: (*Overlapping*) It's not what you know; it's who you know to get in there.

ALICE: (*Overlap continuous*) Why no. Alfred didn't mention that Frederick had moved into Mom's house.

ESTHER: (*Overlap continuous*) It's like who your kids know to get you in here.

BETTY: I don't guess he'd have nerve enough to tell you he'd moved his son in. Maybe afraid you or Aunt Louise would want to move one of your children and family in with him. (*Betty laughs*)

REBECCA: (*Overlapping*) It's costing too much for these nursing homes. I read a piece in the paper the other day. The man is right.

ALICE: Now, Betty. There's none of you that would need to . . .

REBECCA: (*Still overlapping, mumbling almost*) We pay for the water in the bill, we pay for the light bill, we pay for the cleanin' bill. And when we could stay at home and be a lot more satisfied and pay someone to come to our places and care for us. He said we could save thousands and thousands of dollars. (*Rebecca speaks almost continuously and usually only to herself although Esther and Ruth respond to her. Rebecca cannot read or write even though she pretends she reads the paper and the Bible*)

BETTY: Does Grandma know that her least favorite grandchild is . . .

ALICE: I don't see how Grandma would know. Louise would have told me . . . Did you stop in to see Fred?

BETTY: Sure, I went in and met Mary—and her four kids. And little Freddie's fine. (*Betty and Alice fall quiet*)

ESTHER: (*Responding to Rebecca's tirade; continuing to overlap*) Where is he going to get those people to take care of everybody?

REBECCA: A nursing home only takes care of people half way. I know. I wurk'd here.

ESTHER: Did you help anybody?

REBECCA: If they could find somebody to come to m'a hus and tek cer of me. I wanta 'em ta do it!

ESTHER: If they ·could find somebody to do it! Do you know anybody who is satisfied in a nursing home? Ever?

REBECCA: No. Nobody. Never.

ESTHER: No. Nobody. Nobody knows what they want. They can make $500 a week or $100 or $5,000; they don't know what they want. They go there for two years and can't say or do a thing they want.

REBECCA: So some of them die . . .

RUTH: Hell, let us run the country for a day!

(*Orderly leads Martha in; she crosses and sits by Esther; Martha is small, quiet, practical, liked by everyone; loves others*)

ESTHER: Come on Mary Martha, I'm saving a seat for you. (*Orderly exits*)

MARTHA: I went down to the other room.

MARGARET: They chased us out of there this morning, wouldn't let us in.

MARTHA: I asked about you. I brought the *Enquirer* for my sister. I'm still reading yours.

ESTHER: All right.

MARTHA: And I'll bring it when I finish.

ESTHER: It's all right.

MARTHA: I was setting out there at the desk. (*Martha also has poor grammar but she is not illiterate. She has always been terribly poor*)

ALICE: Did you tell Fred I was here? That I was coming to see him? (*Pause*) I should have come here sooner.

BETTY: Yes. I asked Fred why he was living in Grandma's house. What gives him the right to live there . . .

ALICE: Betty, you . . .

BETTY: He said I should know. As *all* the other grandkids know—that the *farm*—remember all of Uncle Alfred's kids always said "our farm"—was Uncle Al's and that Grandpa had signed it over to him and he, of course, gave it to his eldest son—Jesus, if Fred'd ever get off his dead ass and do something for himself!

ALICE: (*Reproachfully*) Betty. Maybe Fred's paying rent and Alfred's saving it for Mom.

BETTY: Don't count on it! He couldn't take care of himself and Freddie before he married this new wife with her four kids. (*Betty crosses to the women*) Do you have a family?

ESTHER: Of course, we all have families.

REBECCA: (*Overlapping*) Jesus' family—we're all part of Jesus' and God's family.

BETTY: How many children?

ESTHER: I was married for nine years before I had my son, and then I had him for nine years before he passed away. In three days.

(*Orderly enters, crosses to Martha*)

MARTHA: No, dear, I left the *Enquirer* by the door.

(*Orderly exits*)

ESTHER: They said it was a mastoid. Meningitis. He got sick at school. He came from school and said he couldn't see. I took him to a doctor and they said it was a mastoid and they operated.

BETTY: And that still makes you sad.

ESTHER: Very. I get along. A handsome boy of nine years.

MARGARET: Anytime we lose someone it's hard.

ESTHER: There's nothing that hurts like losing a child.

MARGARET: I hate to see a child or someone—you know . . . (*Margaret drawls her words*)

ESTHER: A youth . . .

MARGARET: A youth—someone who's just about ready to do something—or not do something have to leave life . . .

ESTHER: (*Drawn out*) Yes.

MARGARET: I hate to see any person have to leave life.

BETTY: I'm sorry about your son.

ESTHER: (*Looks up at Betty*) My daughter in California screams at her children.

(*Orderly enters with* Enquirer *for Martha*)

MARTHA: I had left it at the desk where I had picked up my meal ticket that I lost. Thank you.

(*Orderly exits*)

ESTHER: Thank you so much. This lady supplies me with what I call this "Washer Woman's Gazette."

MARTHA: *The National Enquirer*. I asked this girl at the desk. Do you ever read one of these? Well, I told her, you ought to buy one. They are really amusing.

ESTHER: I could sit for just hours and read all the gossip. I was going to talk about my son.

MARTHA: Pardon me for all the intruding.

ESTHER: I had a son; I lost a son before Blanche was born. He was my only child and I tried to adopt. After a few months I realized I was pregnant so I didn't bother with it—and when Blanche was 17 months they brought this little 3½ year old child that weighed less than my child of 17 months. It was during the depression; I said I can't take her, and my mother, God rest her soul, said, "Take her, take her, where one can eat; two can eat." She is my best daughter today.

(*The following is spoken simultaneously*)

RUTH: She didn't want to know she wasn't your daughter?

ESTHER: She looks like me. Blanche looks like her father. Madge looks like me. One day I walked in unannounced and her friends said: "Madge, your mother's here." (*Esther laughs*)

MARGARET: One of my daughters is in Illinois and one is in Texas and then I has three stepdaughters too and I don't know where all of them is. One of them's in California but I don't know where'bouts. And the other's in Georgia. Her husband just got transferred from the prison here down to Atlanta. So they live down there. I don't hear from them very often. The other one's still in Union County.

ESTHER: I was married for nine years before I had a son and then I had him for nine years and he passed away.

ALICE: Louise said they planted a big garden by the back field across from the horse barn. His new wife must have gotten Fred to do that. Need a garden today with five kids.

BETTY: Good. But on whose land? Certainly not his! God knows it might even be grandma's!

ALICE: No—Alfred bought that land across the road from neighbors of Mom and Dad's a long time ago. Ours just went to the pig lot.

(*Alfred enters*)

ALICE: Now don't say anything to your Uncle yet.

ALFRED: The doc says Mom's about the same. Don't expect her to know you—especially you, Betty. She'll probably think you're Louise or one of the girls.

ALICE: Does she know you?

ALFRED: (*Slightly stumbling*) Well, now I'm not sure she always has. She's pretty senile, you know. Hardening of the arteries, the doctor said.

ALICE: Tim told me last night that she'd know all of us.

ALFRED: Our baby (*Laughs*) brother Tim has always exaggerated. He likes to think she always knows him.

ALICE: He said he comes twice a week.

ALFRED: Yeah, yeah, but I don't think she knows him all the time. He thinks so.

(*Rebecca's following monologue runs throughout the following scene; she pauses and then begins again. It runs parallel to the Alice, Alfred, Betty speeches*)

REBECCA: When I was six years old, I wus pullin' weeds outa' the onion patch. Milkin', hoein', plowin'; use't load wagons; got up at four o'clock in the a.m. and light the lantern. The boys and daddy went to the barn. There wus thirteen of us kids. The kitchen was readied the night before for breakfast. In the mornin' Daddy started the fire, mommy sifted the flour for the biscuits, sister and me cooked a big breakfast: sausage, bacon, fried taters, eggs, biscuits and milk gravy on special mornings.

We stripped cane for molasses. Daddy smoked his meat. He rubbed salt and red pepper, brown sugar—he put holes in it with an ice pick; dipped it in sorghum and smoked it all day with hickory and sassafras roots. Next morning, he'd rub it with honey and black pepper; dip in sorghum. Whoeeee, it wus good . . .

ESTHER: (*At the end of Rebecca's speech*) Is that where you got so fat?

REBECCA: (*Continuing her personal monologue*) Ain't ever tasted country ham like m'daddy could make. Sister and me'd fry that up on special Sundays and serve with red-eye gravy, biscuits, and fried apples with fresh-biscuit sorghum butter on the side. Whoeee, that was good eatin'. (*Sad*) Shor cain't make none of that now.

ALICE: Alfred, he told me she even knew the children—the great grandchildren.

ALFRED: I just don't want you to think she's going to be great, Alice. Now you know we thought we were losing her twice during the winter.

ALICE: Yes. (*Droll*) Thanks for letting me know.

ALFRED: Louise didn't want to call you and got angry with Tim when he pulled the big pneumonia scare.

REBECCA: (*Continuing her monologue*) I married when I wus sixteen; we decided to travel; had eight children; two boys and two girls still living. Found one of my girls dead and we took her to bury and next morning my littlest boy tuk sick at 6 o'clock—by nightfall he wus dead. Went to bury him and came back to find my house burned. Well, the husband decided somethin' was against him and he tole me he couldn't stand it no more, so he left.

I was a widow for seven years 'fore me and Mr. James married. I run him off three times 'fore I decided I wanted him. I have nine step kids—every one of them likes me too.

BETTY: But the doctor did think it was going to be soon, didn't he? Mama called all of us that time. We were all ready to come.

ALFRED: Well, it could still be soon. When you're 100 years old and weigh 86 pounds you've gotta be pretty fragile.

ALICE: (*Overlapping*) Eight-six. No one told me she lost so much weight.

BETTY: I always thought Grandma was strong as an ox.

ALFRED: She lost eight pounds with the flu and then four with the pneumonia before they could get her stabilized. It's a good thing the director here is a business acquaintance and friend of mine. We go duck hunting in Canada together. Now when Louise and Tim first talked to them there was absolutely no room. They only took her because Ham did it as a favor for me.

| BETTY: Just how bad does Grandma . . . | ALICE: How does Mom feel? |

ALFRED: Why—uh—last week when I was here, she looked better than she had in quite a while. Seems to be getting a little strength back.

BETTY: Uncle Al, how often do you and Aunt Josie see her?

| MARTHA: (*Martha tells the story of her family continuously until finished*) I was married in 1917 when I was nineteen. My husband was in the National Guard. He had to go right away to France. He was | ALFRED: Frequently . . . frequently . . . We come every chance we get. We live here. You know how it is . . . Of course, she doesn't always know when you're here, you know. |

in ammunition training. He had five men under him; he was there for the Battle of Verdun.

ESTHER: (*Overlapping Martha's story and the dialogue of the Family*) I had older brothers; one thirteen years older.

REBECCA: Jesus wants us here.

RUTH: (*Overlapping above; a response to Esther's last line*) Did they help at home?

ESTHER: (*Continuing to overlap*) I was a change-of-life baby. That brother brought me up. My brothers were men actually, one was married, one was a bachelor, one was a lawyer.

RUTH: Your brothers?

ESTHER: (*Still overlapping dialogue*) All gone now.

MARGARET: (*Overlapping dialogue with the Family story*) I had four brothers and three

ALICE: I hope she likes what we brought.

ALFRED: Listen Alice, remember what I said. Don't be upset if she doesn't know you. She's failing fast. And she'll tell you I don't visit. That's her way of chastising me for forgetting a couple of months. Why, most people love it. Look how happy those women are. (*He gestures to the window bay*) Why, they play cards and sew . . . (*The women stop what they're doing and look at him when he gestures to them, then they continue*)

BETTY: (*Looking down hall to avoid women's reactions, pause, then*) Here she comes!

(*Alice rushes to greet her mother as the Orderly pushes her to the table. Bertie is petite, frail, but alert and perky. She is an old woman who will probably elude death for some time to come. All speak slightly louder when speaking to Bertie as she is hard of hearing*)

ALICE: (*Obviously taken aback by the wheelchair and the fraility of the tiny woman*) Hello, Mom. Ma, you're looking good. How've you been? How do you feel? (*Alice kisses her mother*)

BERTIE: O.K. O.K.

ALICE: (*Worried*) Ma, you know who I am?

BERTIE: What's the matter? You don't know who you are?

ALICE: It's me, Alice, Ma.

ALFRED: You know who I brought to see you, Ma. See, it's Alice. I told you she was coming.

sisters. Each one of my brothers had three brothers and three, uh, four sisters. (*Pause, then she continues*) I was the oldest girl in the family so I cannot remember when I didn't have to do dishes.

MARTHA: My husband was shell-shocked—you know, they won't tell you much. He told us one story—He had lost his gas mask and there were bombs bursting around him. Well, he found his gas mask. That was about the only tale he'd tell us. (*She alone may have listened to her story but that in itself gives it its merit. She enjoyed telling it to herself*)

MARGARET: (*Overlapping Family dialogue; dominant action is Family dialogue*) No, they don't want to talk about it . . .

ALICE: You know me, don't you? Here, I brought you some soft chocolates. And we have some fruit for you. You got something to peel peaches with? (*Louder*) You want a peach?

BERTIE: O.K. O.K. I know you. Humph. Haven't been here in a long time.

ALICE: School's just out Mom. You know, I've been teaching all year. It's my last year. You know I couldn't come. I wanted to come when you were in the hospital. Tim called me and told . . .

BERTIE: Tim comes to see me. Twice a week . . . Him—humph—he never comes see me. Like you. You never come. My best daughter.

ALICE: I teach during the year Ma and you know it's a long way. I want to come . . .

BERTIE: Humph—you don't come. Lock me up here. Don't come.

ALICE: (*Continuous with the above speeches of Martha and Margaret*) Look who I brought with me, Mom. You know who this is, don't you.

MARTHA: (*Overlapping*) So he was shell-shocked. He was dependent on the veteran's disabled pension. I could live in a Veteran's Retired Home if I wanted to—I had boys in both wars. This oldest one that's with me here was the one whose Daddy was in France when I gave birth. He took headaches while he was in San Antoin. During the World War II. The doctors told him he just imagined his pain. Do you think a person could just imagine that he has pain. But they gave him pain tablets . . .

MARGARET: Seems like that's the kind of thing that causes a lot of people to commit suicide.

MARTHA: (*She continues to speak during the Orderly and Margaret incident*) The other boy that was in WWI didn't get a scratch on him during the war and he came home; he was a sheet metal worker; he slipped and fell twenty feet to a concrete floor and they put him in an ambulance. After he was unconscious for over two months, I said to this brain specialist, "I

BERTIE: Well, I'll be . . . Of course . . . Look who came to see me!

BETTY: Hi, Grandma Bert. (*Bends to kiss her grandmother*) How are you?

BERTIE: I'd be livelier if I could get out of this . . . Hey, I bet you're just the girl who'll get me out of here . . .

ALFRED: Hell, mother · · ·

BERTIE: (*Overlapping—this continues through Ruth, Esther, Margaret, and Martha's stories*) Get me outa here! If you can't do it with tools, get an injunction! (*She laughs at her own joke directed to Betty*)

ALICE: (*Overlapping*) I don't think you're supposed to open it, Ma. They think you need it for support.

(*During the above the Orderly in the white pants uniform comes into the room, moves among the Chorus. Margaret is chewing tobacco; she spits on the back of the Orderly; once, the Orderly does not feel it; the Chorus laughs: twice, she does not feel it; they laugh again; she does not know why they are laughing and does not care; Margaret spits the third time,*

think I'll put him in a Vet. Hospital." He said, "Oh, no. You let those sheet metal people pay for this." He was in for three years and we went to that hospital—traveled 65 miles there every Sunday for those three years.

He had one boy and his boy right now is in Germany. He has made the Air Force his career. Both my girls married chaplains—one was in the Phillipines and the other in Japan for years. She sent me pictures. These kids really get around these days. My husband was in World War I and my sons were in World War II, and I have a grandson who was in Vietnam so there I've been concerned with all our wars.

I raised eight children and then I became a professional baby sitter when I was 76. $100 a month. Worked ten years at that.

the Orderly feels the wetness, goes over and quietly chastises Margaret and then hurries out of the room)

BETTY: That nurse looks like she's just out in her pajamas!

BERTIE: (*Overlapping Martha's speech*) Hell, Alice, let Betty try. They'd never suspect her or you of unfastening it. You're women. They'd think Alfred have to be the one to pry me out of here but, unless he has orders from the Chief Jailer . . .

BETTY: Grandma, you know I can't take you out of there. But I have something here for you. (*Betty hands Bertie some fruit*)

BERTIE: Good. I'd like to eat it now. Bet . . . (*She pulls Betty down and whispers to her*) I need my teeth—go to my room and get my teeth.

BETTY: O.K. Gram. (*Betty exits*)

BERTIE: Alfred, it's nice to see you. Did the President declare this Visit-Mothers-in-Old-Folks-Home Day? You haven't been here since you picked up my checks last month.

MARGARET: (*Overlapping*) My baby sister, she's younger and I—we had cows to feed—milk to churn.

RUTH: (*Overlapping*) I worked in a hospital.

ESTHER: I always wanted a little adoration . . . Now'd be happy to have Leonard here to harp on me.

MARGARET: (*Overlapping*) The doctors wanted me to take something to calm me down.

REBECCA: (*Overlapping—to herself*) Turning . . . turning into my insides . . .

ESTHER: (*Overlapping*) The best cook I ever had in my kitchen was a Chinese

ALFRED: Mom, I was here last week.

BERTIE: (*To Alice*) Seems like months! Only came because he needs my check. (*Loudly, to Alfred*) Did you pay the tax on the house?

ALFRED: Of course, Ma. I've paid the taxes on your house going on seven years now. Smile, Ma.

BERTIE: For you? Why should I smile?

ALFRED: 'Cause you look nice.

BERTIE: I look nice when I don't smile. Alice—do you know women are stronger than men?

ALICE: In spirit, Mom— or physically?

BERTIE: When you reach my age, both! (*Sweeping gesture toward the bay*) They have to be physically. We've always been spiritually. Maybe some of the young ones never were . . .

ALICE: Betty is. (*Betty enters*)

. . . came here when they could still get out . . .

REBECCA: (*Overlapping*) I see my life . . .

RUTH: (*Reading aloud from her book*) "Only the incidental relations of life, such as mother, wife, sister, daughter, which may involve some special duties about training . . .'

BETTY: Here are your teeth. I'm what?

ALICE: Strong—spiritually and physically.

BERTIE: You strong enough to peel the peach?

BETTY: Yep, Gram. Where's the knife?

BERTIE: Alfred, go ask for a knife.
(*Alfred exits, glad to escape even briefly*)

BETTY: Gram, you sound strong, do you feel strong?

ALICE: Betty asks how you feel, Mom. Are you feeling your strength back?

BERTIE: I'm strong enough not to need this damn chair. *Now* Bet, now while he's gone, you undo this chair.

BETTY: Gram, I can't.

ALICE: Mother, now, she can't do that. You know that.

ALFRED: (*Returning with knife*) How's the food this

RUTH: (*Still reading*) "In disarming the sphere of man, we do not decide his rights as an individual, as a citizen, as a man . . ." week, Ma? What did you have for supper last night?

(*Betty peels the peach and feeds small bites to Bertie*)

BERTIE: Awful . . . always terrible. Tasted like crap. Can't cook here. Never cook . . .

BETTY: What did you have, Grandma?

BERTIE: (*Loudly*) Dead beans.

ALICE: What else, Ma? Were they green beans or limas? What with them? Did you have some fresh, yellow squash?

BERTIE: DEAD BEANS. Always, all we have . . . DEAD BEANS. Dried beans for dead people.

ALICE: Grandma, how you carry on . . .

ALFRED: (*Overlapping Alice's speech*) Hear the cook's great here. If Josie doesn't start doing better, I'll move in with you!

REBECCA: (*Overlapping*) First obeying my mom and pap, then obeying my husband . . .

BERTIE: I always relied on myself; even though your Dad tried to make me dependent on him, he was really just dependent on me.

REBECCA: (*Continues overlapping—thoughtfully to herself*) . . . Then obeying my kids. They just told me to come here and I come.

RUTH: (*Reading*) ". . . by his duties as a father, a husband, a brother or son, some of which he may never undertake."

BERTIE: Betty, how's the baby boy?

BETTY: Whose baby boy? My sister's? Grandma, you know I don't have any babies . . . I'm . . .

BERTIE: Hell, I know that . . . or somebody'd tell me. Debbie's boy. Betty, you think I know nothing . . . the little boy. She comes to see me and brings the baby. I tell her to take me home—home to my house so I don't have to eat those rotten beans. Where I can cook good green beans from the garden now. But she's got so much. With the boy—and the baby. You know your cousin is going to have another baby?

BETTY: Yes, Grandma.

BERTIE: Well, I don't care, but I want to know why you don't have any family yet.

BETTY: I'm not going to have children, Grandma. You've got enough grandchildren and great grandchildren already.

ALICE: Ma, we know Debbie's going to have a new baby. So is Betty's sister, Kim . .

BETTY: Here's some pictures of Kim—remember your granddaughter, my sister . . .

BERTIE: Ah, Betty, go on with you. I know you and Kim anywhere. But not you yet, hm, Bet?

BETTY: (*Laughs*) Not for a long time, Grandma. You've got enough grand-kids.

BERTIE: Alice, you come to take me home? I'm glad. I gotta get . . .

ALICE: (*Firmly*) Mom, I'm afraid I can't.

BERTIE: . . . out of here. I dry up in this place with all these old people around me who can't hear.

ALICE: Mom, the doctor says you're not well enough yet.

BERTIE: Which doctor? Who told that? That young Dr. Gruber tell you? Or Alfred tell you that? Alfred doesn't want me to come home. He wants me to rot here where he doesn't have to see me. Where they give me shriveled beans.

ALFRED: (*Overlapping his mother*) Gruber says you got to stay here, Mom. Now, you've just been carrying on. Alice and Betty came 600 miles to see you.

ALICE: Mom, here look at these pictures Betty brought.

ALFRED: I'll take the knife back. (*Alfred exits*)

BERTIE: (*Taking the pictures from Betty, which include a clipping from a newspaper*) I know this fellow?

ALICE: Where are your glasses?

BERTIE: Can't see too well anyway. The cataracts on my left eye are bad again. (*Bertie takes glasses out of robe pocket*)

ALICE: Have you told anyone? Does the doctor know?

BERTIE: I'm too old to fool with changing 'em. I read a little. (*Laughs*) And I see the birds outside my window glass every morning and the new leaves on the trees. (*She looks at pictures*) That's Jack, isn't it?

ALICE: (*Prodding*) Who else? Can you see? Who's behind him?

BERTIE: Sure—there's Katherine—I can tell 'cause she's got her mouth open! When are they coming to see me?

ALICE: I imagine they'll be here in August—before they go back for fall term.

BERTIE: They've done just about everything, haven't they?

ALICE: Yes. (*Pause*) Mom, when did you sign house papers for Alfred?

BERTIE: What? What are you saying?

ALICE: What did you sign for Alfred for the house?

BERTIE: He tell you I did? I think he wants it—but not yet. I'm still here!

ALICE: Tell me about the paper, Mom. When did you sign it?

BERTIE: I signed the paper for him to pay the taxes.

BETTY: Can he sign your checks now, Gram?

BERTIE: I think so. He said it'd be easier if he could just sign my name now I'm here all the time. Alice, I want to go home.

BETTY: Grandma, you've been real sick this past winter. You can't go out to the farm by yourself—and who could come with you?

BERTIE: I know Alfred can't keep me. Your sister Louise works all day, so does Tim and his wife. But Alice—you could come stay with me there now, can't you?

ALICE: (*Kindly*) Mom, I can't come to the farm to live with you.

BERTIE: Alice . . . Please . . .

ALICE: Mom, I have my own house.

BERTIE: No. What'd you say? Where's Betty's man?

BETTY: Out of the blue you say that, Gram. Don't you know? Crawford and I got a divorce, Grandma. We're still good friends.

RUTH: (*Overlapping through the following dialogue with the Family*) My sons are both divorced. One a friendly divorce. One not. They both say they would never marry another woman until they had lived with her awhile. I don't know that it's all bad. I'm going to a big family wedding Saturday. My niece has been living with this man and after a very early divorce and a child—a rather pathetic marriage . . .

BERTIE: Alice, how did this happen?

ALICE: Mom, I think it's O.K. . . . . for the better.

BERTIE: Of all my grandchildren I never thought you and your man'd be divorced. And you a big lawyer. Did you give yourself your own divorce?

BETTY: (*Laughing*) Gram, you can't do that.

BERTIE: Why, Bet, I liked that young fellow.

ALICE: He was a leaf—the first one the breeze blew by when she got through seven years of school.

BETTY: I have a new friend, Gram. When I come back this way I'll stop. He'll be with me.

BERTIE: (*Replying to Betty*) Humph.
(*Alfred returns*)

MARGARET: (*Overlapping*) I think that when one has been married before it pays to be cautious.

ESTHER: (*Overlapping*) I think they find out what a divorce costs.

MARGARET: Some families probably used to stay together because they couldn't get divorced.

RUTH: (*Overlapping*) There's an awful lot of things you can live through too. If you stay together for six months 'cause you say "we can't afford to break up now" after that six months is over, the troubles may be mostly over too.

MARGARET: (*Overlapping*) Some people stay together for children and the children don't benefit.

RUTH: (*Overlapping*) If the relationship is vicious, it should break up. (*Pause*) On the other hand, I have two little great grand-daughters and I can see what a friendly divorce is doing to them.

MARGARET: (*Overlapping*) Young people today have so much greater expectations.

ESTHER: And they're more readily disappointed.

RUTH: (*Overlapping*) They're ready to call it over and begin again.

BETTY: You'll like my new friend, Gram. His name is . . .

BERTIE: (*Cutting her off*) You and this man gonna have a family?

ESTHER: (*Overlapping*) I think family is coming back.

MARTHA: I read in the *Enquirer* it is coming back.

BETTY: I have a family, Grandma. I have *you*, Mom, three sisters and a brother, four nephews, two nieces. I have an enormous family . . . six aunts, four uncles, (*Laughs*) hundreds of cousins . . .

MARTHA: (*Overlapping Betty*) Yes, he told all of them that was living together to go out and get married.

BETTY: I have all them . . . All because of you, Gram.

REBECCA: The Bible says man is head of the house as Christ is head of the church.

RUTH: But you have foolish fathers and wise mothers. Different cases—different solutions.

BERTIE: Take me to the bathroom.

ALICE: I'll get the attendant. (*Alice exits*)

BETTY: Grandma Bert, I'm sorry I won't be here for your birthday, but we'll celebrate when I come back through here next month.

ALFRED: It's going to be a big Fourth of July celebration!

BERTIE: I'm a Yankee Doodle birthday girl. Yep, I'm exactly 100 years younger than our country.

ALFRED: (*Slightly overlapping Bertie*) Yes, sir, we're going to have a pig roast—we'll barbecue a good-sized baby pig in our new barbecue pit at the farm and invite the entire riding club. Late in the afternoon, we'll all go into the horse show at the fairgrounds . . .

BERTIE: (*To Alfred*) Last year on my birthday, you didn't even come to see me . . . and I was 99—why you planning such a celebration this birthday? Special Fourth of July for your horse group?

ALFRED: Now, Ma, everybody can't stay out here all day . . . we'll have the whole family out here for your cake at noon and then in the afternoon while you nap, they can all come over to the farm for roast pork—barbecued—how's that sound, Bet? Maybe even have a friend you'd be interested in seeing.

BETTY: If I were going to be here (*Quietly to Alfred*), I'd prefer staying here with Grandmama. (*She turns to Bertie*) Grandmama, I remember when we celebrated your 75th birthday at the pavilion on the lake. It was the first Fourth of July I ever really remember, the blue sky rockets, the silvery shooting stars exploding in the sky, the red sparklers, and your Fourth of July cake. It had 75 candles, I had never seen so many candles before. They were brighter than all the fireworks. I was holding my breath hoping you would blow out all those candles. Then from the wind the candles caught the icing on the cake on fire. I thought it was going to burn your face . . . I looked through the fire at you trying to blow out all of those candles. Then Uncle Al put out the fire with his fireman's extinguisher. This disappointed little girl was blowing as hard as possible to help you get out the candle fire.

ALICE: (*Returning disturbed*) She said she'd be here soon. (*Softly to Alfred*) She said it doesn't matter. That she's probably already messed when she thinks she has to go to the bathroom.

ALFRED: It's true. I'm sure she has. You wouldn't have believed what she did at the house just before she went to the hospital.

BERTIE: What are you two whispering about?

ALICE: (*Louder*) The attendant's coming to take you to potty, Mom.

BERTIE: They don't come. Tell 'em I've got to take a crap. Now.

BETTY: I'll take you, Gram. Show me the way! (*Betty pushes wheelchair down corridor*)

BERTIE: Better hurry up, Bet. I'm like a baby now.

ALICE: Does this happen all the time?

REBECCA: (*Overlapping*) Billie . . . Billie . . . (*Drawn out "i" becomes "ea" sound*)

ALFRED: That's one of the reasons she's in the chair. I told you it's not good. They have pads in the chair. They'll clean her up. Betty's too late. (*Laughs*) One day Josie and I went over to the house and she'd wiped shit all over the walls upstairs. Got mad trying to clean herself up.

ALICE: Had she been regular taking her medicine? I thought we were paying for someone to stay with her.

ALFRED: Hell, old Mrs. Partridge wanted the money but couldn't do a thing with her. You know Ma! She ran her off with a butcher knife. (*Laughs*) The one she used to cut heads off of chickens. Told us that there was an old man outside with a knife—but she wouldn't let him in. He wanted in; she wouldn't let him. I asked her what he looked like, she described Pa.

REBECCA: (*Overlapping*) Ohhhh, Billie, Come git me, Billie . . .

ALICE: He's been dead sixteen years.

ALFRED: Next afternoon Mrs. Partridge came back and Ma was lying on the floor covered up with a coat. She asked her what happened? Ma said, "I fell down." She was taking a nap on the goddamned floor.

ALICE: Does Mom know Fred's living in her house?

ALFRED: (*Expansively*) Sure she does.

ALICE: She didn't say anything. Neither did Louise.

REBECCA: (*Overlapping*) Ohhh, Billie . . . Oh, Bill . . .

ALFRED: Hell, I told her right after he and Mary moved in . . .

ALICE: I hear you put in a bathroom for them too, and all these years Mom walked down those back stairs to empty her slop jar.

ALFRED: The kids had to have something.

MARGARET: (*Overlapping—to no one*) I tried to reach my dreams; I guess I was always a failure.

ALICE: So should Mom and Dad. What if Betty, one of the other grand-kids, or one of Louise's or Tim's kids wanted to move in too?

ALFRED: (*Laughs*) Why, we could have a young folks home.

RUTH: (*Overlapping*) Watch after 'em care for 'em and give 'em all the love that they'll accept. If you don't have much to eat, love is the best dream you can have. If you've got your children and they love you—what more can you have?

ESTHER: (*Overlapping*) Your hope is your dream? You think you've achieved that, don't you?

REBECCA: (*Overlapping through several speeches*) Billie, Billie, Come here Billie. Ohhhh . . . come here to me . . .

ALICE: Alfred, Mom never got along with Freddie.

ALFRED: Hell, Alice. No one does. This wife he's got now is a saint! She's a change for him and a chance for him to do O.K. Hell, he doesn't even act like he remembers Viet Nam now that he has Mary. You've got to get to know her, Alice.

ALICE: (*To self*) Don't know that a good marriage'll cure Frederick. (*To Alfred*) You know in the summers he always tormented the girls to no end. (*Betty and Bertie enter*) No, I don't think Mom would like it.

BERTIE: What wouldn't Mom like?

ALFRED: (*Effusively*) She pretends she can't hear and just when you believe her, she hears! (*Alfred laughs*)

BERTIE: What wouldn't I like? What you done now, Alfred?

ALFRED: Nothing, Mom. Alice and I were just reminiscing.

BERTIE: About Fred? Betty and I were talking about him. Does he like living in my house?

ALFRED: You bitc—! Did you tell her? ˙

ALICE: I thought she knew . . . said you told her.

BETTY: She knows. I didn't have to tell her.

ALFRED: I'm sure the prosecuting attorney led her to it!

BERTIE: (*In an outrage*) Why else did you want me in here? Only so you could instill that spoiled no-good son of yours in my house. Well, collect the rent. I could use a little cash! Betty offered to handle my legal affairs!

ALICE: (*To Alfred*) She doesn't remember, does she?

BETTY: Well, Unc. You've got some explaining to do.

ALFRED: Mom, now you know I told—asked you—when he and Mary were getting married . . .

BERTIE: Who's Mary? What happened to Tracy—or what was her name after her? I won't stand for anyone living in sin in my house.

BETTY: (*To Alice*) Grandma told me that Uncle Al talked to the Social Security officer and told him that Grandma didn't know what she was doing and that his name was on the deed. The Social Security agent said that it had been sold a long time ago.

ALICE: Alfred, I think you should do something.

REBECCA: (*Overlapping Betty and Alice*) The guy from the Aid for the Aged said that they regarded who had it should turn it over.

ALICE: (*To Alfred*) You've been trying to take over the farm since you made Mom get rid of her chickens by putting your pigs in there.

BERTIE: (*Overlapping*) Dad'd come out and chase the grand-kids out of the flowers for me. Every year. We had a flower garden—calla lilies, peonies, iris, belles of Ireland—late summer mums.

BETTY: Uncle Alfred—I love you, but Gram told me she knew—she said you sneaked Fred into her house. She just doesn't know you're also trying to take it over.

BERTIE: (*Authoritatively*) We're making something out of nothing and what we are making is no good!

(*The others speak as if Bertie is not present*)

ALFRED: (*Ignoring Bertie; to Alice and Betty*) I'm not trying to take it over 'cause the house is mine. I've paid the taxes since Dad died. You two don't live here.

ALICE: You've been trying to take over the farm since you made Mom . . .

ALFRED: (*Cuts her off*) Now Alice, it's not *the farm*, it's not Mom's farm, it's *our* farm.

ALICE: Mom told me that Tim had to get rid of his cow too because you took over the whole pasture for your pigs, and they rooted it all up so it wasn't fit for the cow to graze, just like when they got into the yard. It was no longer serviceable for Mom growing flowers.

ALFRED: The farm's in my name, Alice.

BETTY: Legally deeded as such—transferred?

ALICE: Before, you said seven years you'd paid taxes.

ALFRED: A long time—seven—five—fifteen—I've paid them!

ALICE: How can it be in your name?

ALFRED: Dad signed it over to me.

ALICE: He didn't . . .

ALFRED: Our names are the same, you know. A.B. Goodall. I'm Alfred—the A; he was Ben. We went to the courthouse together.

REBECCA: (*Overlap*) Billie, oh, Billie . . .

ALICE: (*Very softly, but brave speech for her*) Dad didn't intend for that farm to be yours. He told me once that it was to be divided equally, and since Spencer is gone and the oldest brother, then I am to see to it. Betty said she'd do the legal work—or we can hire someone if you want to have power of attorney. We can work it out—but we all have to know.

BERTIE: Don't let those little kids go out to the pig lot. There are wild pigs and horses out there. The kids chase the pigs. Tell Freddie to watch that old sow that's gone mean. Alfred took all her baby piglets from her before she weaned 'em. She's a bad 'un now. Daddy Ben said she beat down all the corn in the back garden last week.

ALFRED: (*Becoming oily*) Alice, Alice, you know I wouldn't take the farm. I've only been kidding you.

BERTIE: (*Overlapping*) Fred's his. If it's your own shit, you just don't smell it.

(*They ignore Bertie*)

BETTY: Yeah—then why's Fred there?

ALFRED: He'll move when Mom dies.

ALICE: (*to Bertie*) Mom, shhh . . . (*Alice pats Bertie's hand; Bertie grabs Alice's hand and holds on tightly*)

BERTIE: Take me home, Alice. I said I want to go home, Alice.

MARTHA: (*Overlapping Bertie—to Chorus in general*) Could you have done this to your family? I couldn't have done that to my daddy.

BETTY: But is he paying rent? Is Gramma getting the money?

ALFRED: I didn't think she'd want him to pay rent.

BETTY: I talked to her; you heard her, she does. I'd be glad to draw up a lease for him.

ALFRED: What have you always had against Frederick? He doesn't have to pay rent. I've paid the taxes for a long time.

BETTY: He didn't pay the taxes.

ALICE: You paid them. I'll pay my share of everything you've paid.

BERTIE: Nobody pays for me. I paid taxes with my checks that I give Alfred.

BETTY: Is that true?

ALFRED: (*Shouts at Betty*) You're not here all the time! Mom, that money goes to keep you in here!

BERTIE: Then take me out! How much can this God-forsaken hole cost?

BETTY: Taxes pay for this, isn't that the system?

ALFRED: I've got to go pick up Josie for lunch. Her car's in the garage.

BETTY: Uncle Al, Mother may do nothing about this; Grandmama can't do anything—but I will do it for her. I will contact Aunt Louise, Uncle Tim, every cousin I have.

ALFRED: (*Cutting her off*) Betty, you always meddled in other's business too much. You don't live here, you know. Now, we've always gotten along. There's nothing for you to do. Legality's on my side. That house is mine. I'll see you all at Louise's for dinner tonight. (*He exits*)

BERTIE: No, and he doesn't need to come either.

BETTY: (*Overlap; calling after him*) And I will tell everyone there what you are doing and have done . . . Jesus, you have to realize that this is my grandmother.

ALICE: Betty, please don't carry on so.

BETTY: Mama, I know you won't. I know Grandma can't, but that farm is not his. It's hers. And she can say what happens to it. I will take him to court and I will win.

ALICE: I don't care about the farm for me, Betty.

BETTY: I know, Mama, but it's what is right. I tried to tell you about him a long time ago, Mama—when I first did his taxes for him. Your brother steals from your mother.

ALICE: Well, I'll talk to Louise and Tim.

BERTIE: Alice, take me home. It's time to get the chickens up for the night. You know, Alice, when I was a little girl I remember when they brought Lincoln's body through here on the train.

ALICE: Mom, Lincoln died before you were born.

MARGARET: (*Overlapping*) I just wanted to be a teacher. I succeeded in doing that, but sometimes I think I did the state a disfavor. My mother was a teacher and my grandmother was a teacher. I never knew much else to do. I knew I could be a nurse and a secretary.

BERTIE: Then I remember my mother telling me about it like it was yesterday. I can still see it.

(*Orderly enters*)

RUTH: That was about it.

BETTY: Grandmother, don't you want to make a will?

BERTIE: Betty, my life's made a difference—cause of six children. Well, seven, one girl didn't make it, she didn't have enough strength. And 23 grandchildren, and 32, well, now 31 great-grandchildren and four great-great-grandchildren. When are you going to have a great-grand-baby for me, Bet?

ORDERLY: Mrs. Goodall, it's time for lunch and nap in bed.

RUTH: (*Overlapping*) My father was a liberated man; anything I wanted to do, he'd back me. But the depression hit and all I could do was all I could afford to do.

BETTY: Grandmother, it's a matter of more than babies.

MARTHA: (*Overlapping*) All I ever wanted was someone to make me smile. I found him, he died.

BERTIE: Time to go to bed—I don't know of anybody I want to get in bed with—not here.

BETTY: Gram, I'll make everything right for you. I promise—and I'll be back here in a month to see you.

ORDERLY: (*Overlapping Martha*) You may visit again from four to six. (*Loudly*) Tell them good-bye for now. Mrs. Goodall.

RUTH: (*Overlapping*) Frankly, I don't want to be the kind of burden on my children that . . .

BERTIE: O.K. O.K. I'll be looking for you and your new young man, Bet.

MARTHA: (*Overlapping*) The whole majority of people don't want that put on the daughters . . .

REBECCA: (*Overlapping*) I think if your daughter loves you enough . . .

RUTH: (*Overlapping*) I love my children too much to ask them to keep me.

ORDERLY: Yes, I know, Mrs. Goodall. Let's go.

MARGARET: (*Simultaneously with Orderly's speech*) Butterfly on your way to death—land on my shoulder.

BERTIE: (*Talking to Orderly as they go down the hall*) Of all my kids—only two aren't living. The baby girl—and Spencer who went several years ago with cancer. Cancer of the brain. He was smart. My oldest son is in the hospital—he should be here—he's a senile old man who can't eat! Alice and Alfred were both here today. They used to be just like twins. The young ones are Louise and Tim—you know them . . .

ESTHER: (*Overlapping Bertie*) That's right, I don't want to depend on them.

REBECCA: (*Overlapping Bertie*) Anyone of my kids'd want me with them.

ESTHER: Why are you here?

RUTH: It's like if we don't die when we're supposed to, then they just put you away and forget you.

MARTHA: (*Overlapping Esther*) My daughter wants me with her.

REBECCA: I'd rather be in a little home by myself, but

when it come to the place, I come here. But I know they want me with 'em.

RUTH: I'd sacrifice myself rather than their families.

BETTY: (*Crossing to her mother and putting her arm around her shoulder*) Mom, let's go now.

MARTHA: Me too.

ESTHER: You'd get along anywhere you were to go.

(*Alice comes back to the chair and begins to gather up her things. Betty crosses to the door to leave; she waits for Alice who vaguely gestures for her to go on*)

MARTHA: Well, I can compromise and make myself fit whatever situation I'm in!

REBECCA: I can too. I've had to make myself satisfied here, but if I wanted to, one of my daughters'd cum and tek me to their home.

(*Betty exits*)

ESTHER: I lived in a one bedroom apartment for two and a half years, and I was never so lonely. I lived in a motel and loved it. I had lots of people.

(*Alice crosses to door, turns to look at the women*)

REBECCA: I wouldn't live in a motel—full of strangers.

ESTHER: Wherever I go, I know everybody; everybody knows me.

RUTH: You *live* here.

(*Alice exits. The lights stream in on the Chorus, and they are bathed in midday sunlight*)

The End

Michael Kassin

TODAY A LITTLE EXTRA

Michael Kassin

Michael Kassin makes his debut as a published playwright in this volume with his touching play, *Today A Little Extra*. Reflecting on its performance by Actors Theatre of Louisville as part of the 1980 New Play Festival (performed with companion piece *Remembrance*), Scott Fosdick of the *Sunday Herald* (Chicago) described the play as "A bittersweet three-character comedy that brings fresh life to the word poignant . . . Among other things, *Today A Little Extra* shows us what we lost when America traded in the bustle of inner city life for the convenience of the shopping center." And William Mootz of the *Courier-Journal* (Louisville) observed "Kassin's play is about survival and endurance and learning to challenge the future with the uses of the past. It's a sweet comedy with a lot of honest sentiment in it. . . . Most of all, however, Kassin's play is about the passing on of traditions from one generation to another. In a world that increasingly seems hell-bent on churning all societies and all ethnic groups into one homogeneous and faceless mass, it dares to ask whether there is still a place for eternal verities." Prior to the Actors Theatre production, the play, first performed in 1977 by Minneapolis Jewish Community Center's Centre Stage, won first place in the Minnesota State Community Theatre Festival.

The author, born in Chicago in 1947, reports that he was raised "in a very kosher home, where my grandfather—my father's father, may he rest in peace—brought home all the beauty of Old World 'extra.'" Undoubtedly, this background is reflected in both the characters and values evident in *Today A Little Extra*.

After majoring in acting at the University of Minnesota, where he received his B.A. summa cum laude in 1969, Mr. Kassin taught high school in Illinois and Minnesota for six years before returning to his alma mater to receive an M.A. in theatre in 1976.

Other produced plays include: *No Mourning After Dark*, a one-act performed by the Centre Stage of Minneapolis, which won the 1975 Minnesota State Community Theatre Festival and was subsequently performed at the Guthrie Theatre; *Brother Champ*, a full-length play performed by the Mixed Blood Theatre of Minneapolis in 1976 and revived a year later at the American Theatre Association Convention in Chicago and later presented by the Shirtsleeve Theatre at the West Side Airlines terminal in New York in 1978; *Sophie and*

Willa, first read by the Playwrights Lab of Minnesota in 1979 and professionally performed as the first play in the First Stage Series at Center Stage, Baltimore, in 1980. Mr. Kassin also has written scripts for a forthcoming PBS children's series, *Great Stone Balloon,* and adapted work for television and radio. Additionally, he has written theatre reviews for the *Minneapolis Star* and the *Minnesota Daily,* and an article for the *Dramatists Guild Quarterly.*

His playwriting has been honored with the Guthrie Theatre Award, a grant from the Minnesota Playwrights Lab, the Oscar Firkins Scholarship, and commissions from the Actors Theatre of Louisville and the Cricket Theatre in Minneapolis.

As an actor, Mr. Kassin appeared in Minneapolis at the Guthrie Theatre, the Guthrie II, and the Mixed Blood Theatre; and in New York at The Richard Allen Center.

Now a resident of Bronxville, New York, Mr. Kassin is at work on a full-length adaptation of *Today A Little Extra.*

Characters:

ZALMAN ABRAMS, *seventy-four, a kosher butcher, probably small, white-haired and stooped, but vigorous and apparently healthy.*

MARK LEVINE, *twenty-seven, future owner of the shop, pudgy, well-dressed, the son of a very successful delicatessen owner, a nice boy, just a little young yet.*

ESTHER FINKELSTEIN, *sixty-eight, plainly dressed but not unattractive. She may be diminutive, but her mouth is as big as she is.*

Scene:

The action takes place in a broken-down neighborhood, once almost exclusively Jewish, in any large city—but preferably New York—in or near the present.

The setting is a butcher shop, old, simple and on the verge of extinction. A picture window with the words, "Zalman Abrams— Butcher," and the Hebrew word for kosher underneath it, is gated at the moment. To the left of the window is the outside door, also gated. Somewhere opposite this wall is a simple white butcher's display case and a counter with a scale on top. Behind the counter is a dial-less phone, and, on the wall near the door is a coin operated phone. Next to the dial-less phone is a sign, "Ask About Credit," and somewhere nearby is the door to the back room in which the coolers, the chicken cages and who-knows-what-else, reside. Somewhere onstage are three old chrome chairs with green vinyl seats—in a row—meant to seat customers who, alas, no longer come.

It is 8:00 a.m., Friday morning. Through the outer doorway comes Zalman Abrams, whitehaired, stooped but apparently healthy. He takes a long look at the shop, he taps the scale with his fingers, he unlocks the gated window and door. He disappears into the back room, reappearing almost momentarily with coat off, skullcap on, bloody apron in hand, pencil behind the ear. He shuts his eyes and says a quick prayer. He opens them again and dons the apron. Again he disappears into the back room. The sound of an old radio is heard, more static than music—the kind you heard in barber shops when you were a kid. He re-enters, broom in one hand, dustpan in the other. He sweeps, hums, mutters. The phone rings. He watches it for a moment. It rings again. He crosses to it, picks it up.

ABRAMS: Boo-tcher!   . . . Who?   . . . Candy's Massage Parlor? . . . No, I'm sorry, this is kosher meat . . . (*He hangs up and starts back for the broom. A second ring. He pauses, crosses back to the phone, answers*) Hallo . . . You again? Look, I don't know from Candy, but if you can reach her at 8:00 a.m., she's in the wrong business . . . (*He starts to hang up*) . . . Who? Max Levine? It didn't sound like you . . . It didn't sound like me either? . . . What do you know, a stranger could make a good living talking to you . . . So how's the delicatessen? . . . From you either, they don't buy kosher meat? Well, at least you got "trayfe" meat you can sell to make a living. Must be good for the pocketbook to be a liberal . . . So, how should I feel on the last day? . . . Ya, big plans. Monday I'm running off with an eighteen-year-old girl. A real "tzatzke" . . . Why? We're good for one another. With what I got, and what she's got, we'll get along like Richard Burton and Shirley Temple . . . So what can I do for you? . . . Ya, I'll be out today. Who you sending over? . . . The boy? I haven't seen him, maybe fifteen years. If he's like you, I wouldn't let him in . . . *He's* taking the shop? We'll see. A little test I'll give him . . . (*Mark appears at the window, and Abrams notices him*) I think that's him now outside . . . How do I know? Same guilty look you had before you got rich. I'll talk to you . . . (*He hangs up*) . . . Goodbye . . .

(*Mark Levine enters. He is about twenty-seven, fairly well-dressed—except that his suit is a little too tight on his chubby body. He's a good boy, trying to look too old. He carries a cardboard sign with him—"Under New Management," and a topcoat tucked under one arm. Abrams has him sized up in three seconds*)

LEVINE: Mr. Abrams . . .

ABRAMS: (*Pretending to be startled*) Yes? . . . Don't tell me. Your wife sent you early you shouldn't wake the guests . . .

LEVINE: Mr. Abrams . . .

ABRAMS: . . . and the A&P ain't open yet, and besides, they ain't got kosher like Zalman Abrams got kosher so you come by me to get the best. You're new in the neighborhood?

LEVINE: No, I . . .

ABRAMS: I know, don't say it. You had a fight. You didn't

want to spend extra, and your wife sent you anyway. We dicker, ya? Like in the old days. I cheat you, you starve me. You're my first customer, I gotta sell you. What do you want? Chicken? I got special this morning, let me tell you, so plump I had to circumcise the door to bring them in . . .

LEVINE: No thank you . . .

ABRAMS: How about beef? Brisket I got so lean, so tasty . . .

LEVINE: Please.

ABRAMS: Forget it. I know what you need—(*He moves behind the counter*)—Duck! (*He shows Levine*) . . . You start now, maybe it would be ready for Shabbos. So much pleasure you'll get from eating this bird, you wouldn't look at your wife for a week . . .

LEVINE: Please . . .

ABRAMS: You don't like so fancy? I give you steak. Good, simple steak. Like the goyem eat. No class, but very tasty.

LEVINE: Just let me . . .

ABRAMS: (*Helpfully*) Think about it? Of course you think about it! Go call your wife. Go, go, go. There's a phone. (*He gestures*) You have guests, a happy meal this should be. You want everything? I make you a special price. This is my last day you know.

LEVINE: (*Spotting his chance*) I know.

ABRAMS: (*"Surprised"*) You know?

LEVINE: (*Extending his hand*) I'm Mark Levine.

ABRAMS: YOU'RE LEVINE? (*Mark smiles*) But Max Levine . . .

LEVINE: . . . is my father.

ABRAMS: Max said he would send by me the new manager.

LEVINE: (*Glowing*) And owner.

ABRAMS: And Manny?

LEVINE: Manny will stay at Pa's shop and help when I need him.

ABRAMS: Manny don't get the shop?

LEVINE: Manny didn't want the shop. Manny has a bad heart.

ABRAMS: And you got the shop, huh? (*He looks at Mark*) How old are you?

LEVINE: Older than you when you started.

ABRAMS: How do you know?

LEVINE: Pa told me.

ABRAMS: Your Pa counts like he weighs meat. No wonder he's got such a big business. He and I started the same age.

LEVINE: That's not what he said.

ABRAMS: Who you gonna believe, your father or an honest man?

LEVINE: Can we get down to business?

ABRAMS: Ya, what can I do for you?

LEVINE: Can we talk seriously?

ABRAMS: Wait a minute . . . (*He exits to the back room for a moment. The radio is turned to solid static, and the volume is turned up. He reappears*) Ya?

LEVINE: Uh, can we turn that off so we can start?

ABRAMS: I thought you wanted to talk serious?

LEVINE: I do.

ABRAMS: So why are you making me play games with the radio?

LEVINE: (*Exasperated*) Please—

ABRAMS: You want me to turn it off?

LEVINE: Thank you, yes.

ABRAMS: Okey-dokey . . . (*He disappears. A long pause. Mark tries to busy himself around the shop. Silence. Mark becomes worried*)

LEVINE: Mr. Abrams . . . (*No response*) . . . Mr. ABRAMS . . . (*Still nothing. He starts to look*) MR. ABRAMS!

ABRAMS: (*Offstage*) Not yet, my tuchas ain't got ears! (*He re-enters, sits*) Now, Mr. Levine

LEVINE: Mr. Abrams, I thought—

ABRAMS: So did I. You come tomorrow, ya? The shop is yours tomorrow. It's in the papers.

LEVINE: *Please.* I've planned this very carefully.

ABRAMS: So have I. Thirty-four years I been in this shop, and on my last Friday, I close an hour before sundown. Like always. You come tomorrow, ya? The shop is yours tomorrow sundown. It's all in the papers.

LEVINE: The thing is, if I can get an early start, I could maybe be open Monday.

ABRAMS: Monday you want to be open?

LEVINE: Yes.

ABRAMS: So work on Sunday.

LEVINE: Who works on Sunday?

ABRAMS: Kind men who don't kick Alta Kakers out before the time has come. Listen to me. Today you go and think some more. Tomorrow you pray the shop should keep you like it's kept me. Sunday you do extra, ya?

LEVINE: Thirty-one years Pa's run his shop, even a delicatessen, he's *never* worked on Sunday.

ABRAMS: So?

LEVINE: Sundays Manny runs the shop.

ABRAMS: You got a Manny to run for you?

LEVINE: I have a *shop*. Sundays I don't work.

ABRAMS: And a year from Sunday you go broke. You want to be ready Monday? Sunday you do extra.

LEVINE: Today I'll do extra. Tomorrow I'll do extra. Sunday I don't work.

ABRAMS: But Saturday you work?

LEVINE: Saturday I work. Saturday is a big day for us.

ABRAMS: (*Playing on it*) I know. Saturday I *don't* work.

LEVINE: Yeah, and look at you—(*He stops himself, realizing what he has just said*)

(*Abrams is silent. He moves to the window, and, with great patience, motions to Levine*)

ABRAMS: Come here, sonny boy. Come. Look across the street. See? With the windows boarded, with the words I'm trying not to read? Thirty-four years ago it was Mandelman's Grocery Store. Mandelman dies and young Mandelman takes over. Six years. Then it's Warshawski's Sausages and Fine Meats. Nineteen years maybe. Warshawski retires. Now it's Young's Rib-Tips-With-Extra-Hot-Sauce. Three years. Young is robbed twice in a month. He sells to Lopez. I don't know what Lopez sells. I can't read the sign. Lopez is evicted by the city, who make it an office for a nice boy with too much hair and not enough sense. The office is burned. Now it sits empty. Thirty-four years I'm here, and I don't work Shabbos. Listen to me. Sunday you do extra. Today you leave me alone, ya?

LEVINE: Look, Mr. Abrams, in half an hour they're making a delivery from my father's shop. I thought if I could . . .

ABRAMS: (*Incredulous*) They're making a delivery? Today? In *my* shop?

LEVINE: Yes.

ABRAMS: What kind of delivery?

LEVINE: What do you think?

ABRAMS: From your father's shop it could be pigeon parts in chili sauce.

LEVINE: My father sells good meat.

ABRAMS: With his customers, who would know the difference?

LEVINE: Look, I'm not going to argue with you. I just want to know . . .

ABRAMS: Is it kosher?

LEVINE: What?

ABRAMS: This meat they're delivering? Is it kosher?

LEVINE: Who's going to buy kosher meat in this neighborhood anymore?

ABRAMS: (*Shrugging*) I don't know. Must be a rich phantom kept me in business so long.

LEVINE: Please. This is the only time I can get him to deliver.

ABRAMS: You have him deliver tomorrow, ya? I'll be in the synagogue. I wouldn't look.

LEVINE: He's not working tomorrow.

ABRAMS: I'm glad to see SOMEBODY there has got some sense.

LEVINE: Look, I won't be in your way. You can sell what you want. In twenty-four hours it'll be my shop anyway, so what's the difference?

ABRAMS: What's the difference? In five minutes will come Esther Finkelstein to buy for Shabbos, who has been my customer since before her husband died. Twenty-six years she's come to me because I run a kosher shop. Three blocks away is the A&P which is selling kosher meat for cheap maybe ten years now, from which she DON'T buy because also they sell trayf. Tomorrow there will be no place and she will be your problem. Today there is still a place, and after twenty-six years, she is still MY problem, and I want it that way.

LEVINE: Mr. Abrams . . .

ABRAMS: No.

LEVINE: Just listen for a minute.

ABRAMS: The answer is no.

LEVINE: She'll be gone before he gets here with the delivery, so what's the problem?

ABRAMS: She'll be back. You don't know the ritual.

LEVINE: The ritual?

ABRAMS: Stick around.

LEVINE: Look, what does she care what's being delivered?

ABRAMS: *I* care. And I ain't gonna disappoint her.

LEVINE: Look, can I use your phone?

ABRAMS: You gonna cancel the delivery?

LEVINE: No.

ABRAMS: Then use the one on the street. Cost you ten cents. Unless maybe the kids fixed it again. Then it's free.

LEVINE: They do things like that in this neighborhood?

ABRAMS: What do you mean, "in this neighborhood?" In Queens they don't cheat the phone company?

LEVINE: If you'll excuse me.

ABRAMS: It's all right.

LEVINE: I'll be back very soon.

ABRAMS: Take your time, I got all day.

LEVINE: We'll see.

ABRAMS: What? You'll get your father after me? What can he do? By the time he gets his lawyer, I could elope with Mrs. Finkelstein. And what's the point of that? We're both sterile. Relax, boychik. Monday you'll be open anyway, and this will all seem funny when you think about it.

LEVINE: You think so?

ABRAMS: Ya. With a pest like you around, your papa will either get by you the meat or cancel your birth certificate. Go make your call.

LEVINE: I'll be back.

(*He starts to exit. Abrams watches him. Stealthily, determinedly, Levine crosses to the window and deposits his "Under New Management" sign. But he is not quick enough. Before he can leave, Abrams has snatched it from the window and handed it back to Levine. The two men glare at one another. Then Levine exits in a huff, depositing the sign on the* outside *of the window as he hurries up the street. Abrams rushes to the door and watches Levine, shouting after the boy. He moves to the window and removes the sign. He crosses inside, wondering what justice he can bestow on it and its owner. He has it. He crosses to the back room, returning with the broom. He puts the sign down and sweeps all the garbage onto it. Then he takes both into the back room. He returns, thinking a moment. Then he grabs a dime and crosses to the pay phone. He dials*)

ABRAMS: Hallo, Max?. . .Look, your boy just left me . . . Ya, he said he'd be right back . . . I don't know. I think he's probably trying to call you now . . . Why? If he don't learn to open his mouth, he'll be out of business in a week . . . Ya, he's a nice boy, but he don't know how to talk . . . How hard on him could I be? If he thinks I'm bad, wait 'till he hears the Wailing Widow . . . (*And who should appear at the door*) Huh. Mention the devil and she taps you on the shoulder. I'll talk to you. (*He hangs up*) Goodbye . . . (*An elaborate ritual follows, in which he bangs the phone to get his dime back. The dime returns. Esther Finkelstein enters. She is a small, not unattractive woman of sixty-eight. She is dressed simply in overcoat, dress and hat. He watches her*) Today, of all days, you had to be first?

(*A pregnant pause. Esther looks around*)

FINKELSTEIN: Wait. I'll stand back from the door I shouldn't get trampled. (*She takes a deep breath*) Oy, such a crowd is here you could die of suffocation.

ABRAMS: Very funny.

FINKELSTEIN: Funny? *I'M* funny? With what you sell me, I don't know whether to cook it or have it arrested. What do you got for me fresh?

ABRAMS: Take a number and find out.

FINKELSTEIN: What's to take a number for? There's no one here.

ABRAMS: You want to spoil the system?

FINKELSTEIN: No, I can see how well it's working. (*She takes a number*) Here. Five. You happy now?

(*Abrams looks at his number machine, then looks around*)

ABRAMS: TWO! Where is two please?

FINKELSTEIN: You mean I gotta wait? I'll be back in half an hour.

ABRAMS: Don't take so long. You'll lose your place in line.

FINKELSTEIN: I'm going by the A&P.

ABRAMS: Why?

FINKELSTEIN: I need eggs.

ABRAMS: I got eggs fresh.

FINKELSTEIN: Your fresh eggs are already on pension.

ABRAMS: I'll give you fresh as I got. Why are you going by the A&P?

FINKELSTEIN: Why? Next week will be a new owner here and I'll have to go anyway. I thought today I would practice.

ABRAMS: You can't practice later?

FINKELSTEIN: I can practice now while I'm waiting for you.

ABRAMS: I'll bring out another tray. I'm sorry, I ain't had time yet.

FINKELSTEIN: Why not?

ABRAMS: The new owner was in.

FINKELSTEIN: (*Brightening*) Really? What does he look like?

ABRAMS: You're too old for him . . . You're finally giving up on me?

FINKELSTEIN: What hope have I got? Twelve years I'm trying to get you to come for Shabbos dinner at my apartment, and every week it's a different excuse. So what is it this time?

ABRAMS: What is it? I'm too old for fast women.

FINKELSTEIN: Tomorrow you'll be younger?

ABRAMS: Have a seat. I'll be right back.

FINKELSTEIN: Take your time. The A&P ain't open yet . . . Huh. It would serve you right if I left and bought from them.

ABRAMS: (*On his way out*) Have a seat and rest your mouth. (*She sits*)

FINKELSTEIN: The way you talk, anyone would think we were married.

ABRAMS: (*Offstage*) The way you talk back, anyone would know better.

FINKELSTEIN: In your house a wife can't speak her piece?

ABRAMS: (*Returning with a tray of meat*) In my house, my wife ALWAYS spoke her piece. So did I. She's dead fourteen years and I'm still around . . . Here . . . (*He motions to the trays*) You want fancy on the last day, or just the usual?

FINKELSTEIN: I can't afford the usual. Why should I pay extra for fancy? (*Smiling*) Unless, of course, you're making me a special price?

ABRAMS: Special price? I'll give you a special price. You still owe me from before. On the last day, you'll maybe pay the balance?

FINKELSTEIN: On the last day I'll maybe pay the balance if you'll give me extra.

ABRAMS: I'll give you "extra." If you don't pay up today, I'll come over and collect.

FINKELSTEIN: (*Smiling*) Twelve years I been waiting to hear you say that.

ABRAMS: (*Caught*) What do you want extra?

FINKELSTEIN: Let me see maybe a nice piece chuck.

ABRAMS: Chuck? (*He removes a roast from the tray, puts it on the counter*) I got for you a chuck roast, let me tell you . . .

FINKELSTEIN: You told me. Twelve years you're telling me.

Keep it a while. You'll give it a Bar Mitzvah. (*He starts to put it away. She stops him*) No, let me see . . . (*He hands it to her. A long ritual as she inspects it*) Huh . . . The cow that gave you this is still laughing. Where is the meat? All I see is bone, and where the bone ain't, the gristle is.

ABRAMS: On your credit you were expecting eye of the rib?

FINKELSTEIN: On my credit I was expecting something I could swallow. (*She hands it back*) Let me see chicken. (*He starts to remove one from a hook*) Uh-uh. Let me see FRESH.

ABRAMS: (*Resigned*) Wait a minute . . . (*He disappears into the back room. She looks around, crosses to the scale, taps it*)

FINKELSTEIN: Once, just once on the last day, you'll give an honest weight? (*Pause*) Ah, what am I talking? You're like he is. Too old to change. (*Abrams re-enters, chicken in hand. He spots her*)

ABRAMS: What are you doing with my trusty scale?

FINKELSTEIN: Trusty scale? If God weighed like you weigh, we'd have nine Commandments . . . Let me see your scrawny hen . . . (*He hands it to her. Another elaborate ritual as she runs her hands over it, pinching and fingering it*)

ABRAMS: What are you gonna do, eat it or molest it?

FINKELSTEIN: This from a kosher butcher?

ABRAMS: You don't like? I got others.

FINKELSTEIN: Let me see FRESH.

ABRAMS: You mean LIVE? You'll have to wait for the shochet. He ain't here to slaughter 'em.

FINKELSTEIN: When will he be?

ABRAMS: I don't know, maybe an hour. Huh. It used to be he was here all day Friday. Now he gives me a couple of hours when he can spare them.

FINKELSTEIN: And what about your customers?

ABRAMS: There ain't so many any more. And them what takes, take like you take.

FINKELSTEIN: How can you run a business like that?

ABRAMS: I can't. That's why I'm retiring . . . You want to look at another?

FINKELSTEIN: Ya. Something with some meat on it.

(*He removes one from a hook. She starts to object*)

ABRAMS: It's all right. It's fresh from yesterday. Here. (*He hands it to her. Again the inspection*)

FINKELSTEIN: This is better, but it ain't so clean . . .

ABRAMS: Missus, you should pass such a physical.

FINKELSTEIN: This all you got?

ABRAMS: Tell you what. You take this one, I give you a dozen eggs free.

FINKELSTEIN: Sold! . . . Wait. Let me see the carton . . (*He hands it to her*) Three of them is broken.

ABRAMS: What do you want from a bargain chicken? If they were unbroken, I'd sell them. You gonna take or not?

FINKELSTEIN: All right, all right, throw in the eggs and this one I'll take . . . Abrams, what is three unbroken eggs on the last day?

(*Pause*)

ABRAMS: You're right . . . (*He replaces the carton*) Now you got a dozen good eggs free . . . (*He shows her*) and a chicken without a gizzard. (*He shows her that, too*)

FINKELSTEIN: I give up. Cut for me the chicken please.

ABRAMS: All right. (*He starts to*)

FINKELSTEIN: (*Stopping him*) Ah-ah! You won't forget to weigh for me please?

ABRAMS: (*Sighing*) All right. (*He puts the chicken on the scale. She puts her nose up to the scale and watches very carefully*)

FINKELSTEIN: Fingers away from the scale please . . . (*Grumbling, Abrams obliges. Then he sneaks his fingers back onto the scale the moment she looks away. She looks back. He removes them. He backs away. She checks the scale, reading the numbers first on her side, then his, then her own again*) How come on my side is three pounds and yours is only two-and-a-half?

ABRAMS: Must be the way you're staring. I got here a sensitive machine. You give a dirty look, it cheats.

FINKELSTEIN: (*Resigned*) Cut for me the chicken . . . (*He does so, the old way, with a large knife*) And don't forget any parts like last time.

ABRAMS: (*As he is wrapping it*) How could I? Three days afterward, the gizzard yelled at me in your voice. What kind of power you got over chickens? (*He finishes wrapping*) Three-fifteen, please.

FINKELSTEIN: (*Incredulous*) Three-fifteen? How much a pound is chicken?

ABRAMS: (*Not looking at her*) Same as last time.

FINKELSTEIN: Then how come it don't cost like last time? Twenty-six years the chickens have been getting smaller, and the prices bigger, and always the cost is "same as last time." Who are you kidding?

ABRAMS: I ain't kidding. It don't cost more. It's the taxes. If you don't like, take your chicken to City Hall and get back the difference.

FINKELSTEIN: A lot of good that would do me. One look at us, they'd put the chicken in a rest home and me on relief . . . Ah, just once, I wish I could afford a nice roast.

ABRAMS: Why not? With what you owe already, a little more ain't gonna break either of us.

FINKELSTEIN: What's the sense of it? A chicken already lasts by me a week. How long do you think a roast would keep?

ABRAMS: Invite a guest . . . (*She looks at him*) I mean one who would come.

FINKELSTEIN: What's the use? Them what aren't dead are cowards like you.

ABRAMS: You cook it, small wonder.

FINKELSTEIN: You sell it, you should talk.

ABRAMS: Here's the eggs. I gave you extra. This is maybe enough for one Friday, or you'll be back like usual?

FINKELSTEIN: You want to spoil the ritual?

ABRAMS: No, I know too well . . . (*Levine re-enters*) Uh, Mrs. Finkelstein, this is Mark Levine. The new owner.

(*She sizes him up*)

FINKELSTEIN: Owner? I thought maybe a new delivery boy. What's a pisher like you doing in a business like this?

LEVINE: (*Smiling*) Trying to make an honest living.

FINKELSTEIN: That's what Abrams says. And look at his business. And he cheats GOOD. You don't look like you cheat so good.

LEVINE: I won't need to.

FINKELSTEIN: Why not? Your daddy's name is Rockefeller? Boychik, believe me, in a business like this, you do a little extra. What they don't know don't hurt them, and what they DO know, they usually accept. Right, Abrams? (*No response*) Well, I see you . . . (*She starts to go*) So, Mr. Levine, you'll have kosher for me next week? If not, I got no place to go . . . (*Again she starts to leave*) And HEALTHY. Not like Abrams sells. You look at his hens, you don't know whether to eat them or adopt them . . . Well, I see you. (*And she is gone. Abrams and Levine stare after her*)

LEVINE: You have many customers like her?

ABRAMS: No, thank God. She's all I can afford . . . Well?

LEVINE: Well what?

ABRAMS: You couldn't wait until tomorrow?

LEVINE: That's what I wanted to talk to you about. I spoke with my dad—

ABRAMS: So did I.

LEVINE: You DID?

ABRAMS: Ya. Before you got here. And after. In fact, he told me you were coming.

LEVINE: So why did you pretend . . .

ABRAMS: A little test I gave you. You failed. You're not ready to run a shop. Listen to me. Manny could help for a little while . . .

LEVINE: Manny can't get away right now. Not for that long. A day or two, maybe, but you're talking months. Dad couldn't spare him that long.

ABRAMS: How about Herschel?

LEVINE: Herschel retired two years ago.

ABRAMS: (*Surprised*) He did? (*Pause*) Well, I could help. (*Levine looks at him*) A few months . . .

LEVINE: You? You're retiring. I thought you were sick of this.

ABRAMS: After five minutes of the Wailing Widow, I'm too angry to be sick. Anyway, with two of us here it wouldn't be so bad. You could deliver—

LEVINE: I'm not going to deliver. The delivery boy will deliver. How am I going to learn the business if I'm out delivering?

ABRAMS: Okay, so we'll hire a delivery boy. Simpler yet. Three to do the work of one. Think what a business we can build.

LEVINE: We?

ABRAMS: You and me. I can teach you shortweight, who to cheat and who not, how to cut skimpy . . .

LEVINE: What I need, I can learn from Dad. And what's this "we" business? The shop is mine, isn't it?

ABRAMS: (*Low*) Ya, the shop is yours.

LEVINE: So sooner or later, I'm going to have to learn from my own mistakes, right?

ABRAMS: Right.

LEVINE: So it might as well be sooner. Like today, right?

(*No answer*) Now. I talked to my Dad. The way we figured it, between your delivery boy and our delivery boy, we could . .

ABRAMS: What delivery boy?

LEVINE: You mean you don't have a delivery boy?

ABRAMS: Ya, I have a delivery boy. I've had eight delivery boys in two years. Now I have no delivery boy. Six months maybe. Why do you think I'm selling?

LEVINE: Why didn't you say something? Dad could have worked something out.

ABRAMS: Why should he waste his time? Anyway, what difference does it make? If I had said something, you wouldn't have a shop.

LEVINE: I'd have waited a year to two.

ABRAMS: (*Laughing*) A year or two? Boychik, if I'd had help I could trust, they would bury me in this shop. You think I give up that easy?

LEVINE: No. (*Pause*) What makes you so stubborn?

ABRAMS: What makes me so stubborn? You think through Mandelman and Warshawsky and Young and Lopez that Abrams would have stayed if he hadn't been stubborn? You think I'd last two minutes with Mrs. Finkelstein if I wasn't stubborn? (*He winks at Levine*) Stick with me, boychik. I'll make you so stubborn your worst enemies would buy from you extra. And LIKE it.

LEVINE: Mr. Abrams, I've—(*Pause*) Look. All right. So our delivery boy will deliver. If you haven't delivered in six months, there can't be so many . . .

ABRAMS: Please . . .

LEVINE: Do you have a list?

ABRAMS: Ya, I got a list . . . (*He goes behind the counter and produces a small, battered pocketbook*)

LEVINE: Let me see . . .

ABRAMS: (*Jerking it away*) Ah-ah! It ain't up to date yet . . . (*He thumbs through*) . . . Abramowitz . . . Huh. She passed away six months ago . . . Aronberg . . . They moved to Florida . . . On what I don't know . . . They still owe me $26.37 . . . Levy . . . Ah, they come on and off . . .

LEVINE: Mr. Abrams, do you KNOW how many you've got?

ABRAMS: What's the sense of counting till they've bought? If they come, I got chickens enough. If not, let it rest. It's between them and their souls . . . (*Pause*) What do YOU got, boychik? You got kosher? (*He taps his heart*) In here, I mean. (*No answer*) So how can you sell to them what has? How can you run a shop for them? How can you take "Zalman Abrams—Kosher" and make it "Mark Levine—Trayf".

LEVINE: (*A little hot*) Mr. Abrams, I'm taking over a BUSINESS. You make it sound like I'm turning a synagogue into Burger King.

ABRAMS: (*A wry smile*) Not bad, not bad. You're not as dumb as I thought.

LEVINE: Look, Mr. Abrams, what's so terrible about trying to make a buck?

ABRAMS: Boychik, your father bought for you a shop in a lousy neighborhood. WHY? You think he wants you to turn it into another B. Manischevitz and Company?

LEVINE: Is it such a sin to try?

ABRAMS: He wants you to learn a BUSINESS, right? So someday you can run HIS business, right? Now why would he pick a dying shop in a lousy neighborhood . . . (*He is interrupted by Mrs. Finkelstein, who appears at the door*) Now you had to come, ya? I'm trying to make sense to this pisher, who don't want to keep a kosher shop. What do you want, another chicken or more eggs?

FINKELSTEIN: Neither. Give me the stringy chuck roast please.

ABRAMS: (*Incredulous*) Instead of the chicken?

FINKELSTEIN: Who said a word about the chicken? The chicken is mine. (*She looks at Levine*) If the pisher ain't gonna sell kosher, I got to stock up.

ABRAMS: You're only planning on living another week?

FINKELSTEIN: In another week I'll find another place. At least this way I got time to think. (*To Abrams*) Go, go, give me. Charge me what you want. On the last day, I ain't even gonna argue . . . (*Levine looks at Abrams as if to offer help, but Mrs. Finkelstein stops him*) Let him, boychik. It's still his shop. You and I will talk a minute, ya? (*She leads him away*) Boychik, let me tell you about Abrams . . . (*She shrugs*) All right, so he shortweights. So once in a while we shortchange in return. It balances out . . . (*Abrams looks at her. She continues*) Look at this neighborhood. Believe me, the pocketbooks look like the buildings. Them what has, leaves when they can. Them what hasn't, stays. So who would want to run a business in this? You never get ahead. Always they owe you . . . With what they owe Abrams, he should have a house in Florida by now . . . (*Pause. She smiles*) With what he charges, he should own the state . . . You know what? "So they owe me," he says. "Let it rest. They have a good Sabbath and I have a good business. Over pennies you don't break a friendship." (*Pause*) So, for all of us, today I buy from him extra . . .

(*By now Abrams has weighed the meat and is wrapping it*)

ABRAMS: Four thirty-six please.

FINKELSTEIN: Here. (*She hands him a ten dollar bill*) Keep the change.

ABRAMS: Esther . . .

FINKELSTEIN: What? I know what I'm doing.

ABRAMS: I know better. This is grocery money for the week. I can't take this.

FINKELSTEIN: Take.

ABRAMS: I can't.

FINKELSTEIN: *TAKE!* (*Her voice is fierce*) So for one week I'll skimp on milk and spend on meat. For me there will be other weeks. This much I can do . . . (*She looks at Abrams and smiles*) Five dollars extra. Is that so much? . . . Twenty-four years ago you took my son off the street and made an apprentice out of him. You took a boy out of jail and gave me back a Mensch . . . (*Pause. To Levine*) My son died in Korea. At the end . . . I got a medal for his death. I gave the medal to Abrams . . . (*To Abrams*) You still have it?

ABRAMS: I still have it.

FINKELSTEIN: So you see? For a few ounces extra, I forgive. (*Pause. She starts to go*) Abrams, you thief you. For five dollars extra you'll maybe come tonight for Shabbos dinner? I'll be waiting. I'm going home now to start . . . (*She starts for the door. As she gets to it, she turns to Abrams, as if for the last time. There is a quaver in her voice*) Old man, I love you . . .

(*And she exits. A long pause. Abrams, tears in his eyes, begins to sweep again—for want of something to do. Levine stands for a long moment looking at Abrams. Then he moves to the phone and dials*)

LEVINE: Hello, Dad? It's Mark . . . Fine, fine . . . Listen. Have Ziggy hold up on the delivery . . . What? . . . No, no problems. I'll explain it later. Ya, fine, fine. Ya, sure, everything's okay. No, no time now. I'll see you. Goodbye. (*He hangs up. He and Abrams look at one another*)

ABRAMS: Well?

LEVINE: Mr. Abrams, I want you to come in next week. I want you to come in as often as you like. Please . .

ABRAMS: You'll be out of business in a month.

LEVINE: I'll make it.

ABRAMS: You? You don't know what kosher is.

LEVINE: I do . . . (*He taps his heart*) Really.

(*He smiles. Pause. Now it is Abrams' turn to smile. He moves toward Levine, then past Levine to the telephone. He bangs on the phone. The coin returns. He hands it to Levine. They stand frozen as the lights fade out*)

End of Play

John Olive

MINNESOTA MOON

John Olive

John Olive's *Minnesota Moon* enjoyed a successful run as a touring production of the Playwrights Lab of Minneapolis before its lauded New York production at the Circle Repertory Theatre in January and February of 1979. Directed by Carole Rothman, the Circle Rep production was described by Eileen Blumenthal in the *Village Voice* as "a sensitive, naturalistic sketch of lives disentwining. In the pre-dawn hours, Al and Larry break into a neighbor's fenced field to share a few beers before Al leaves for college in Minneapolis. Beneath their devil-may-care horseplay is the closeness and affection of years of friendship—growing up together in a small town, sharing one buddy's death and another's military enlistment (it is September 1968)." Edith Oliver in the *New Yorker* continues, "By the time this unpretentious, haunting play is over, we realize that their youth is over, and that the friendship has perforce come to an end." Mel Gussow in the *New York Times* comments, "It is as if the characters are living a moment that will too soon prove to be a subject of nostalgia. Even as they leave the farmyard, we can feel the scene receding into their memories. Their encounter is as evanescent as the bright Minnesota moon that gives the play its title . . . the playwright succeeds in evoking an atmosphere of wistfulness and eagerness." Other productions of *Minnesota Moon* have been presented at the 1979 Edinburgh Fringe Festival in Scotland, the Soho Poly Theatre in London, and the BoarsHead Theatre in Lansing, Michigan. The play makes its publishing debut in this volume.

Residing in Minneapolis, John Olive has been produced frequently by groups in the Twin Cities area. His productions include: *The Silver Fox*, an opera for young people with music by Libby Larsen, produced in St. Paul in 1979; and his adaptation of *The Gift of the Magi*, toured by a professional children's theatre group for two years. He has been Playwright-in-Residence with the Actors Theatre of St. Paul, a Working Resident with the Playwrights Lab of Minneapolis, and he has received a grant from the Minnesota Arts Board for general support of his playwrighting career.

In 1977 Mr. Olive was invited to participate in Dale Wasserman's Midwest Playwrights Laboratory with the play *Texas Dry*. Recommended by the Laboratory to the Eugene O'Neill Theatre Center National Playwrights Conference at Waterford, Connecticut, Mr. Olive continued work on *Texas Dry* in the summer of 1978.

His play *Standing on My Knees* received productions at the North Light Repertory Company in Chicago, the Ensemble Studio Theatre in New York, and at the Mark Taper Forum in Los Angeles. *Earplay,* a division of National Public Radio, commissioned him to write a radio drama, *Pentecost,* and also recorded a radio adaptation of *Minnesota Moon.*

Mr. Olive's most recent play, *Clara's Play,* has been presented in both a one-act and a full-length version by Actors Theatre of Louisville and was aired on BBC in the fall of 1981.

Characters:

LARRY, *eighteen*
ALAN, *eighteen*

Scene:

The moonlit yard of an old deserted farmhouse in southern Minnesota.

We see the front of the house and a good portion of the yard. The house is made of crumbling grey wood, except for the door and windows which have been boarded up with fresh yellow pine. There is a chain lock on the door and a huge NO TRESSPASSING (sic) has been spraypainted across a window. The yard is full of junk: old automobile tires, rusted farm machinery, crates, etc. It is September, 1968.

Alan and Larry enter, carrying a couple six packs of beer.

LARRY: Oh no!! (*Alan laughs. Larry runs up to the boarded up door, pounds on it, pulls at the chain*) He boarded it up! The scurvy old sonofabitch!

ALAN: You'd think he didn't want us in there.

LARRY: (*Exiting around the side of the house*) Pisses me off.

ALAN: Where are you . . . ?

LARRY: Jesus! Every window in the place!

(*We hear loud rhythmic crashing from offstage*)

ALAN: Hey, Larry! Larry!

LARRY: (*Still offstage*) Goddamit!!

ALAN: Larry!! Forget it.

LARRY: (*Entering*) Old man Pearson . . .

ALAN: It's nicer out here. Cool and clear.

LARRY: It's right by the road.

ALAN: We're a good hundred yards from the road.

LARRY: They'll see us.

ALAN: This time a' night? Naw.

LARRY: That asshole, I'm gonna let the air outta his tractor tires.

ALAN: Ya' can't blame him. We been partyin' out here all summer, probably afraid we'll burn the place down.

LARRY: There's an idea.

ALAN: Naw, I think we should turn it into a shrine.

LARRY: Yeah, a church and a statue.

ALAN: Fountain running with beer.

LARRY: Gotta jackknife? Let's carve our names.

ALAN: We already did that, remember? Night before Winkie left.

LARRY: I don't recall too mucha that night. Hey, lookit this. (*Picks up an empty beer can*) I remember drinkin' this can. (*Alan laughs*) Some good times here, eh?

ALAN: Yeah.

LARRY: (*Suddenly hurls the can against the house*) Goddam you, Pearson! I'm gonna piss all over your soybeans! (*Exits. From offstage*) Think they'll miss us at the party?

ALAN: Who cares. Jesus, it's beautiful out here.

LARRY: (*Offstage*) Yeah. Ahhhhhhhhhhhhhh. . . .

ALAN: I know what you mean.

(*Larry re-enters, grabs a beer, opens it, sits*)

LARRY: Beer's gettin' warm.

ALAN: (*Overlapping Larry's line*) Lookit the moon.

ALAN & LARRY: What? (*Pause. Again simultaneously*) I . . .

LARRY: You.

ALAN: I said: lookit the moon.

LARRY: Oh, yeah.

ALAN: (*Makes a toast*) Ah, milady, my blue lady of the breezes.

LARRY: To the man a' the moon

ALAN: What'd you say?

LARRY: To the man a' the moon.

ALAN: I mean before that.

LARRY: Oh, beer's gettin' warm.

ALAN: Tragedy.

LARRY: Next time hafta bring one a' them little yellow styrofoam coolers. Don't cost but a buck. Saw 'em over at . . .

ALAN: Next time, right.

LARRY: Here's to the next time. (*Pause: they sip their beer and belch contentedly*) Heh.

ALAN: What.

LARRY: Thinkin' 'bout Winkie.

ALAN: Don't think about Winkie. It's a waste a' good beer.

LARRY: Wonder what he's doin'.

ALAN: Sleepin'. It's way past midnight.

LARRY: You gotta be home?

ALAN: Naw.

LARRY: Your folks . . .

ALAN: What're they gonna do, ground me?

LARRY: Ya' gotta get up and pack?

ALAN: No, I'm all set. Gotta eat lunch with the grandparents and then: bye-bye Maple Lake.

LARRY: Lucky bastard.

ALAN: You work tomorrow?

LARRY: Yeah, shit.

ALAN: In the mornin'?

LARRY: Fuck it, it's such a half-ass job I can do it half asleep.

ALAN: Hey. Whatcha hear from Sharon?

LARRY: Sh!

ALAN: (*Laughs*) There's ears in the cornfield!

LARRY: I don't wanna talk about . . .

ALAN: She's nice.

LARRY: Oh, yeah.

ALAN: And for a fat girl she didn't hardly sweat at all.

LARRY: She called me!

ALAN: What'd she call you?

LARRY: Cindy'd rip 'em off me with her teeth if she found out about . . .

ALAN: "Larry, Larry-baby, I just can't get you off my mind."

LARRY: Yeah!

ALAN: She say that?

LARRY: Yeah. Well, not in those words but . . .

ALAN: "It's your eyes. They glow like hot steel."

LARRY: Hey, fuck you.

ALAN: "That Cindy, she may know what you need . . ."

LARRY: Hey.

ALAN: "But, honey, I know what you want."

LARRY: You make that up?

ALAN: Yeah. What of it?

LARRY: You got yourself a smart mouth, boy. I'm liable to fatten it up for ya'.

ALAN: Yeah? Who you gonna hire?

LARRY: I'll fix it so's you can watch the sun rise and the sun set without turnin' around.

ALAN: Yeah? I'll hit you so hard when you wake up, your clothes'll be outta style.

LARRY: Alright, you little tit, I've had it . . . (*Alan bursts out laughing*) I'll pop ya one.

ALAN: Tit . . .

LARRY: You're playin' with fire. Hey.

ALAN: Tit . . .

LARRY: (*Insistent*) Hey, Al. A car. (*Crouching*) Al. A car. Come on.

ALAN: (*Still laughing*) What're you whispering for?

LARRY: Will ya' get down? They'll see us.

ALAN: They won't see us.

LARRY: They could if they was lookin'. Will ya' just get down.

ALAN: (*Complying*) Jesus.

LARRY: It ain't the sheriff, I don't think.

ALAN: Tit.

LARRY: It's old man Pearson. A dumb shit if there ever was one.

ALAN: (*Waving*) You dumb shit.

LARRY: Probably had a heavy date tonight with his new heifer.

ALAN: Yeah.

LARRY: Farmers.

ALAN: Now Larry, don't be unkind.

LARRY: Hayseeds.

ALAN: Shit-kickers.

LARRY: Heifer-humpers.

ALAN: That's good! It's poetic.

LARRY: Yeah, it's . . . literation.

ALAN: Alliteration.

LARRY: That's what I said.

ALAN: (*Exiting upstage*) Hey, you hear about Sharon's cousin, up at the U. of M., majoring in animal husbandry?

LARRY: Sharon's got a cousin?

ALAN: (*Offstage*) Yeah, majoring in animal husbandry.

LARRY: What about him?

ALAN: They caught him.

LARRY: Yeah? Caught him doin' what?

ALAN: (*After a pause, still offstage*) Never mind.

LARRY: Caught him doin' what?

ALAN: I'm takin' a leak, don't bug me.

LARRY: Hey.

ALAN: You dumb shit.

LARRY: I'll pop ya' one. (*Alan starts laughing*) Okay, tell me. Why am I a dumb shit?

ALAN: Forget it.

LARRY: No. Now tell me. Why am I a dumb shit?

ALAN: Because (*Re-entering*) Sharon doesn't have a cousin.

LARRY: Oh.

ALAN: Dumb shit.

LARRY: I'll pop ya' one. (*Pause: they drink beer, belch thoughtfully*) Ain't so cold.

ALAN: No wind.

LARRY: That's right. Be real cold if there was any kinda wind.

ALAN: It's perfect. Right now. The stars, the moon, the beer, no wind. You feel it? Everything . . . is . . . perfectly . . . still.

LARRY: You feelin' that beer at all?

ALAN: I dunno. Lemme check.

LARRY: Plus we had the whiskey. You should definitely be feelin' it.

ALAN: Wait a second. Yep. I'm feeling it.

LARRY: Me too. (*With a certain passion*) Whiskey and beer, never fear. Beer and whiskey, now that's risky.

ALAN: What?

LARRY: So ya' don't hafta worry. That's a poem sayin' that it's okay that we drank the whiskey. Before the beer.

ALAN: What?

LARRY: Don't gimme no smartass. You heard it.

ALAN: Yeah, but . . .

LARRY: Whiskey 'n beer, never fear.

ALAN: Beer 'n whiskey, that ain't risky. Whiskey 'n beer, now that's somethin' to fear.

LARRY: What?

ALAN: You heard me.

LARRY: Fuck you.

ALAN: You dumb shit.

LARRY: I'll pop ya' one. Hey.

ALAN: What.

LARRY: You need a beer.

ALAN: Thanks for tellin' me, Jesus. I was naked and I didn't even know it.

LARRY: Here.

ALAN: Sustenance. Sweet cool sustenance.

LARRY: Drankin' beer.

ALAN: In the middle of a cornfield. A pleasure for sure.

LARRY: In the winter time, that's when I like it. Drivin' around in the hot car with the fan blowin', everybody yellin' and laughin'. Pissin' in the snowbanks.

ALAN: Ice cold moonlight.

LARRY: Yeah, and Winkie pukin'.

ALAN: When did . . . ?

LARRY: You remember, you was there. After the dance when Estelle cracked him one.

ALAN: Oh, yeah, yeah.

LARRY: You're an alkie already, you can't remember that.

ALAN: I remember.

LARRY: Drank an entire six-pack, first time he ever laid lips on the stuff.

ALAN: Sixteens?

LARRY: Twelves.

ALAN: My first time, I drank a whole six-pack a' sixteens.

LARRY: Fuckin' puked all over the side a' the car an' after we took him home we hadda drive all the way to Mankato to find a carwash that was open. Fuckin' Winkie. Didn't he look great? With his basic training hairdo?

ALAN: He was a regular traffic hazard.

LARRY: A paratrooper, shit. I don't believe it. Remember breakin' into the old bowling alley, before they tore it down? (*Alan laughs*) Terry turned off the flashlight and started rollin' balls down the alleys.

ALAN: Winkie went nuts.

LARRY: "Mama! Mama!"

ALAN: And then: "Hey, you guys."

LARRY: Yeah, right. "I bet you guys thought I was scared." This is the guy they're trainin' to jump outta airplanes.

ALAN: And be a commie-killer.

LARRY: He'll shit his shorts, first time they shoot at him.

ALAN: No, he won't.

LARRY: You don't think so?

ALAN: Winkie'll be a good soldier.

LARRY: Fuckin' Winkie.

ALAN: Some good times.

LARRY: Over now.

ALAN: Here's to the good times.

LARRY: Hey, remember that time Jim and Terry went over to Kasota?

ALAN: Yeah, yeah.

LARRY: And Terry tried to buy beer from that weird old lady in the . . .

ALAN: Yeah, I remember, Larry.

LARRY: And he . . .

ALAN: (*Sharply, angrily*) I remember.

LARRY: (*Somewhat taken aback, after an awkward pause*) Know who your roommate's gonna be?

ALAN: Now how would I know that?

LARRY: I just asked.

ALAN: They asked me if I wanted a smoker or a non-smoker. I said I could care less. I think they put guys together by what their major is. Mine's undecided, so God knows what they'll stick me with.

LARRY: Guy about three hundred pounds, picks his toenails with a jackknife.

ALAN: (*Laughs*) Shit . . .

(*Pause*)

LARRY: Nice out. No skeeters.

ALAN: Eh?

LARRY: There ain't any mosquitoes. (*Pause*) Hey, you hear about Mr. Findler?

ALAN: What?

LARRY: Got cancer.

ALAN: Really?

LARRY: Got it in the stomach. That's why he always used to burp in soc class, and then he'd cross his eyes.

ALAN: Really?

LARRY: Found when he went to the Mayo Clinic. Couldn't a' happened to a better guy.

ALAN: What's gonna happen?

LARRY: Gonna die.

ALAN: That's true of a lotta people.

LARRY: First he has a big operation, then he dies.

ALAN: How'd you find all this out?

LARRY: From Cindy.

ALAN: Wow.

LARRY: Best fuckin' news I've heard in a long time.

ALAN: It's too bad.

LARRY: (*After a slight pause*) Yeah, it is too bad. He ain't that old. Guess that's what you get for goin' to bed every night at ten. (*Pause: they drink beer and belch pensively*) Goin' up to the "cits", eh? Minneapolis. Saint Paul. Bloomington. Gonna be a lot different than around here.

ALAN: I 'spect so.

LARRY: Gonna hafta come up and visit ya', check that place out.

ALAN: You been there.

LARRY: Yeah, but only with my folks and you know what a gas that is.

ALAN: Yeah.

LARRY: Same thing, every time. Shoppin' at Dayton's but practically never buy nothin' and then . . . What's the name a' that Chink restaurant across the—

ALAN: Nankin.

LARRY: Right. And then have dinner at the Nankin. Big deal.

ALAN: Sure, come on up. There'll probably be room on the floor underneath my bed.

LARRY: You think you'll be able to find somebody to buy you beer? I'd like to drink a bunch a beer and then go up to the top a' that Foshay Tower.

ALAN: Say hello to God for me.

LARRY: Huh?

ALAN: Why don't you move up?

LARRY: Move up?

ALAN: Sure. Find a job and we'll get a place together.

LARRY: Where the hell am I gonna get a job in the cities?

ALAN: They got plenty a' gas stations up there. I seen 'em.

LARRY: Probably hafta work with niggers.

ALAN: (*Laughs*) Jesus . . . Well, how 'bout it?

LARRY: You serious?

ALAN: Sure.

LARRY: I couldn't do that.

ALAN: Why?

LARRY: I dunno.

ALAN: What would your parents say?

LARRY: Yeah, right.

ALAN: What would Cindy say?

LARRY: Shit!

ALAN: Huh?

LARRY: Maybe lookin' forward to a smelly roommate ain't much, but it's lookin' forward to a helluva lot more 'n I got.

ALAN: What?

LARRY: Must be nice, gettin' a scholarship, for tuition and books and your dorm and everything. And Terry with his track scholarship and Winkie in San Diego. You get to go away, to a city with people. Me, I gotta stay here, in this fucked-up, two-bit burg, pumpin' gas at Winklers.

ALAN: "I gotta stay here." Bullshit.

LARRY: What am I gonna do? Ain't got the smarts or the dough to go to school nowhere.

ALAN: Bullshit!

LARRY: Fuck you.

ALAN: Fuck yourself. You're just too stupid to know what kinda' smarts you got. You get a job, your first full time job and then it's this-is-what-I'm-gonna-do-for-the-rest-of-my-life. Shit.

LARRY: I didn't say that.

ALAN: You want outta this graveyard of a town? Then leave. That's all . . .

LARRY: It ain't that easy, Al.

ALAN: It is easy. What's keepin' you here? There's nothing for you . . . (*Pauses*) Oh, Jesus, no.

LARRY: And she's gettin' weird, too. Sayin' shit like "I wish I had a place a' my own." And "The Hinikers got a house and three acres for rent cheap."

ALAN: Subtle.

LARRY: "Oh, honey. I don't wanna ever let you go."

ALAN: Yeah, I get the picture.

LARRY: And then all the time with this . . . this . . . look, in her eyes. This . . . look in her eyes.

ALAN: And you don't do anything to encourage . . .

LARRY: No! All I wanna do is . . . what I'm doin'. And I don't even wanna do that. I don't know what I wanna do. But I know what I don't wanna do.

ALAN: Like move into a house and three acres with Cindy.

LARRY: Right, don't wanna do that.

ALAN: Maybe you oughta tell her?

LARRY: Shit, I can't talk to her about that kinda stuff. She gets weird on me, cries, and tries to jump outta the car. (*Alan laughs*) Fuck you. It ain't funny, Al. It ain't funny!

ALAN: (*Stops laughing, pauses*) You been seein' a lotta her, these days.

LARRY: What the fuck else is there to do!? You spend all your time with your nose in a book, Winkie's gone, Terry's—

ALAN: (*Slight pause*) Yeah.

LARRY: How come you read so much, anyway?

ALAN: (*Mimics Larry*) What the fuck else is there to do!?

LARRY: Yeah. (*Sees something offstage*) Al. A car. (*Crouches*)

ALAN: (*Gets down*) Yeah, I see it.

(*Pause: they watch the car pass*)

LARRY: Gonna miss you, man.

ALAN: Wouldn't waste a lotta time missin' me.

LARRY: Well, I'm gonna. Shit.

ALAN: Well, fuck. Are you gonna get all depressed and feelin' sorry for yourself on our last night together?

LARRY: No.

ALAN: "No." Are you gonna get up, crack yourself open another beer and start talkin' dirty like the Larry we all know and love?

LARRY: Yeah.

ALAN: "Yeah."

LARRY: Yeah!

ALAN: Yeah!

LARRY: Yeah!

ALAN: Alright!

LARRY: (*Opens beer*) To whom it may concern. I'm horny.

ALAN: But you're always horny.

LARRY: Yeah, but I'm really horny this time.

ALAN: Yeah.

LARRY: I'm so horny.

ALAN: So tell me about it already.

LARRY: I'd fuck anything right now. I'd fuck leaves. Let's go over to old man Pearson's and steal a nice fat chicken.

ALAN: Yeah!

LARRY: I could fuck a baked potato.

ALAN: A watermelon.

LARRY: Right! A squishy, soft, rotten watermelon.

ALAN: Oh, ish! You're making me sick, please stop.

LARRY: Hey. Lesse' that beer. Just what I thought, it's empty. You been holdin' an empty can a' beer, you fuckin' wimp.

ALAN: Don't hit me.

LARRY: Keep that up and I'm liable to get pissed. Hey, Al.

ALAN: Hm?

LARRY: You gonna smoke pot when you get up there?

ALAN: First chance I get.

LARRY: Really? Let your hair grow, down to your ass?

ALAN: Beards 'n beads 'n bells 'n feathers.

LARRY: Yeah!

ALAN: Boy, could I meet girls.

LARRY: Yeah! Did you see that *Life* magazine thing? There was some real sharp chicks smokin' those funny yellow cigarettes.

ALAN: Joints.

LARRY: Reefers. You gonna?

ALAN: Guys at the frat'd never have me. Ya gotta be blonde and pure.

LARRY: I'd do that for sure.

ALAN: Sharp chicks, eh?

LARRY: Hubba-hubba. Hey, you hear about Danny Shiner?

ALAN: Who?

LARRY: Danny Shiner, you know. From Good Thunder.

ALAN: With the tattoo.

LARRY: Right, and he tried to rape Winkie's cousin. That's what she said, anyway. God, he musta' been horny.

ALAN: Anyway.

LARRY: Anyway, he got arrested for possession a' pot.

ALAN: Well, I'm definitely gonna try it then 'cause Danny Shiner has always been my idol.

LARRY: Wonder if you can drink when you're on it.

ALAN: Beer 'n pot, your gut'll rot. Pot 'n beer . . .

LARRY: Never fear.

ALAN: Ruin your career.

LARRY: LSD?

ALAN: Soar like an eagle.

LARRY: Say hello to God for me.

ALAN: If I can find Him.

LARRY: You scared at all?

ALAN: Scared? 'Bout leavin' Maple Lake and goin' up to the big city where I don't know anybody to study at a university with fifty thousand other students where I don't know what I'm gonna study and where I'll live in a dorm with a total stranger who'll be overweight and fart a lot and where I'll be lucky to have enough spending money to buy a pack of Juicy Fruit on Saturday night?

LARRY: Really scared, eh?

ALAN: No.

LARRY: Bullshit.

ALAN: I'm not really. Just kinda numb, layin' back, sayin' "Let's see how the kid handles this one." I ain't scared, just very interested.

LARRY: Well, good luck, Al.

ALAN: Thanks.

(*Pause: they sip their beers and belch serenely*)

LARRY: Been thinkin' 'bout my tax money.

ALAN: Your tax money.

LARRY: Gonna be close to five hundred dollars if I can get some overtime in over Christmas.

ALAN: And you're gonna put it in your car.

LARRY: Damn right. Mags 'n headers.

ALAN: Big tires.

LARRY: Right.

ALAN: Fancy hubcaps.

LARRY: Hubcaps, fuck. I'm talkin' 'bout mags. And chrome headers 'cause I can use the torque wrench at the station.

ALAN: What's a torque wrench?

LARRY: A special kind a' wrench with a gauge that lets you measure how tight you got a bolt in. Sometimes you gotta be careful 'cause if a bolt's too tight, the engine heat'll snap it off or if it's too loose . . . if it's too loose, you could loose oil pressure or the engine'll corrode up on ya.'

ALAN: "I can't do anything. I'm stuck in Maple Lake. Ain't got the smarts to go to . . ."

LARRY: Hey.

ALAN: "I can't get the grease off my hands, or the hay-seeds outta my hair."

LARRY: I never said . . .

ALAN: Shit.

LARRY: Come on.

ALAN: You know how cars run. You can take 'em apart and fix 'em.

LARRY: Everybody can do that.

ALAN: I can't do it.

LARRY: Well, you're stupid.

ALAN: That's what I'm trying' ta tell ya'.

LARRY: Hey, got a new dance step.

ALAN: Cindy taught you?

LARRY: Yeah, watch this. (*Stumbles*)

ALAN: Drunken fool.

LARRY: Fuck you, I can do it. It's tricky, is all. (*Dancing energetically and singing off key*)

"Hot time, summer in the city.

Back a' my neck gettin' dirty and gritty.

Cool cat, isn't it a pity,

Gonna dance in every corner of the city."

ALAN: Yeah, alright! You could quit your job at the gas station and become a go-go boy.

LARRY: Remember the dances, Al? (*Alan laughs*) You 'n me, Terry, Winkie, Jim. What a bunch of rowdies. The time Terry decided he was gonna dance with every girl in the place. Where was that?

ALAN: (*Still laughing*) I can't remember. Somewhere by Lake Crystal.

LARRY: Five minutes and two fights.

ALAN: You looked real sexy with your fat lip.

LARRY: What a crazy fucker Terry was.

ALAN: Really.

LARRY: With his practical jokes, his runnin'. He had . . . he had . . .

ALAN: Creativity.

LARRY: He had a lotta that, yeah.

ALAN: The most creative person I ever knew. Everything he did, he did his way, his style.

LARRY: (*Counting on his fingers*) May, June, July—

ALAN: Four and a half months.

LARRY: Huh?

ALAN: It's been four and a half months.

LARRY: Since Terry . . . (*Still counting*) Yeah, right. Four and a half . . . (*After a pause*) Alan?

ALAN: Yes, Lawrence?

LARRY: Hey, fuck you.

ALAN: What.

LARRY: I sorta wouldn't mind talkin' 'bout Terry. (*Pause: Alan gets up and opens a beer*) Because I think about him all the time and maybe one a' the reasons I don't know what the fuck I'm doing is because I can't get Terry off my mind.

ALAN: Yeah, yeah, yeah.

LARRY: I mean, it shouldn't take four and a half months to . . .

ALAN: You want one?

LARRY: Huh? No, I got half a' one here. You miss him as much as I do? Al?

ALAN: Whadda ya' think?

LARRY: You pissed?

ALAN: No.

LARRY: Seen his ma lately?

ALAN: Yeah, today. Went over to say good-bye.

LARRY: Yeah? How is she? How's the place look?

ALAN: She's fine, place looks like shit.

LARRY: Nobody around to . . .

ALAN: She's gonna sell it and move up with her daughter.

LARRY: In California?

ALAN: No, the one in Duluth.

LARRY: Oh, yeah. So . . . You said good-bye.

ALAN: Yep.

LARRY: She cry, or anything?

ALAN: Hey.

LARRY: What.

ALAN: You think life's a movie?

LARRY: I dunno what life is.

ALAN: Just somethin' for you to . . .

LARRY: All I asked . . .

ALAN: It was a private . . .

LARRY: (*Overlapping*) Did she . . . ?

ALAN: . . . conversation! Jesus.

LARRY: Okay, you don't have to tell me. I ain't your friend, I wasn't Terry's friend, I'm just a nosy sonofabitch who can't keep his mouth shut.

ALAN: (*After a pause*) We talked about Minneapolis, about how hard I would have to study and would I have enough money.

LARRY: You talk about Terry?

ALAN: Yes, we talked about Terry.

LARRY: And?

ALAN: She's against motorcycles and how there should be a law, like in Florida, that cyclists always have to wear helmets.

LARRY: She say that?

ALAN: Yes.

LARRY: Helmet wouldn't a' helped Terry. That truck squashed him flat.

ALAN: Well, maybe she didn't know that.

LARRY: Why? Didn't she . . . ?

ALAN: They didn't give her the gruesome details or maybe she didn't ask.

LARRY: But didn't she read the . . . ?

ALAN: Larry.

LARRY: "You dumb shit."

ALAN: Yeah.

LARRY: Anything else?

ALAN: None of his scholarships came through.

LARRY: What!? Shit! He was good, man. The hurdles, the dashes, every time he ran the 880 he cleaned up.

ALAN: He got beat.

LARRY: Well, there was just that nigger-guy from Rochester.

ALAN: Maybe the "nigger-guy" got the scholarships.

LARRY: He was good!

ALAN: Guess he'll just hafta work his way through college.

LARRY: Pisses me off.

ALAN: The dinky schools we usually ran against didn't . . .

LARRY: But he was . . .

ALAN: Good, yeah. He really was. He was a runnin' fool.

LARRY: Shit, you too. Both of you crazy fuckers were always . . .

ALAN: Impromptu foot-races.

LARRY: Slam on the brakes, out the door and, bam, you were off.

ALAN: Middle a' winter.

LARRY: You guys really scared the shit outta Winkie that one time.

ALAN: Terry lived for that. Running and laughing and yelling and running. He'd let me get ahead, then I'd hear this "Whoo! Whoo! Whoo!" behind me and he'd be shootin' past, yellin' with every stride. Collapse into a snowbank, laughing, barking huge clouds of white breath up at the cold moon, the air like fire in our lungs.

LARRY: Yeah. Hey, how fast he do the hundred?

ALAN: Hm? Oh, I dunno. Ten somethin'.

LARRY: I could never break twelve.

ALAN: I never tried.

LARRY: Fucker could run.

ALAN: Fucker could run.

LARRY: What's it feel like to be dead? What're you lookin' at me like that for?

ALAN: I'm not . . .

LARRY: One chuckle and I'll stomp yer ass.

ALAN: Hey.

LARRY: Okay, okay.

ALAN: When you're dead, you don't feel. Question is: what's it feel like to die?

LARRY: I guess that's what I meant.

ALAN: Maybe you don't feel anything. Maybe your body sees it comin' and just . . . shuts down. You're fallin' and fallin' and your body sees the ground rushin' up and it transmits a message to every cell: "This is it, guys." Bam, you're dead. Dead before you even hit the ground.

LARRY: Yeah?

ALAN: Yep. Your body'd never let you suffer alla that pain. It'd kill itself for you, put you outta your misery.

LARRY: You think that's what happened to Terry? Died even before the truck hit him?

ALAN: Sure.

LARRY: (*After a pause*) Musta hurt like a bastard.

ALAN: Yeah.

LARRY: Shit.

ALAN: Drink your beer. (*Pause*) Notice how quiet it is? That's because all the bugs 'n birds're depressed. Let's change the subject.

LARRY: You were pretty good in that play.

ALAN: Aw, shucks.

LARRY: You were. I gotta admire you for that. I mean, I'm a pretty gutsy guy but . . . (*Alan laughs*) I'd a' shit my shorts if I hadda get up in front of all those people and . . . do that.

ALAN: I didn't shit my shorts. I puked.

LARRY: You puked? I guess I didn't see it that night.

ALAN: I mean before.

LARRY: Before the play?

ALAN: Yeah, right.

LARRY: You puked before the play? How?

ALAN: You want a demonstration?

LARRY: I mean where?

ALAN: Jesus.

LARRY: And when? I mean, since you're revealing all your innermost secrets you might as well fill me in on the juicy details.

ALAN: About five or ten minutes before curtain I'd get a nervous stomach and throw up, just a little.

LARRY: Every night.

ALAN: Except the last night.

LARRY: I'll be a sonofabitch.

ALAN: You are a sonofabitch.

LARRY: That what you're gonna study maybe? Play-act-ing?

ALAN: I think electrical engineers have more fun.

LARRY: Yeah, they don't puke before they go to work.

ALAN: Not usually, no.

LARRY: Where'd the moon go?

ALAN: Over there now.

LARRY: What a nice night.

ALAN: Warm and clear.

LARRY: Pretty soon, gonna get cold. Shit. Another god-dam Minnesota winter. Betcha winter's colder in the cities. Farther north.

ALAN: I don't mind the winter. It'll be a good time to study.

LARRY: Hey, Al?

ALAN: Yeah?

LARRY: You gonna go on peace marches up there in the cities?

ALAN: Sharp chicks.

LARRY: (*Chants*) The whole world is watching! The whole world is watching! (*Laughs*)

ALAN: You thought that was very funny.

LARRY: It was. Them Chicago cops, man. They kicked some ass. Wham! (*Pauses*) You gonna?

ALAN: Maybe. Why?

LARRY: You against the war?

ALAN: Aren't you?

LARRY: I . . . don't much think about it.

ALAN: You should.

LARRY: Why are you against it?

ALAN: Do we have to talk about it?

LARRY: Because I know you're probably against it, you queer.

ALAN: Gimme a reason for bein' for it.

LARRY: Gotta stop Communism.

ALAN: Why?

LARRY: Because, well, shit. There's no freedom and be-sides, next thing you know.

ALAN: What? Next thing we know there'll be little bare-footed Viet Congs runnin' around this cornfield?

LARRY: Fuck you.

ALAN: It's just that . . .

LARRY: What?

ALAN: I been thinkin' about it a lot, ever since Terry died.

LARRY: Why? You're goin' to school, you got a 2-S.

ALAN: That's not it, Larry. I mean, what if Winkie dies over there?

LARRY: He won't.

ALAN: He might.

LARRY: He don't even know for sure he's goin'.

ALAN: He'll go.

LARRY: How do you know?

ALAN: Because I know. And he'll die, too.

LARRY: (*Rising*) Jesus? What're ya sayin' that for?

ALAN: It's possible.

LARRY: But you don't hafta talk like it already happened. Fuck you.

ALAN: I wasn't prepared for Terry. From now on, I'm gonna be prepared. That's my motto.

LARRY: I don't wanna think about it.

ALAN: If you're serious about wantin' to get away from Maple Lake, you should think about some a' the nasty things that can happen to you out in the world. Life's more complicated than beer, girlfriends and gas stations.

LARRY: Fuck you, Al! Who the fuck're you? Makin' all those those big shit predictions and you don't even know what you'll be doin' one week from now. Givin' everybody advice. I'm stupid for stickin' around, tryin' to keep somethin' goin' with Cindy, Winkie's stupid for enlisting, Terry's stupid for bein' dead. You're fulla bullshit, Al. Bullshit.

ALAN: You're right there.

LARRY: Shit, how'd you like a torque wrench up the wazoo?

ALAN: It's all true. I'm fulla bullshit.

LARRY: Well, I'm sorry I'm so dumb. I'm sorry I think about my car a lot. I'm sorry I'm not a neat, sensitive person. Maybe I should be a priest.

ALAN: Hey.

LARRY: I'm sorry that knowin' what you don't want ain't the same as knowin' what you do want but all I know is that

. . . (*Shouts*) Maple Lake sucks! And I want out, in the worst fuckin' way. And up yours.

ALAN: Didn't mean to insult you. I'm sorry.

LARRY: You really think Winkie was stupid to join the army where they pay you good money, give you a place to live, food to eat, teach you a skill?

ALAN: Why? Larry? Are you . . . ?

LARRY: Because . . .

ALAN: Goddamit!

LARRY: Don't gimme no shit.

ALAN: If you enlist, if you do that, I swear to God I'll follow you all the way to Saigon, cram a rifle down your throat, kill you personally. Jesus Christ, I don't believe it. You're not really . . .

LARRY: I'm just thinkin' 'bout it. I didn't say . . .

ALAN: Larry . . .

LARRY: . . . I was goin' for sure.

ALAN: Larry, don't . . .

LARRY: I was readin' this booklet . .

ALAN: Oh, shit.

LARRY: And it says you can take your pick of . . .

ALAN: Larry!

LARRY: What.

ALAN: Don't do it. Just don't do it.

LARRY: I'll join a branch where there's no chance a' gettin' killed.

ALAN: That ain't it.

LARRY: The Coast Guard.

ALAN: That ain't it.

LARRY: Then what is it? Al?

ALAN: I don't know. It's just that bein' in the army ain't somethin' I want my closest friend to do.

LARRY: Pretty selfish.

ALAN: I suppose.

LARRY: And you're leavin'. Maybe we ain't friends any more.

ALAN: What did ya' have ta say that for?

LARRY: Because it came into my head.

ALAN: So you wanna be a grunt.

LARRY: A what?

ALAN: That's what they call enlisted men. Grunts.

LARRY: Well . . .

ALAN: What about Cindy?

LARRY: Shit. Shit, shit, shit!

ALAN: Larry.

LARRY: This goddam town. Ain't nothin' left. You're gone, Terry's dead, Winkie. Everybody who's worth a shit is takin' off. 'Cept me. I'm gonna be an old man, pumpin' gas at Winklers, a fuckin' tourist attraction.

ALAN: No, you won't.

LARRY: Probably.

ALAN: No. Towns like Maple Lake're dying out, Larry. Ain't no use in fussin' about it and there ain't no use in hangin' around either. Maple Lake ain't a place to live, it's a place to leave.

LARRY: (*After a pause, smiles*) Hey, that's almost poetic.

ALAN: Not to mention true.

LARRY: Yeah, well . . .

ALAN: How you feelin'?

LARRY: I'm having trouble with my vision.

ALAN: Me too. We're outta beer.

LARRY: I'm so tired a' waitin' for somethin' to happen. I just want it to happen now, good or bad, I want it now.

ALAN: Maybe it is happening now. Right now. Listen.

LARRY: For what?

ALAN: Sh. Hear it?

LARRY: What.

ALAN: I think it's happening.

LARRY: You crazy fucker. Here, help me finish this beer.

ALAN: Hey, lookit that.

LARRY: It's called false dawn.

ALAN: Well, false or not, it's gettin' bright. That's tomorrow rising up over the Millers' back section. Soybean dawn.

LARRY: I'm sorry I threatened to stick a torque wrench up your ass.

ALAN: I'm sorry I offered to cram an M-16 down your throat.

LARRY: I ain't sorry I said fuck you.

ALAN: Me either.

LARRY: Fuck you.

ALAN: And a fuck you to you too.

LARRY: Well. Here's the good-bye we been workin' toward. Good-bye and good luck up there, Al.

ALAN: Yeah, thanks.

(They start to shake hands but instead embrace clumsily. Brief tableau. They break the embrace and, slightly embarrassed, gather up their jackets and start to exit)

LARRY: Remember the time we put those sparrows in Winkie's locker? (*Alan laughs*) Fuckin' fainted dead away.

ALAN: I still don't know why he couldn't hear 'em jumpin' around in there.

LARRY: (*As they exit*) You think he's still a virgin?

ALAN: They take virgins in the army?

LARRY: (*Offstage by now*) Oops.

ALAN: Steady on there.

LARRY: Hey, I heard a pheasant croak.

ALAN: That was me.

LARRY: Al. Look at the moon.

Blackout

John Guare

IN FIREWORKS LIE
SECRET CODES

John Guare

When John Guare's *In Fireworks Lie Secret Codes* opened at the Mitzi E. Newhouse Theatre at Lincoln Center in New York in March of 1981, Michael Feingold, critic for the *Village Voice*, extolled it: "Guare handles all the old-homey notions with the uneasy conscience of an urban contemporary who knows that modern life has disrupted them to the point where they are no longer workable. Out of this, and the situation of five well-heeled people at a Fourth of July party, Guare weaves a piece of word-music that gains strength by staying on the surface; the moments when its depths open up are more memorable for being unexpected." On the same bill with Jeffrey Sweet's *Stops Along the Way* (in *Best Short Plays 1981*) and Percy Granger's *Vivien* (elsewhere in this volume), the production of *In Fireworks Lie Secret Codes* was staged by its author with the lyrical precision of a classical ballet.

One of America's most highly acclaimed and original playwrights, John Guare has been awarded many major honors for his work, starting with an Obie Award for *Muzeeka* in 1968. The following year he received another Obie Award as New York Drama Critics's Most Promising Playwright for *Cop-Out*, and in 1971, the coveted New York Drama Critics Circle Award for best American Play for the zany and touching play *The House of Blue Leaves*. This was quickly followed with another Drama Critics Circle Award for Best Musical in 1971–72 for *Two Gentlemen of Verona*—additionally twice-honored by also receiving the Tony Awards for both Best Musical and Best Libretto. In 1977 he received the Joseph Jefferson award for playwriting for *Landscape of the Body*, and in 1981 he received the American Academy and Institute of Arts and Letters Award for his full-length plays. His *Bosoms and Neglect* was cited as the Best Play of 1979 by *The Soho Weekly*, and in 1980 his screenplay for Louis Malle's film *Atlantic City* won the Grand Prize at the Venice Film Festival. Most recently he has been a Visiting Andrew Mellon Fellow at the California Institute of the Arts, which produced his play *Marco Polo Sings A Solo*.

Active in organizations which assist the playwright, Mr. Guare is a council member of the Dramatists Guild, representing the interests of 4000 American and British dramatists. He was a founding member of the O'Neill Foundation, which conducts an annual summer workshop for new plays, and of the New Dramatists Committee, founded to help apprentice playwrights develop their talents.

Born in New York in 1938, Guare's education includes an A.B. from Georgetown University in 1961 and an M.F.A. in 1963 from Yale School of Drama, where he studied with the late John Gassner. Guare rejected, however, the emphasis on logic and traditional construction which Gassner proffered, but responded enthusiastically to his later instructor Arnold Weinstein, who encouraged Guare to disregard both logic and the conventional modes of playwriting.

Guare started writing plays at the age of eleven, and has written a play every year since 1956, when he was eighteen. Enthusiastic about writing, Guare has commented, "I'm very obsessive about work . . . Work for me is all voyaging, a kind of emotional serendipity. I write to get objectivity on things that have happened. Life is the unconscious, writing the conscious."

In Fireworks Lie Secret Codes is the second short play from Mr. Guare to appear in this series. His earlier work, *A Day For Surprises*, was published in the 1970 edition.

The author dedicates his play: "For Adele."

Characters:

1, *a man*
2, *a woman*
3, *a man, English accent*
4, *a woman*
5, *a man*

Scene:

The terrace of a penthouse on the West Side of Manhattan looking over the Hudson River. Night. Fourth of July.
  Everyone is enthralled. Music. Thunder.

1:   Were you here the tall ships day? Fourth of July, 1976. The Bicentennial. The tall ships sailed up the Hudson. People in New York were happy for a year after that. They had predicted riots and bombings and general terror, but nothing went wrong that day. Right up that river all these tall sailing ships from all over the world sailed. Up. Up. Sometimes even today if I find myself stuck in an elevator or the subway that has broken down and you're there in the pitch black, I'll scream out to the darkness, "Remember the day of the tall ships." And one or two people will always scream back, "*Yes!*"
4:   Wasn't that a day!
2:   Pink. Blue.
1:   Pink center! Green. Blue white.
2:   Green center. Blue! White! Gold spill!
1:   Green, blue, white.
2:   Red, blue, green.
3:   Bougainvillaea.
5:   Where?
3:   The spill.
5:   Bougainvillaea?
3:   Perhaps wisteria.
5:   Ahhh. Wisteria.
2:   Wisteria?
3:   The spill.
2:   Ahhh.
3:   Gone.
1:   Pink, white, blue. Silver dribble-down.

3: Wisteria. Pure and simple.

5: Not bougainvillaea.

4: Was it in your lease that Macy's would have to do this in the river right off your terrace?

3: Oh, yes. Right in the lease. Clause 12, triple B. Macy's fireworks right in line with my terrace.

1: Look down below.

5: Right in *our* lease. It's *our* lease and when the building goes co-op, it'll be *our* bill of sale, *our* deed.

4: I don't want any talk about co-op bargains. Only stories where people are gypped, cheated or overcharged.

2: Usually they say penthouse, but all they show you are rooms on top of an expensive building with a window box you can barely stand on. But here! This! This—*pent*house! Four sides. You can walk around. You could plant wheat and grow grass. Do they let you bring cows up on the elevator? You could get farm subsidies.

4: Red! Blue! Green! Green!

2: And you must always ask me back here. Not wait for holidays. We could have quilting parties and sewing bees.

5: We could bundle!

2: Yes! Blue! Blue! Gold! White!

1: Blue! Blue! Gold! White!

2: We'd have 4-H Club meetings!

4: Red! Red! Blue! White! Gold! White! Green!

2: And all the roots from all your crops could travel down all the stories of this building and pass through every apartment and absorb every family up onto this roof in a harvest of urban photosynthesis and these city people will step out of their blossoms and see weathervanes and silos and tractors.

4: Blue! Red! Green! Green! Gold!

3: You make this simple asphalt roof sound like Kansas.

2: Kansas or Oz. Oz or Kansas. With me, it's always been Kansas or Oz. But here tonight—this roof—the eternal dilemma finally and irrevocably resolved. Everything here. I'd never have to leave.

5: But you'd have to.

2: Red! Blue! Green! (*Looks at 3*) Perhaps. Perhaps not.

4: (*To 1*) I don't like to get too close. Don't lean over!

1: Thousands of people.

4: West Side Highway closed for miles. Don't lean over so!

2: Or did all those people used to be automobiles?

3: Chrysanthemums!

4: Yes!

5: Where? Missed! Damn!

2: Holiday headline: Frog Kisses Buick. Turns it into Person.

1: Pink, white, blue. Sun burst! Dazzle!

4: I feel guilty watching this. I never buy anything at Macy's and here they are, paying for all this.

3: Those ones whistled. Very nice whistle!

4: I *only* go to Bloomingdale's and they never do anything for the city. I've never even stepped foot in Macy's.

2: They *are* the world's largest store.

4: But they seem pathetic. 34th Street. Down there. West side.

3: They *do* do the Thanksgiving Day parade. Miracle on 34th Street. All those great balloons.

4: I know. I know. But I comfort myself this way. I say Macy's does today and Thanksgiving Day; Bloomingdale's does the other 363 days of the year. An interesting person's like a holiday, don't you think? Anytime you see an interesting person on the street, that person is a commando sent out there by Bloomingdale's. Bloomingdale's decorates the streets of New York. Macy's just does windows and two holidays a year. But Bloomingdale's does everything in between. I say to myself that Jacqueline Kennedy would have moved years ago to Greece, but Bloomingdale's signed her to a lifetime contract to stay in New York. And Robert Redford lives in New York on upper Fifth Avenue. Bloomingdale's owns him. And Bloomingdale's brought Nixon here, even though he's no holiday. And they do the U.N. and the hostages and the graffiti on the subways. No, Bloomingdale's does lots. Thanks, Macy's, but no thanks. I won't turn on Bloomingdale's. They make every day a holiday.

2: See the last of the sunset over New Jersey.

5: Don't distract us with New Jersey. New Jersey is the worst state in the union. New Jersey blows poison nuclear gases over the river. I wish these fireworks were weapons I could turn back on New Jersey.

2: Everybody has transistors.

5: You need holidays just to stay alive. Just to breathe.

2: Today I can breathe.

4: Don't lean over.

2:   What's that playing?

3:   *Star Wars.*

2:   *Star Wars!* Make it the *National Anthem.* Take it back—*Rhapsody in Blue!* Make that the *National Anthem.*

1:   Pink! Green! Silver!

3:   Chrysanthemums again!

4:   Yes!

5:   Where? Missed! Damn!

3:   I was in the south of France one Bastille Day and they had the International Fireworks Exhibition and Red China put on a show in the sky: Chairman Mao instructing the peasants and dreaming of a new world order.

5:   All in fireworks?

3:   Not like this Macy's rubbish. (*To 4*) Don't be guilty, dear.

1:   Yellow! White! Purple!

4:   Don't make me so dissatisfied. I am so satisfied at this moment.

5:   (*Imitating 4*) Don't get so close to the edge.

2:   When *I* was a kid, my parents took me to the Christmas show at the Music Hall called *Holiday Inn* and Bing Crosby and Fred Astaire opened a nightclub that was only opened holidays and Irving Berlin wrote a song for each holiday.

1:   White! Blue! Blue! Blue!

2:   Bing and Fred fought over the same girl, and she'd be in love with either of them on each holiday so there was always suspense.

3:   What did they do between holidays?

4:   The Music Hall never delved that deep.

2:   (*Sings*) "I'm Dreaming of a White Christmas . . ."

3:   That was the Christmas song.

2:   I always felt rotten because I had to spend holidays with my family, and I could never go to that inn which was always packed. Holiday Inn. Not the fake one that there's always sixteen miles to the next. No, the real Holiday Inn. In that Music Hall pageant. Blue! Blue! Green!

(*All sigh*)

1:   The best holiday I ever spent was in Bethlehem. Christmas! I went swimming in the Dead Sea and it's true.

5:   What's true?

3:   Green! Gold! Ahhh.

1:   That it's hard to go under. I floated right on top of the water. And that afternoon I went to the camel races in Bethany and I went into the bar and King Hussein was sitting at the bar having a drink with a few people. This will show you how long ago it was. Jerusalem was still in Jordan. And that night we went on a pilgrimage to Bethlehem and went to the Three Wise Men Cafe and the Manger Cafe and the Star Cafe. We brought our own wine because we were travellers, hitchhikers, student wanderers. And the management had us arrested and thrown out because it was their big night to make money which is one of the things holidays are about. They let us go, the cops, because it was Christmas and we were from all over the world. South Africa. Brazil. We went to the Church of the Nativity and I was up very close for the mass because I didn't want to get claustroid which I am.

4:   Don't lean over!

1:   The incense during the mass was very thick and it made me sick. I climbed over the altar rail because it was too mobbed to get out through the church. I didn't want to throw up in the Church of the Nativity. I went backstage of the altar, I don't know what you call it, to get fresh air. A radio crew was there. I said what's this? They were from the BBC broadcasting the mass all over the world. "Ahh," I said. I went out through another door where the air was even fresher. The bell tower. An old man was holding on to the ropes. I asked, "Could I help?" He said, "Help? You can do it." The equivalent in Arabic and sign language. The red light went on. The old man signalled me to start pulling the bell. I yanked it down. A loop was on the rope and the old man showed me how to hook my hands into the rope. I began pulling and the bells started ringing, slowly at first, even softly as if I were doing something wrong, but I kept pulling and the bells got louder and wilder and lifted me off the ground. I swung way up in the air and crashed down, way up in the air, crash down. Up. Down! Up. Down! High! Low! High! Low! Twelve minutes. I found out later that the bells rang from the Sanctus to the Communion, which is a pretty long time, and I realized, "Hey, I am ringing the bells for the midnight mass from Bethlehem and I am being broadcast all over the world. Hello, world! This is me! Parents! Girlfriends! Enemies! Loves! Wives! Ex-wives! Husbands! Ex-husbands! Teachers! Everyone who ever tried to stop me!"

4:   Don't lean so close!'

1:   And I went way up, came way down. The old man grabbed on to my legs to stop the motion of the bells.

3:   Pink! Red! Orchid!

1:   Gradually the bells quieted. Quiet. Quiet.

5:   Pink center! Green. Blue, white.

2:   Green center. Blue! White! Gold spill!

1:   Green, blue, white.

2:   Red, blue, green.

3:   Bougainvillaea.

5:   Where?

3:   The spill.

5:   Bougainvillaea?

3:   Perhaps wisteria.

5:   Ahhh. Wisteria.

2:   Wisteria?

3:   The spill.

2:   Ahhhh.

3:   Gone.

1:   Pink, white, blue. Silver dribble-down.

5:   Blue, green. Pink center.

ALL: Ahhhh.

3:   Last May thirtieth—your Memorial Day—I was going over to Brooklyn to one of your houses.

2:   Which of you had a party and didn't invite me? Shame. Shame.

3:   I looked around the subway car and saw a Spanish man reading *El Diario*. A dark Medea of a woman asleep, a Greek newspaper folded over her breasts. I was carrying a week old copy of the *London Times* so I felt everyone in that car had the correct newspaper. All reading the news of the world in the proper language.

5:   Except there was that one man you pointed out. Fantastically un-ethnic. Blonde. Why was he reading the *Manila Journal*? Urgent headlines: "President Marcos Assaulted." We moved to another car.

3:   As I said, we remembered all this because it was Memorial Day. And I was feeling so at home in the world, in that subway. A policeman right by us.

5:   And then we heard the scream.

2:   Scream?

3:   Yes. A scream. Scream for me.

(*2 screams*)

3: Yes. Like that. Only imagine that scream pulled through despair and fear.

2: I did scream with fear and despair. I always scream with fear and despair. Why else would you scream if it weren't fear and despair.

4: Don't get so close to the edge!

1: (*Simultaneously with 4*) Pink! Blue! Look! Look!

3: As I said, imagine that scream with fear and despair and the woman who screamed ran up the subway aisle to the policeman standing by me.

2: What do I say?

3: You say to the policeman, "That man down there, he put his hand on my . . . On my . . ." And then cry.

2: "That man down there. He put his hand on my . . On my . . ." I don't want to make fun of her.

3: Oh, this story makes fun of nobody. You'll see.

5: This story is a photograph. Subway snapshot.

3: Unbeknownst to the woman with the 78 RPM voice, the man who had put his blank on her blank had run out of the car when the subway stopped at Wall Street.

5: The crazed capitalist of Wall Street!

4: Please. The edge. The edge.

3: A Chinese cook gets on at the stop and sits in the crazed capitalist's seat. He opens a Chinese newspaper—all dressed in white, his chef's cap folded out of Chinese newspaper.

5: Fitting in perfectly with our car.

3: The woman drags the copper back as we descend under the river to Brooklyn. She stands in front of her place. "That's him," she says.

2: That's him.

3: The Chinese cook looks up. No English.

5: No English-ee.

3: She begins hitting him. "You touched me," she cries bitterly.

2: I won't do that.

3: You touched me. The Chinese cook holds his Chinese newspaper in defense. Other passengers tell the cop what happened. We speed away under the river from the violation left behind on Wall Street.

5: Where is the crazed capitalist now, I thought! Running up Maiden Lane. Snatching at ladies' parts on Beaver Street. Run! Run!

3: The cop understands what happened. He pulls the lady back to protect the Chinese cook. Everyone begins to laugh.

5: Everyone laughed wildly. It was fantastic to see!

3: Distance under rivers gave us all the terrible objectivity found only in the plays of Moliere.

5: The woman began screaming at us all: "Are you all sick? Are you all sick?" but we couldn't help it.

3: Her pain was worthy of the *Bacchae* out of Aristophanes via Menander passing to Terence.

5: She was in such panic, she couldn't hear the explanation that this Chinese man was not the blank who put his blank on her blank.

3: The policeman holds her back. The Chinese cook transforms into Buster Keaton and flees to another car. One of us—Feydeau? Noel Coward? held the door open for a more nimble escape.

5: "Are you all sick?" she cried at us.

3: We come out from under the river, still underground, but at least underearth. We come to the Clark Street stop. "He touched me."

2: He touched me.

3: The cop tried to explain. She'll hear nothing of it. "I don't even want your badge number."

2: I don't even want your badge number.

3: "I don't want anything to do with any of you."

2: I don't want anything to do with any of you.

3: "If this is the human race . . ."

2: If this is the human race . . .

3: She won't let anyone speak to her—give her explanation.

2: Don't speak. No explanation.

3: The doors open. She gets out at Clark Street. We watch her on the platform. She gets back on the train. But moves to other cars. Pushing people out of the way.

5: Just pushing people. Pushing them.

3: People back to the newspapers of their native language. Some people still laughing. Others no longer laughing. But the laughter had purified nothing. Our laughter had only helped anguish move into anecdote. (*Pause*) Which I give to you right now.

(*Pause*)

2: Pink. Blue.

1: Pink center. Blue! White! Gold spill!

2: Green center. Blue! White! Gold!

1: Green! Blue! White!

2: Red. Blue. Blue. Blue. Green.

3. I've made a great decision. (*Then to* 2) Pass the drinks. That's a dear.

2: Down there. What do you suppose all those thousands of people are saying.

4: Don't get too close.

2: I went to New Orleans once and had a city map that showed a street called Mystery Street. I was sure it was an ordinary street but I wanted to see it just the same. I asked the policeman, "How do I get to Mystery Street?" And he said, "You just march up two blocks to Canal Street and you wait for a streetcar marked *Desire*." The way he said, "Marked." I always thought Tennessee Williams was a poet. He just wrote down the way people spoke.

5: In England I rode a bus in from Kensington. Two women sat in front of me. I didn't think they were together 'til one turned to the other and said, "Hilary had another suicide attempt this weekend." The other woman said, "Oh. What did her husband say this time?" The other woman said viciously, "Oh, Hilary's not telling anyone about *this* episode." And they resumed their silent strange ride. I always thought of that bus line as the Harold Pinter bus line. That's all poetry is. Pinter understood the neighborhood on an ordinary day. A day that's not a holiday. The lingo of the streets. The way the rhythm of the town fits on the tongue. On an ordinary day. Not an hysterical day like a holiday. No poetry on holidays. (*A la Pinter*) Decision? You've made a decision?

1: Pink. Green. Lavender. Mauve.

5: Blue, green. Pink center.

3: I'm leaving America. It's not my holiday. It's not my home. I've lived here twelve years now. I'm not an American. I want to go back to England. The biggest myth in the world is that England and America are alike. We share a language but I don't understand it. I am in the streets and I don't understand what is being said. I want to understand the rhythms in the street. There is a shorthand in the streets. A shorthand in the way people speak. I don't understand America. I don't understand what anyone says. I want to go home and reclaim my language. In fireworks lie secret codes. I've decided it. I'll be back in England by the first of September. I love holidays. I just find it difficult to survive on the days that are not holidays.

1: (*Pause*) Pink. Green.

3: 1976. The tall ships day. I came here in 1965. My God. I have lived one third of my life in New York. I'm just adding it up. One third. I never meant to stay here. And now it is home. One third. My God.

1: The bells swung up. The bells swung down.

5: You can't leave America. Are you doing April Fool? You can't leave New York. You know I can't leave. When you say you're going and announce it like that, I know you're assuming I am not going with you. I teach. I can't up and leave. We have put so much work into this apartment. I can't afford it myself. What am I going to do? I couldn't live here with anyone else. This is our home. We found this place. We made it what it is, we made it the showplace it is, we made it the place where our friends can come and watch holidays. We had Easter dinner right here on this terrace even though it was cold. We ate Thanksgiving Dinner here because that was the day we met. I can't up and leave America. My parents are here. My work is here. My connections are here. I am *from* here. I just can't up and leave. You can't move away—make decisions like that and just announce it.

3: You'll have summer holidays. You can visit me then.

5: It's not the same.

2: And with the budget flights. It's like commuting.

4: Not so close to the edge!

3: I was going to ask you if you wanted to sublet it.

4: Sublet? I can't even look over the side.

1: Stardust. Blue. That's a great one. That's a great one!

3: They're playing *Rhapsody in Blue.*

2: Make that the *National Anthem.*

4: Red!

(*Silence. Dark*)

1: (*Pause*) Come on.

3: That's not it?

2: Is it all over?

1: They just stop it?

5: Screw you, Macy's. We want a finale.

4: There we are. (*To 1*) Pry our car loose from down

there. I dread the elevator ride down. (*To 3*) I'm embarrassed to tell you . . . We're moving to New Jersey. A house. Green. New Jersey's not really poison. Is it? We're buying. We've bought.

2: One-third. One-third of my life.

1: Twelve minutes . . . Up . . . Up . . .

3: That fireworks festival in Nice, the Chinese ended with a silver vase and then they put gladiola buds in the vase and then the gladiolus blossomed and then the petals fell off and then the gladiolus withered.

1: All in fireworks?

3: Unforgettable.

1: Where was Chairman Mao?

3: Nothing political. Just beauty.

1: I'll always remember these blues tonight. Everytime I see wisteria I know I'll think of tonight.

Slow fade to black

Jane Martin

TWIRLER

Jane Martin

Without a doubt, the crowning jewel of the Fifth Annual Festival of New American Plays presented by the Actors Theatre of Louisville was the seventeen-minute monologue *Twirler*. Appearing here under the pseudonym "Jane Martin," the actual author of the script is shrouded in mystery with the true identity known only to a couple of tight-lipped administrators of the company.

Each year, in addition to sponsoring the well-publicized Great American Play Contest open to all American writers and bringing in around four thousand scripts for consideration, the Actors Theatre also solicits one-act plays from anyone involved with their own organization. Entries come from all quarters—from artistic directors to ushers to wives of board members. *Twirler* was originally submitted—unsigned and poorly typed—to this in-house contest, and it won! But when the time came to present the one hundred dollar award, the modest author did not identify herself (himself?).

The monologue, then selected for the Fifth Annual Festival and enchantingly performed by Lisa Goodman, drew accolades from the press. Kathie Beals in the *Gannett Westchester Newspapers* described her impression: "*Twirler* is, as they say in Kentucky, something else again. Recited by a girl wearing a baton twirler's costume of red sequins and cowboy boots. . . . It is a haunting piece that uncovers religious-mystical feelings in the unlikely person of a small town girl who takes up twirling and gets into the nationals. The words ring so true, as if they have just come direct from a revival meeting." Mel Gussow, writing in the *New York Times*, called *Twirler* "the unqualified hit of the festival," while William B. Collins in the *Philadelphia Inquirer* declared, "It was extraordinarily funny and it was heartrending . . ."

Producers and directors inquired eagerly about performance rights—but there was no author or agent willing to step forth to claim responsibility.

Luckily, arrangements have been made with Jon Jory, Producing Director of Actors Theatre of Louisville, and Alexander Speer, Administrative Director, to publish the script in this collection and to handle inquiries regarding productions. But as for Jane Martin, she (or he?) continues to prefer anonymity.

Characters:

APRIL MARCH

A young woman stands center stage. She is dressed in a span-gled, single-piece swimsuit, the kind that is specially made for baton twirlers. She holds a shining, silver baton in her hand.

APRIL: I started when I was six. Momma sawed off a broom handle, and Uncle Carbo slapped some sort of silver paint, well, grey really, on it and I went down in the base-ment and twirled. Later on, Momma hit the daily double on horses named Spin Dry and Silver Revolver and she said that was a sign so she gave me lessons at the Dainty Deb Dance studio where the lady, Miss Aurelia, taught some twirling on the side.

I won the Ohio Juniors title when I was six and the Mid-west Young Adult Division three years later and then in High School I finished fourth in the nationals. Momma and I wore look-alike Statue of Liberty costumes that she had to send clear to Nebraska to get, and Daddy was there in a T-shirt with my name, April . . . my first name is April and my last name is March. There were four thousand people there, and when they yelled my name, golden balloons fell out of the ceiling. Nobody—not even Charlene Ann Morri-son—ever finished fourth at my age.

Oh, I've flown high and known tragedy both. My daddy says it's put spirit in my soul and steel in my heart. My left hand was crushed in a riding accident by a horse named Big Blood Red, and though I came back to twirl, I couldn't do it at the highest level. That was denied me by Big Blood Red who clipped my wings. You mustn't pity me though. Oh, by no means! Being denied showed me the way, showed me the glory that sits inside life where you can't see it.

People think you're a twit if you twirl. It's a prejudice of the unknowing. Twirlers are the niggers of a white Univer-sity. Yes, they are. One time I was doing fire batons at a night game, and all of a sudden I see this guy walk out of the stands. I was doing triples and he walks right out past the half time marshalls, comes up to me . . . he had this

blue bead head band, I can still see it. Walks right up, and
when I come front after a back reverse, he spits in my face.
That's the only, single time I ever dropped a baton.
Dropped 'em both in front of sixty thousand people, and
he smiles see, and he says this thing I won't repeat. He
called me a bodily part in front of half of Ohio. It was like
being raped. It shows that beauty inspires hate and that
hating beauty is Satan.

You haven't twirled, have you? I can see that by your
hands. Would you like to hold my silver baton? Here, hold
it.

You can't imagine what it feels like to have that baton up
in the air. I used to twirl with this girl who called it blue-
collar zen. The "tons" catch the sun when they're up, and
when they go up, you go up too. You can't twirl if you're
not *inside* the "ton." When you've got 'em up over twenty
feet it's like flying or gliding. Your hands are still down, but
your insides spin and rise and leave the ground. Only a
twirler knows that, so we're not niggers.

The secret for a twirler is the light. You live or die with
the light. It's your fate. The best is a February sky clouded
right over in the late afternoon. It's all background then,
and what happens is that the "tons" leave tracks, traces,
they etch the air, and if you're hot, if your hands have it,
you can draw on the sky.

Charlene Ann Morrison . . . God, Charlene Ann! She
was inspired by something beyond man. She won the nationals nine years in a row. Unparallelled and unrepeata-
ble. The last two years she had leukemia and at the end you
could see through her hands when she twirled. Charlene
Ann died with a "ton" thirty feet up, her momma swears on
that. I did speed with Charlene at a regional in Fargo and
she may be fibben' but she says there was a day when her
"tons" erased while they turned. Like the sky was a sheet of
rain and the "tons" were car wipers and when she had
erased this certain part of the sky, you could see the face of
the Lord God Jesus, and his hair was all rhinestones and he
was doing this incredible singing like the sound of a piccolo.
The people who said Charlene was crazy probably never
twirled a day in their life.

Twirling is the physical parallel of revelation. You can't
know that. Twirling is the throwing of yourself up to God.

It's a pure gift, hidden from Satan because it is wrapped and disguised in the midst of football. It is God throwing, spirit fire, and very few come to it. You have to grow eyes in your heart to understand its message, and when it opens to you, it becomes your path to suffer ridicule, to be crucified by misunderstanding, and to be spit upon. I need my baton now.

There is one twirling no one sees. At the winter solstice we go to a meadow God showed us just outside of Green Bay. The God throwers come there on December twenty-first. There's snow, sometimes deep snow and our clothes fall away and we stand unprotected while acolytes bring the "tons." They are ebony "tons" with razors set all along the shaft. They are three feet long. One by one the twirlers throw, two "tons" each, thirty feet up, and as they fall back, they cut your hands. The razors arch into the air and find God and then fly down to take your blood in a crucifixion, and the red drops draw God on the ground and if you are up with the batons you can look down and see him revealed. Red on white. Red on white. You can't imagine. You can't imagine how wonderful it is!

I started twirling when I was six, but I never really twirled until my hand was crushed by the horse named Big Blood Red. I have seen God's face from thirty feet up in the air and I know him.

Listen. I will leave my silver baton here for you. Lying here as if I forgot it and when the people file out you can wait back and pick it up, it can be yours . . . it can be your burden. It is the eye of the needle. I leave it for you.

(*The lights fade*)

Cumulative Index 1968–82